OUR OLDEST ENEMY

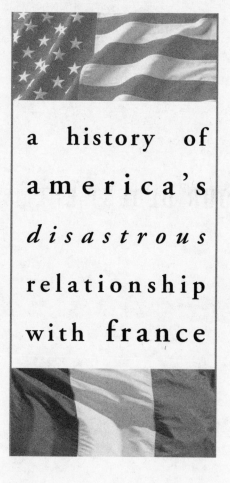

a history of
america's
disastrous
relationship
with france

BROADWAY BOOKS
New York

OUR OLDEST ENEMY

JOHN J. MILLER
&
MARK MOLESKY

Book design by Nicola Ferguson

The Library of Congress catalogued the hardcover edition as follows:
Miller, John J., 1970–
Our oldest enemy : a history of America's disastrous relationship with France / by John J. Miller and Mark Molesky. — 1st ed.
p. cm.
Includes bibliographical references and index.
1. United States—Foreign relations—France. 2. France—Foreign relations—United States. I. Molesky, Mark. II. Title.

E183.8.F8M55 2004
327.73044—dc22   2004047756

ISBN 0-7679-1755-3

1 3 5 7 9 10 8 6 4 2

For my parents,
Eugene and JoAnne Miller
—JJM

To the memory of
Camille Shaffer Dorn,
beloved great-aunt and mentor
—MM

CONTENTS

INTRODUCTION

"A WAR WITHOUT DEATH"

WHEN FRENCH PRESIDENT Jacques Chirac learned on September 11, 2001, that terrorists had toppled the World Trade Center, smashed a fiery hole into the side of the Pentagon, and plunged a plane full of passengers into a Pennsylvania field, he broke off a tour of Brittany and rushed back to Paris. "In these terrible circumstances," he said, "all French people stand by the American people. We express our friendship and solidarity in this tragedy."[1] A week later, he stood next to George W. Bush in the Oval Office. "We are completely determined to fight by your side," he promised the president. "France is prepared and available to discuss all means to fight and eradicate this evil."[2] The following day, he became the first foreign head of state to visit Ground Zero in Manhattan.

Chirac's words and actions were both strong and stirring. They were also expected from a leader whose country had survived the ravages of the twentieth century in large part because of the leadership and sacrifice of the United States. On September 12, France's newspaper of record, *Le Monde*, added its support with a front-page editorial featuring the headline *"Nous Sommes Tous Américains"*—We Are All Americans. The U.S. media turned this simple and poignant phrase into a rousing refrain. America's oldest ally was reasserting its close historical and cultural ties in a moment of national catastrophe.

Or so it seemed. From the beginning, cracks in Franco-American relations were apparent. As Bush began to speak of a war on terror—"a new kind of war," he called it—Chirac expressed reservations. "I don't know whether we should use the word *war*," he cautioned during his visit to the White House on September 18.

Over the next year and a half, semantic disagreements gave way to open conflict as France waged a vigorous campaign of obstruction and harassment against the United States and its war on terror. As the Bush administration set out to take preventative action against the tyrants, organizations, and foot soldiers who had already murdered thousands and were busy plotting future attacks, France was generous with aid and information. But when the United States decided to end the outlaw regime of Saddam Hussein in Iraq as well, Chirac and his government did everything in their power to thwart American efforts.

Not content with simply voicing their opposition, the French actively fought the Americans at every turn. They delivered condescending lectures on the arrogance of the United States and the sanctity of Iraqi sovereignty. They insisted that the Bush administration proceed only with the approval of the United Nations—and then threatened to use their veto power on the Security Council to block effective military action. They went so far as to form a new political axis with Germany and Russia and tried to rally the world against the American resolve. They insulted and bullied countries that chose to defy Paris and support the United States. They publicly declared the nations of Africa to be opposed to an invasion of Iraq, though their claims were based on pledges that had not in fact been made. In a provocative and totally unprecedented move, they endangered a cornerstone of Western security by attempting to block a request from fellow NATO member Turkey for defensive military equipment to be used in the event of an Iraqi attack. France's entire foreign policy seemed driven by belligerence toward the United States.

Chirac's top deputy in this anti-American offensive was Foreign

Minister Dominique de Villepin. An amateur poet and historian with oily good looks and a condescending manner, Villepin became the leading French spokesman at the UN and in the media. For all his charms, he had great difficulty hiding the deep resentment he felt toward the United States and its policies. While American soldiers and their allies were battling Saddam's henchmen inside Iraq in the spring of 2003, Villepin could not even bring himself, under direct questioning, to say that he hoped for a U.S. victory.

Chirac and Villepin were hardly alone in their anti-Americanism. In a speech to the French legislature, Prime Minister Jean-Pierre Rafarrin scolded Americans for their "simplistic view of a war of good against evil." One wonders whether the prime minister views America's crusade to drive Hitler from France sixty years earlier in a similar light. Although Rafarrin chose not to address such complexities, he did add a quintessentially French flourish to his remarks: "Young countries have the tendency to underestimate the history of old countries."[3] Americans have become accustomed to such patronizing from the French. In this instance, however, the prime minister might have benefited from a history lesson. After all, which country is older? The one with a durable and long-lived constitution or the one that currently calls itself the Fifth Republic? Perhaps the youthful regime of France was guilty of underestimating its older, wiser, and more experienced democratic cousin.

Then there was the matter of what *Le Monde* really meant when it declared "We Are All Americans." This much-celebrated headline sat atop one of the most-cited but least-read newspaper editorials ever written, for beneath that catchy phrase was an anti-American diatribe of extraordinary virulence and rage. Penned by publisher Jean-Marie Colombani, it worried that the United States would turn "Islamic fundamentalism" into "the new enemy." After the Oklahoma City bombing in 1995, wrote Colombani, Americans had succumbed to an "anti-Islamic reflex" consisting of "ridiculous, if not downright odious" behavior. He further asserted that 9/11 had occurred because the United States dominates a world "with no counterbalance." The terrorist atrocity was the predictable result "of an America whose own cynicism has caught up with it" in the person of Osama bin Laden, whom he interpreted as the villainous invention of the Central Intelligence Agency. Anything but a declaration of solidarity, the famous editorial was constructed around a particularly ugly and outrageous slander: "Might it not then have been America itself that created this demon?"[4]

Credited in the world press with a sympathy for America that it had not expressed, *Le Monde* made certain in the days to follow that none of its readers would misinterpret its true beliefs. "How we have dreamt of this event," wrote the eminent intellectual Jean Baudrillard, referring to 9/11. "How all the world without exception dreamt of this event, for no one can avoid dreaming of the destruction of a power that has become hegemonic. . . . It is they who acted, but we who wanted the deed." Colombani also did his best to make sure no one in the future would mistake him for an admirer of the United States. In subsequent writings, including a book called *Tous Américains?* (*All Americans?*)—in which he retreated from his original headline by adding a question mark—the illustrious publisher stooped to present an old and vicious caricature of America as a country controlled by crazed Christian dogmatists who excelled at oppressing their black neighbors. He further argued that the United States was hypocritical to protest the consequences of Islamic radicalism when it still embraced that supposedly primitive instrument of legalized brutality, the death penalty.[5]

Although millions of Americans found the behavior of the French exasperating, many initially responded in a characteristically American way: with humor. "You know why the French don't want to bomb Saddam Hussein?" asked television comedian Conan O'Brien. "Because he hates America, loves mistresses, and wears a beret. He *is* French, people." Every evening seemed to bring a new late-night laugh. "I don't know why people are surprised that France won't help us get Saddam out of Iraq," joked Jay Leno. "After all, France wouldn't help us get the Germans out of France." Even politicians joined in: "Do you know how many Frenchmen it takes to defend Paris?"

quipped Congressman Roy Blunt of Missouri. "It's not known. It's never been tried." Jokes were a way for Americans to express their frustration with the behavior of a country they considered a friend.

As the quarrel intensified, however, American feelings toward the French shifted from bemusement to betrayal. From a cafeteria in Congress to diners and eateries across the country, french fries were transformed into "freedom fries." Restaurant owners poured bottles of French wine down drains and promised to stock only American vintages or those from countries that supported the war on terror. On the popular television program *The O'Reilly Factor*, host Bill O'Reilly launched a nationwide and much-publicized appeal to boycott French products. Internet sites posted long lists of brand-name items owned by French companies: Bic, Evian, Michelin, Perrier, and Yoplait. The U.S. presence at the renowned defense-industry confab, the Paris Air Show, was really more like an absence (as a French deconstructionist might say). The economic impact was immediate. French wine exports to the United States dropped like guillotines during the Reign of Terror. American tourists avoided France, where government officials calculated losses in the billions. Before the terrorist attacks of 2001, 77 percent of Americans held a favorable opinion of France and a mere 17 percent held an unfavorable one. In March 2003, on the eve of the invasion of Iraq, these feelings were reversed. Only 34 percent of Americans saw France in a positive light, while fully 64 percent viewed it negatively.

In the United States, earnest pundits lamented the rift between the two countries. "Franco-American friendship goes back a long way," warned Kevin Phillips on National Public Radio.[6] If the bitterness continued, it might erase a cherished legacy of goodwill and harmony. "We run the risk of losing this long friendship, a history built up over time and adversity," wrote Josephine Humphreys in the *New York Times*. "Do we really want a divorce?"[7]

Such sentiments assume, of course, that there had been a marriage in the first place—a marriage allegedly consummated when France rushed to the aid of desperate American colonists during their War of

Independence. That's where the oft-told story of Franco-American friendship usually begins, with tributes to the valor and idealism of the Marquis de Lafayette, the gallant aristocrat who offered his services to General Washington and the American cause. Within a few years of his arrival, the French provided decisive naval support at the battle of Yorktown, securing American liberty. Next comes the Louisiana Purchase of 1803, commonly understood as a benign real-estate transaction in which Napoleon generously sold vast tracts of North America at rock-bottom prices to his friend Thomas Jefferson. In the decades to follow, the French aristocrat Alexis de Tocqueville toured the United States and gazed in wonder at its political achievements, leaving the impression that it was the French who had discovered the genius of American democracy. Later in the century, France made a gift of the Statue of Liberty to its sister republic and became America's tutor in the ways of art and culture. In the twentieth century, American doughboys fought in the trenches beside French troops in the First World War and symbolically repaid America's debt to Lafayette and his country. A generation later, GIs valiantly stormed the beaches of Normandy, liberated freedom-loving France from the Nazis, and, as their reward, enjoyed the gratitude of comely French maidens. During the Cold War, the United States and France stood shoulder to shoulder as they stared down the Soviet menace. Sure, Charles de Gaulle could be prickly and pompous at times, but he remained a steadfast ally of America when the chips were down. And in the early 1990s, when Saddam Hussein invaded Kuwait, the French once again went bravely into battle alongside their American cousins.

Isn't that how the story goes? Deep down, underneath their berets and black turtlenecks, don't the French really love us?

Au contraire. This familiar and comforting narrative can be found in our history books. French politicians eager to advance their country's interests have nurtured it. American statesmen have been seduced by its charms. Yet this feature of our popular imagination is in fact a figment of our imagination. The tale of Franco-American harmony is a long-standing and pernicious myth. The French attitude toward the United

States consistently has been one of cultural suspicion and political dislike, bordering at times on raw hatred, as well as diplomatic friction that occasionally has erupted into violent hostility. France is not America's oldest ally, but its oldest enemy.

The true story of Franco-American relations begins many years before the American Revolution, during the French and Indian Wars. Lasting nearly a century, these conflicts pitted the French and their Indian comrades against seventeenth- and eighteenth-century American colonists. French military officers used massacres as weapons of imperial terror against the hardy men, women, and children who settled on the frontier. At the age of twenty-two, George Washington nearly fell victim to one of these brutal onslaughts and was reviled in France as a murderous villain for many years (an opinion sustained by French propaganda and reversed only when the American Revolution made it politically necessary). Amid this tumult, the first articulations of a recognizably American national consciousness came into being. Indeed, America's first authentic sense of self was born not in a revolt against Britain, but in a struggle with France.

Although the French provided American colonial rebels with crucial assistance during their bid for independence, direct French military intervention came only after the Americans had achieved a decisive victory on their own at Saratoga. The French crown regarded the principles of the Declaration of Independence as abhorrent and frightening. French aristocrats viewed Lafayette with contempt and branded him a criminal for traveling to America against King Louis XVI's explicit command. The king and his government overcame their revulsion to the young republic only because they sniffed an opportunity to weaken their ancient rival Britain. To be sure, France did become an ally to the colonists for a few years in the late 1770s and early 1780s when American sovereignty served French geopolitical aims. But then the French believed that double-dealing against their erstwhile friends after Yorktown served their interests as well. During the peace talks, France sought to limit American gains because it feared the new nation might become too powerful. If the

French had achieved all of their objectives in the Treaty of Paris in 1783, the United States today might be confined to a slender band of territory along the eastern seaboard, like a North American version of Chile.

In 1998, French defense minister Alain Richard declared that "France and the United States never fought each other."[8] This is manifestly untrue. Within a generation of Yorktown, French and American forces were exchanging deadly fire during the little-known Quasi-War of 1798–1800—during which France earned the dubious distinction of becoming the first military enemy of the United States following the ratification of the Constitution. Shortly before these hostilities, France supplied the United States with its first foreign subversive: French ambassador Edmond Charles Genet, better known as "Citizen Genet." In 1796, a Genet successor, Pierre Adet, meddled in the presidential election in a desperate but failed attempt to prevent John Adams from becoming commander-in-chief.

During the Napoleonic era, France posed a constant threat to the United States and its westward expansion. Napoleon himself longed to invade North America with a powerful army. He agreed to sell the Louisiana Territory only after suffering a military disaster in the Caribbean and hearing threats of war from Thomas Jefferson. The War of 1812 was very nearly fought against France rather than Britain, and the Monroe Doctrine was written with France clearly in mind. In the 1830s, Andrew Jackson came close to declaring war on France for its persistent refusal to make good on promised reparations for French naval crimes during Napoleon's reign.

Whenever French politicians want to generate feelings of goodwill among Americans, they invariably appeal to the memory of Lafayette and Yorktown. They neglect to mention the French role in the Civil War, when Napoleon's imperial nephew supported the South and incited disunion, carried out the first major transgression of the Monroe Doctrine, and engaged in what General Ulysses S. Grant considered acts of war against the United States.

In the twentieth century, France welcomed American help to end the First World War. During the subsequent peace negotiations, however, the French fought the United States over how to treat the vanquished Germans and conceive a postwar world. By rejecting the advice of Woodrow Wilson and insisting on crippling and humiliating reparations, France fatally undermined the fledgling German democracy and planted many of the seeds of the Second World War—a conflict for which the French required another American rescue. Before that liberation could occur, however, American troops landing in North Africa in 1942 encountered stiff resistance from the soldiers of Vichy France. The GIs literally had to fight their way through the French to get to the Nazis.

More than 60,000 Americans who gave their lives in these two world wars lie buried in French soil. Yet it was not long after the Second World War had ended that many in France forgot this sacrifice. Anti-Americanism metastasized as a whole generation of French intellectuals embraced the West's totalitarian enemy, the Soviet Union. During the Cold War, French misrule in its Southeast Asian colonies made Ho Chi Minh's Communist movement possible and set the stage for an American debacle. Indeed, if the French had followed the advice of Franklin Roosevelt and granted Vietnam its independence after World War II, the Vietnam War might not have been necessary, and today Vietnam might be a prospering democracy like South Korea.

During the presidency of Charles de Gaulle, France became the source of strife within the Western alliance as it undermined NATO and downplayed the Soviet threat—and even refused to rule out aiming its own nuclear missiles at the United States. In 1986, when the United States obtained positive proof that Libyan strongman Muammar Qaddafi was behind a fatal terrorist bombing in Berlin, the French rejected American requests to let U.S. warplanes fly through their airspace on a mission to retaliate against a sinister forerunner of Osama bin Laden and Saddam Hussein.

At times, Americans have reacted with passionate indignation at French hostility and intransigence. In the 1790s, during the infamous

XYZ Affair, the public was outraged when French officials demanded huge bribes from U.S. diplomats. In the 1960s, de Gaulle's shrill anti-American harangues and his dramatic decision to pull French troops from NATO resulted in boycotts of French products across the United States. Yet the myth of Franco-American friendship remains so tenacious that when each new generation of Americans encounters French enmity, it reacts with shock and disbelief.

The French themselves have harbored considerably fewer misapprehensions. "We are at war with America," declared François Mitterrand shortly before his death in 1996. "A permanent war . . . a war without death. They are very hard, the Americans—they are voracious. They want undivided power over the world."[9] Indeed, anti-Americanism has deep roots in France, especially among its political and intellectual elites. Fueled by an abiding belief in French superiority, this attitude at times has assumed odd shapes: As a diplomat in Paris in the 1780s, Thomas Jefferson tried to disabuse French thinkers of their strange insistence that North American animals were smaller and weaker than those native to Europe. More often, however, the French have sought to contrast their Old World refinements with what they have regarded as New World vulgarities. As French prime minister Georges Clemenceau put it, "America is the only nation in history which miraculously has gone directly from barbarism to degeneration without the usual interval of civilization."

Yet the French have been victims of their own illusion: a mirage of grandeur and entitlement based on the belief that because France was once a powerful nation, it should always be a powerful nation. This has produced a national character dominated by nostalgia for a glorious past that simply cannot be recovered. French national decline began in the middle of the eighteenth century and has progressed almost without interruption. The single exception came during the reign of Napoleon, when the French made an audacious and bloody bid for European dominance. Their failure has haunted them ever since. Time and again in the last two centuries, France has refused to come to grips with its diminished status as a country whose greatest general was a foreigner, whose greatest warrior was a teenage girl, and whose last great military victory came on the plains of Wagram in 1809. Instead, it projects a politics of chauvinism and resentment—with much of its animus aimed at the United States, a nation whose rise to prominence in global affairs presents almost a mirror image of French decline.

Indeed, the very word *chauvinism* derives from the life and attitude of the legendary Nicolas Chauvin, an officer in Napoleon's *Grande Armée* who was severely wounded seventeen times during his military service. Years after Waterloo, he refused to give up his fierce loyalty to his former general and the French dream of empire. In time, the French public made Chauvin's excessive patriotism an object of ridicule and derision. Plays satirized the disfigured ex-soldier and his undying loyalty to the imperial cause. Yet if the French had looked more closely at themselves, they would have seen that Chauvin was less of an eccentric than an exemplar. As French power and influence withered, the French public remained true to the alluring vision of a great and transcendent France—just like Napoleon's gallant soldier. Unfortunately, a foreign policy built on a fantasy is bound to stumble when it encounters hard realities. Much Franco-American friction over the last century and a half has come from the French reluctance to accept a new role in a democratic world order led by the United States.

But Americans, with all their own cultural insecurities, have more often than not chosen to overlook French arrogance and condescension, preferring instead to revel in France's considerable artistic and intellectual achievements. From Henry James's enthusiasm for the subtleties of French manners and conversation to the many African-American writers and musicians who found acceptance and creative inspiration in Paris's Montmartre and Montparnasse, Americans of taste and discernment have long been drawn to the rich cultural tradition of their European brethren. Even during moments of serious discord, Americans have refused to turn their backs on the great lights of French civilization. The Beaujolais Nouveau may be poured down the drain, but Rabelais, Balzac, and Camus remain on the shelves.

The French often disguise their contempt for America with false affection. In the fall of 2003, former prime minister Lionel Jospin paid the United States a typically backhanded compliment: "The French love America so much that they'd often like it to be different."[10] This is rather like saying that the French love apple pie so much they wish it were escargot. Although the French masses have welcomed American movies, music, and literature, French elites such as Jospin frequently display xenophobic suspicion of American cultural influences. Take the word *email*. In 2003, the French government banned it from official documents because of its American provenance. Writers are told instead to use a made-up word, *courriel*. Although the word *mail* actually entered the English language by way of the Norman invasion, the French seem to believe that Anglo-Saxon usage over the course of a millennium has corrupted it. The French have even allowed their cultural protectionism to assume violent forms. When a mob of vandals attacked a McDonald's restaurant in the south of France in 1999, Chirac applauded.

Throughout the recent differences over Iraq, the French have continued the charade of pretending that they are America's best friend—"its ally forever," as Chirac said in the wake of September 11.[11] But true friends and allies of the United States do not behave the way the French did. Despite the British public's misgivings about the wisdom of invading Iraq, Prime Minister Tony Blair acted with a solid appreciation of America's positive role in the world and a firm understanding of common values and mutual interests. Where Britain has transformed itself from an old enemy into a true ally, France has failed to do the same. Perhaps this is simply a reflection of French political experience. Historically dominated by a pendulum swinging between the extremes of right and left—the very concepts of "Right" and "Left" come from the French Revolution—modern France simply has not developed a sufficiently deep foundation in liberal democracy that would lead it to believe, along with the United States and Britain, that a successful foreign policy can be based on common ideals. The hypernationalist French continue to jockey for global supremacy much as they did three hundred years ago. And while it is no sin for a government to pursue a foreign policy of national interest—all nations owe this to their citizens—the French have failed to realize that the United States does not pose and, in fact, never has posed a threat to their country. In the words of the French novelist and critic Alphonse Karr: *Plus ça change, plus c'est la même chose.* The more things change, the more they stay the same.

ONE

OLD FRANCE IN THE NEW WORLD

Who can tell what sorrows pierced our souls?
—Reverend John Williams [1]

THE PEOPLE OF Deerfield, Massachusetts, didn't know what danger lurked just outside their little village before dawn on February 29, 1704. Yet dozens of them had only hours to live. For most of the rest, it would be the worst day they would ever witness.

They certainly weren't blind to the risks of residing in the wilderness of western Massachusetts. At the start of the eighteenth century, Deerfield sat precariously on the edge of the American frontier. Many of its residents lived within the walls of a small fort, and even more crowded in each night. Patrols checked the surrounding countryside. A night watchman kept vigil. There was a good reason for these precautions: The previous summer, French and Indian raiders had destroyed the village of Wells, Maine, as well as a few smaller outposts. In October, Indians allied with the French had captured a pair of men from Deerfield itself. [2]

Winter was supposed to be a season of relative calm, with the bitter cold and three feet of snow providing a blanket of security found at no other time of year. The people of Deerfield probably had gone to bed the night before thinking they would wake up to a chilly morning like any other, except for the trivial fact that it would be a leap-year day. Yet somewhere in the darkness, between two hundred and three hundred French and Indian marauders were descending upon the town. Led by Sieur Hertel de Rouville, they had braved the severe conditions, trudging 300 miles south from Canada on snowshoes, to spread terror among the American colonists and capture hostages who might be exchanged for French prisoners.

As the sun disappeared on February 28, the French and Indian expedition halted a mile or two north of Deerfield and began to probe the little town. Throughout the night, scouts crossed the frozen Connecticut River and observed their unsuspecting target. A little after midnight, one of them returned to the camp and informed his companions that a watchman was making his rounds. A few hours later, however, a second reconnaissance found no trace of him. The man apparently had nodded off. At about four o'clock, the attackers approached the sleeping hamlet.

The harsh weather that had hampered their progress from New France now became a friend to the French and Indians. Drifts of snow pressing against the walls of the fort created ramps that allowed a few to clamber over the twelve-foot-tall barriers. Once inside, they opened the main doors of the fort for their comrades. The killing was about to begin.

As bloodcurdling war whoops echoed through the cold air, attackers burst into the home of the Reverend John Williams, the village's most prominent citizen. He had been marked for capture, not death. Two of his young children, however, were not as fortunate: John junior, age six, and Jerusha, a six-week-old baby who could not even hold up his head, were murdered before his eyes. The children's nursemaid, a black servant named Parthena, was also slaughtered.

Outside, a massacre raged. In all, seventeen homes were put to the torch. One family of five suffocated in their cellar as a fire burned above them. The inhabitants of another dwelling, the brick home of Benobi Stebbins and his family, put up a fierce resistance. For several hours, French and Indians laid siege to it, but their numbers dwindled as members of their party quit the fort to lead captives away. At about nine in the morning, reinforcements from the nearby towns of Hadley and Hatfield managed to push the attackers beyond the walls of Deerfield only to break off their pursuit when they clashed with a larger French and Indian force that already had left the village.

When the men returned to the smoldering town, they surveyed the magnitude of the disaster. Nearly 300 people had gone to sleep in the village the night before, but only 133 remained. Forty-four residents had been killed, including ten men, nine women, and twenty-five children. Five soldiers garrisoned at the fort lost their lives, as well as seven men from Hadley and Hatfield, for a total of fifty-six fatalities. Another 109 people had been herded off as captives.[3]

The French and Indians had displayed enormous cruelty in deciding whom to kill and whom to capture. Children age two and under were slain at an exceptionally high rate and those between three and twelve at a somewhat lower one, while all of the older children survived.[4] It seems the French and Indians were making judgments about which villagers would be able endure a forced march through the wintertime wilderness to Canada and which might slow them down. They had designated the weakest and most vulnerable members of the Deerfield community for death—and they did not think twice about slaughtering infants. Leaving the little ones behind for others to rescue does not seem to have entered their thinking.

Many of the captives faced a similarly grim fate. In the first three days of the march, the French and Indians killed nine of their prisoners, including "a suckling child" and three elderly women.[5] One of the victims was Eunice Williams, the minister's wife. During the trek, she fell into a river and injured herself, thus becoming a liability to the raiders. "The cruel and bloodthirsty savage who took her slew her with his hatchet at one stroke," wrote her husband of the incident. Her body was abandoned, leaving the Reverend Williams to pray that somehow "she might meet with a Christian burial and not be left for meat to the fowls of the air and beasts of the earth."[6] (His wish was granted: Searchers recovered her body a few days later and buried it in the Deerfield graveyard.)

In all, some twenty-one captives perished during the journey north. One of them was the pregnant Mary Brooks, murdered after she slipped on the ice and miscarried her child. Another was a four-year-old girl, whose Indian porter had struggled under the weight in the deep snow and decided his pack was more important than the child. By the middle of April, a full six weeks later, the survivors at last reached New France.

Over the next forty months, the governor of Massachusetts, William Dudley, pleaded with his counterpart in New France, the Marquis de Vaudreuil, to release the captives. Most were let go after more than a year in Canada, although twenty-nine of the youngest members never returned because the French had successfully convinced (or coerced) them to join their community and convert to Catholicism. John Williams was one of the last to be released. Vaudreuil considered him the most valuable captive, and would exchange him only for Jean Baptiste, a notorious French pirate confined to a Boston jail. At first Dudley refused to give up this dangerous criminal, but as the months dragged on, he finally relented. By the beginning of 1707, the widower Williams was back home in Deerfield, almost three years after he had been forced to leave at gunpoint.

But the French had not yet had their fill of bloodshed—and New England would not know peace for many decades. The year after Williams returned, violence again visited the recovering village when Indians allied with the French captured one resident and killed a Hatfield man. In April 1709, they seized another from Deerfield. Two months later, some 140 French and Indians attacked the town once more. This time, however, sentries raised an alarm and succeeded in hustling most of the locals into the fort. Two people were killed and another pair captured, but Deerfield survived.

The Deerfield Massacre was merely an episode in what the colonists would collectively refer to as the French Wars—a series of brutal conflicts that eventually came to be known as the French and Indian Wars. There were four of them in all—King William's War (1689 to 1697), Queen Anne's War (1702 to 1713), King George's War

(1744 to 1748), and the eponymous one known as *the* French and Indian War (1754 to 1760). Each was part of a larger imperial struggle between Britain and France, with American colonists bearing the brunt of the violence. Only the last of these conflicts proved decisive in toppling the New World empire France had been trying to build for more than two centuries. It also set in motion many of the resentments and jealousies that would animate French attitudes toward Americans in the years to come.

Like the British, the French were latecomers to the Western Hemisphere. Spain had already conquered the Aztecs in Mexico and was well on its way to subduing the Incas in Peru when King Francis I decided that his country needed to make its own claims in the New World. In the 1530s, he commissioned Jacques Cartier to search for gold in faraway lands. An intrepid navigator, Cartier explored the Gulf of St. Lawrence. Although he found no treasure, he did raise a thirty-foot-tall cross bearing the fleur-de-lis at Gaspé. This action served as the initial basis for French territorial claims in North America. Later Cartier ascended the St. Lawrence River to the site of modern-day Montreal. One day, he came upon an encampment the natives called Canada. An effort to start a colony failed, and Canada—as the entire region came to be known—would remain virtually untouched by Europeans until the first part of the seventeenth century.

In 1608, Samuel de Champlain founded the city of Quebec. A man of common birth, he was a remarkable leader who formed alliances with local Indian tribes, raided others, and began to establish the fur-trading networks that would come to dominate life in New France. With the exception of Catholic missionaries devoted to the conversion of natives, almost everyone participated in this industry. Population growth already was impaired by the severe winters, but fur trading made it even more difficult because it drew men away from the farms that formed the backbone of any seventeenth-century community. France compounded the problem by both failing to invest significant financial resources in Canada and banning Protestant settlement. In time, French colonists came to rely heavily on the goodwill of local Indians. Intermarriage was common. A hundred years after Champlain's arrival, immigration had dwindled to the point where the majority of French people in New France had been born in North America.

Despite its drawbacks, fur trading did encourage the exploration of an unknown continent. In the 1660s and 1670s, Father Jacques Marquette traveled extensively in the Great Lakes region and eventually made his way to the Mississippi River. In 1682, Robert La Salle became the first European to descend the Mississippi to the Gulf of Mexico, claiming all the lands whose waters flowed into the huge river for Louis XIV and giving them a name that stuck: Louisiana. Within a generation, France was sending colonists to the area, where they traded in furs or started indigo plantations. By the 1720s, the city of New Orleans had been founded and became the capital of the province.

New France now formed an enormous crescent from the mouth of the St. Lawrence to the delta of the Mississippi. With so few people, it was no economic powerhouse. Yet the government in Paris recognized its geopolitical importance. Along the eastern seaboard of North America, the British had founded a string of thriving colonies, which France was determined to keep from expanding west of the Appalachians. It would be a difficult task. By the 1750s, there were a mere 55,000 colonists living in New France, compared to the 1.3 million colonists and 300,000 slaves in British North America.

What the French lacked in population, however, they tried to compensate for in good tribal relations. Indians formed alliances with both French and British colonists, but a clear majority of those who fought in the French and Indian Wars did so on the side of the French. This gave France a distinct advantage in the guerrilla combat of an untamed continent. It also forced tremendous suffering upon British colonists who were trying to create a new life in the New World. Indians aligned with the French were responsible for the vast majority of raids and massacres against North American settlers. To be sure, the British did not have entirely clean hands when it came to Indian atrocities, but their crimes simply did not compare with what France was willing to tolerate in its name. The French were far more effective at exploiting and directing Indian violence.

From this bloodshed, it is possible to glean the beginnings of an American national identity forged in opposition to the constant threat from New France. As the distinguished twentieth-century historian Crane Brinton observed in the late 1960s: "For New Englanders and New Yorkers the existence of a French menace on their northern borders was for years a very real thing, more real than any acute danger from a foreign power was to seem to Americans until the Russians acquired their own atomic bomb."[7] The French and Indian Wars were not merely a series of British efforts to defeat an imperial adversary—they were a set of joint American efforts to defend against a common foe. The famously fractious colonists demonstrated an ability to band together during times of trouble. During Queen Anne's War, as French and Indian raiders plundered Deerfield, Connecticut sent troops into Massachusetts. Such cooperation became a routine practice during the eighteenth century and played a crucial role in persuading the colonists that they shared common interests.

Although these early Americans did not create a formal union until later in the century, they began to think about it seriously for the first time during the French and Indian Wars. At the Albany Congress of 1754, when representatives from seven colonies gathered to discuss increased cooperation, Benjamin Franklin observed that their "disunited state" actually encouraged French aggression. The French, said Franklin, "presume that they may with impunity . . . kill, seize and imprison our traders, and confiscate their effects at pleasure (as they have done for several years past), murder and scalp our farmers, with their wives and children, and take an easy possession of such parts of the British territory as they find most convenient for them."[8]

Franklin issued his warning at the dawn of the fourth, final, and decisive French and Indian War. While the first three had erupted in Europe before making their way to America, this new war would be different. Starting in the New World, it quickly expanded into a global conflict. It was triggered by a young Virginian who unwittingly put his name to a document that had him admitting to a monstrous act in the forests of Pennsylvania. His name was George Washington.

Late in the evening of July 3, 1754, the man who would become one of his country's greatest generals found himself staring at surrender documents handwritten by his French enemies. Unable to speak or read French, he certainly did not understand their precise meaning. He could barely even see them in the flickering candlelight of Fort Necessity. What he did know, however, was that French soldiers surrounded his tiny stockade and outnumbered his troops. They had battled all day. By nightfall, about a third of Washington's men were dead or unable to fight. The rest were exhausted. Ammunition was running low and food was scarce.

Things would soon get worse. When Washington reluctantly agreed to discuss surrender terms, the French commander, Captain Louis Coulon de Villiers, sent a formal proposal across the lines in the hands of Washington's own courier. There was also an unwritten message from Villiers: Indian reinforcements were on the way, and the French refused any responsibility for their behavior in the event of Fort Necessity's capture by force. This was a less-than-subtle way of informing Washington that if he failed to sign the surrender, Villiers would step aside and permit the Virginian and his men to be massacred.

Just a few months earlier, Robert Dinwiddie, the governor of Virginia, had recruited the twenty-two-year-old Washington to lead a company of soldiers into the Ohio River valley. Although Washington's youth made him an unconventional choice, the governor must have perceived the young man's extraordinary potential. A tall and gallant figure full of ambition and self-confidence, he appeared to have the brightest of futures. Perhaps more important, he also knew the area, having scouted it for Dinwiddie the previous fall. In any event, Washington's mission was critical. Colonists in Virginia and elsewhere wanted room to expand. France had its own designs on the

Ohio River valley. A clash was inevitable—and Washington boasted that he would drive the French all the way to Montreal.

His orders were to occupy a position at the fork of the Ohio River, where Pittsburgh now stands. On his way there, however, Washington encountered a party of Virginians whom Dinwiddie had sent ahead to begin the construction of a fort. A large group of French soldiers had chased them off and begun building their own fort—called Fort Duquesne—at the river junction. This was exactly the sort of French military activity Washington was supposed to prevent.

Washington stationed his men at Great Meadows—"a charming field for an encounter," as he described it—about sixty-five miles southeast of the new French fort.[9] In late May, he received reports of French soldiers camped in a hollow just a few miles from his position. Why were they hiding off the main trails? Why hadn't they tried to make contact with him? Washington grew suspicious. He assembled forty of his men and marched them through a rainy night, under the guidance of Indians, to a place that would become known as Jumonville's Glen.

Exactly what happened there on the morning of May 28 is a matter of some controversy. It's clear that the French were caught by surprise. They had posted no sentries, and Washington approached them as they awoke. Someone squeezed off a shot. Washington maintained that it came from the French, who raised alarms and grabbed their weapons as they saw him draw near. The French insisted that they had been ambushed and merely returned fire. Whatever the case, the immediate result is not in dispute: Washington and his men poured two deadly volleys upon their adversaries, reducing the French detachment of about thirty-five soldiers by fourteen while suffering only four casualties of their own. One of the dead was the commander, Joseph Coulon de Villiers de Jumonville, the younger brother of Louis. By Washington's own estimate, the skirmish lasted about fifteen minutes. "I heard the bullets whistle and, believe me, there is something charming in the sound," wrote Washington—perhaps a bit too easily charmed—in a letter to his brother.[10]

After their surrender, the surviving French soldiers claimed to be on a mission of peace. Their only aim, they insisted, had been to warn Washington and his troops to leave French territory. Although Jumonville's body carried documents that appeared to confirm this story, Washington remained skeptical because the French had chosen to hide in a remote area rather than head straight for his camp.

The tense situation became even more complicated when Tanaghrisson, an Indian leader who had led Washington to the glen, scalped Jumonville in plain view of everyone. As if acting on cue, Tanaghrisson's men then set upon the French wounded, killing all but one. Washington was helpless to stop the slaughter, though he did succeed in hustling away his twenty-one captives as the Indians began to mutilate the bodies that were left behind. One Frenchman did manage to escape. He had slipped away during the firefight and headed straight to Fort Duquesne, where he reported his harrowing story to Louis Coulon de Villiers.

After the engagement, Washington returned to Great Meadows and built a circular fort of split logs, which he believed could hold off as many as five hundred attackers.[11] Named Fort Necessity, it was about fifty feet in diameter and could accommodate only a small portion of the three hundred men under Washington's command. Its primary purpose was to store food and ammunition. During a battle, most of his soldiers would have to crouch in shallow ditches surrounding the stockade.

Toward the end of June, Washington learned that more than a thousand French and Indians under the command of Villiers had departed Fort Duquesne. On the morning of July 3, they arrived at Great Meadows. The fighting began almost immediately. As casualties mounted, Fort Necessity's many weaknesses became apparent. A rainstorm flooded the trenches, and Washington's men struggled to stay afloat amid streams of water mixed with blood. Yet they put up a spirited fight during the daylight hours. The kegs of rum inside the fort undoubtedly played their part.

When night fell, the French offered to discuss terms, and Washington sent one of his men to the enemy lines. The temporary truce gave Washington a chance to stretch his six-foot-four frame and survey the scene. For all their pluck, his troops had taken a severe beating. Further resistance would only lead to more killing and delay the inevitable defeat. The situation was worse than Washington probably realized: For all of the punishment his own men had taken—thirty dead, seventy wounded—they had killed only three Frenchmen.[12]

Villiers' surrender terms, by themselves, were generous. Washington and his men would be allowed to depart the next day with their personal belongings, including their weapons. They simply had to release their French prisoners, promise not to return to the region for a year, and provide two of their own officers as hostages. There was one further condition, which appeared to be a formality: Washington would have to put his name on a piece of paper agreeing to the arrangement.

Only a handful of Washington's men spoke any French at all. They grasped the general meaning of the surrender terms, but the document had been written so hastily that it was difficult even for fully literate readers to decipher it. To make matters worse, Washington and his men felt the intense pressure of an ominous threat. They must have believed that the alternative to signing was death—and perhaps death of an especially brutal nature.

And so on July 4, 1754, Washington signed the document and led his tired troops back to Virginia. The triumphant French promptly destroyed Fort Necessity and left Great Meadows, delighted to have ousted their foes from the newest part of New France—and also to have in their possession a propaganda tool of enormous value, for the capitulation agreement held Washington personally responsible for the "assassination" of Jumonville. In short, it had him admitting to the cold-blooded murder of a diplomat operating under a flag of truce.

Later on, Washington would deny that the word *assassination* had ever crossed the lips of his translators. He recalled being told only that the passage in question referred to the "death or the loss of" Jumonville. When Washington's supposed confession became known across the ocean, however, these fine points were not part of a story that would bedevil him at home and abroad for many years. All across France, Washington's supposed crime aroused French patriotism for the coming war with Britain. "The assassination of Jumonville is a monument of perfidy that ought to enrage eternity," declared one French poet. "Every moment should be utilized for perpetuating its memory; and, since for the human race there is no tribunal where one can summon culpable nations, at least let posterity, recognizing that fact, set a stamp of disgrace on them, and let the fear of infamy at least checkmate them."[13] An Englishman commented that Washington had approved papers that "were the most infamous a British subject ever put his hand to."[14] Many of Washington's fellow colonists, however, were more sympathetic, believing that he had done as well as any commander might have under the circumstances. There was also some feeling that he had been the victim of French trickery and bullying. Villiers admitted as much in a later statement: "We made them consent to sign that they had assassinated my brother in his camp."[15] Twenty years later, the French would revise their negative appraisal of Washington when it became expedient for them to do so. During the American Revolution, they would celebrate him as a nationalist hero.

The episodes at Jumonville's Glen and Fort Necessity sparked the final French and Indian War—known in Europe as the Seven Years' War. In addition to North America, fighting raged across Europe, the Indian subcontinent, and the Caribbean. The conflict was probably unavoidable, given the old rivalry between Britain and France, plus a tangle of messy alliances with other powers. "Such was the complication of political interests that a cannon shot fired in America could give the signal that set Europe in a blaze," commented Voltaire, evidently unaware that no cannons were used at either Jumonville's Glen or Fort Necessity in 1754.[16] Although wrong on the specifics, he was correct on the big picture: A small battle on the frontier of two empires had ignited a worldwide conflagration pitting Britain, Hanover, and Prussia against France, Austria, Russia, Saxony, Spain, and Sweden. In the end, the war would go as poorly for the French as the skirmish at Fort

Necessity had gone for Washington. Before it was over, however, Villiers' gruesome threat of Indian violence at Great Meadows would prove to be more than idle words.

In 1757, at the southern end of Lake George in New York, Fort William Henry guarded the northern entrance to the Hudson River valley. If invaders from New France were to force their way past the fort and on to Fort Edward a few miles away, nothing would stand between them and Albany. Below Albany lay an even bigger prize: New York City.

The ordeal of Fort William Henry started much as the Deerfield Massacre had half a century earlier, with a large body of French and Indians using the cloak of winter to head south and surprise a foe. Yet the 1,600 raiders who crossed a frozen Lake George were a far more formidable force than the one that had attacked Deerfield. The defenses were stronger as well, with 350 troops manning a fort built to survive an assault or a siege long enough for reinforcements to arrive.

When the French attackers appeared in March, one of them, François Le Mercier, delivered a frightening message to the fort's defenders: If the men inside resisted, "the Cruelties of the Savages cou'd not altogether be prevented."[17] Threatening barbaric slaughter had become standard operating procedure for the French. In a world of muskets and swords, Indian massacres were not merely instruments of terror—they were weapons of mass destruction capable of inflicting catastrophic damage on large numbers of helpless victims. And the French were not above using them for purposes of blackmail. "Nothing," declared the governor-general of New France, "is more calculated to disgust the people of those Colonies and to make them desire the return of peace."[18]

Despite such a horrible threat, the defenders of Fort William Henry chose to stand and fight. Perhaps they recalled the fate of Fort Oswego. Less than a year earlier, the Marquis de Montcalm had surrounded this stronghold on the shores of Lake Ontario, in New York, with a mixed force of professional French infantry, French Canadian militia, and Indian allies. The fort was still under construction, and its defenders were outnumbered by nearly three to one. When an opening cannon shot decapitated Oswego's commanding officer, the troops lost all hope and surrendered. Ever attentive to the military etiquette that ruled his life as a soldier in Europe, Montcalm determined that their resistance had been too brief to warrant generous surrender terms. Rather than allowing the men of Oswego to march away with their colors, as Villiers had permitted Washington to do at Fort Necessity, Montcalm decided to make them his prisoners of war. According to the strict code of conduct that Montcalm professed to uphold, this meant that he would be responsible for their safety. His Indian compatriots, however, had different plans. Greedy for the spoils of victory, they ransacked a hospital, seized captives, and scalped the wounded—as many as a hundred soldiers and civilians were murdered. Ashamed of what he had allowed to happen, Montcalm arranged ransoms for many of the captives, though he neglected to mention the incident in his official report to France's minister of war. Such an event, however, could not be whitewashed from the memories of those who witnessed it. The massacre left a permanent stain on Montcalm's reputation and blackened the American assessment of French military honor.

After Oswego, the troops at Fort William Henry knew there were no guarantees. Luckily for them, their attackers lacked cannons. Without artillery, any assault was bound to fail—as this one did after only four days. Yet the French and Indians did succeed in destroying all of the fort's outbuildings as well as a sloop that would have been critical to its defenses once the lake cleared of ice. Thus, they laid the foundation of a more vigorous effort in warmer weather.

In the spring, Lieutenant Colonel George Monro assumed command at Fort William Henry. By June, he had 1,500 men under his command—a sizable force, but puny compared to the 8,000 French and Indians that Montcalm had assembled at Fort Carillon (now Ticonderoga), which sat between the north end of Lake George and Lake Champlain. On July 23, a large squad of soldiers sent from Fort William Henry to burn French sawmills met with disaster when a group of Montcalm's Indians surprised them and captured some 200 soldiers. "The rum which was in the barges and which the Indians immediately drank caused them to commit great cruelties," wrote Montcalm's aide-de-camp, Louis-Antoine de Bougainville. "They put in the pot and ate three prisoners, and perhaps others were so treated."[19]

Bougainville was a brilliant man of high culture and intellectual distinction. Before traveling to the New World, he had written a book on calculus. After the war, he went on to fame as the first Frenchman to circumnavigate the globe. (The flowering bougainvillea plant and the largest of the Solomon Islands, in the Pacific Ocean, are named for him.) In a letter, the amateur ethnographer described the indigenous allies his general was gathering for a renewed assault on Fort William Henry: "Indians, naked, black, red, howling, bellowing, dancing, singing the war song, getting drunk, yelling for 'broth,' that is to say, blood, drawn from 500 leagues away by the smell of fresh human blood and the chance to teach their young men how one carves up a human being destined for the pot. Behold our comrades who, night and day, are our shadows. I shiver at the frightful spectacles which they are preparing for us."[20]

Indeed, Bougainville understood what it meant to make war with Indian allies. Here is how he put it in a letter to his godmother, sent just before Montcalm ordered his army south:

> Your son shudders with horror at what he is going to be forced to witness. It is with great difficulty that we can restrain the Indians of the far west, the most ferocious of all men and cannibals by trade. Listen to what the chiefs came to tell M. de Montcalm three days ago: "Father, don't expect that we can easily give quarter to the English. We have some young warriors who have not yet drunk of this broth. Raw flesh has led them here from the ends of the earth; they must learn to wield the knife and to bury it in English hearts." Behold our comrades, dear mama; what a crew, what a spectacle for civilized man.[21]

For all of his private outpourings of disgust, the cultured Bougainville never shrank from the actual practice of unleashing Indian massacres upon British soldiers and American colonists. He may not have enjoyed it, but he was willing to overlook the carnage so long as it served French interests. In Bougainville's view, North America was a hopeless moral cesspool to be shunned rather than confronted and reformed: "The air one breathes here is contagious," he said of North America, "and I fear lest a long sojourn here makes us acquire the vices of a people to whom we communicate no virtues."[22]

So much for the French Enlightenment's idealization of the Indian as a noble savage whose pristine innocence was contrasted with the stifling morality and corrupt civilization of Europe. The experience of North America should have taught the French that Rousseau's ideas about human nature and social cohesion were fundamentally flawed. Although he never met a savage, noble or otherwise, Rousseau nonetheless felt confident in making audacious claims about mankind's inborn goodness and perfectibility—opinions based more on wishful thinking and fantasy than on firsthand observation. As a well-educated French officer in North America, Bougainville was uniquely positioned to rebut these sweeping assertions. He was certainly aware of the sensation his contemporary was causing in France with his enticing visions of utopia. Bougainville also had more direct knowledge of human behavior in a state of nature than virtually any other member of Rousseau's nodding readership. It might even be said that he was the leading French authority on the subject. Had he challenged Rousseau, Bougainville would have performed an enormous service to European thought.

Yet such was the radical and flawed nature of the French Enlightenment that its disciples tended to deny or overlook the stubborn persistence of natural facts, especially those involving human nature. (By contrast, the American revolutionaries would find greater use for the more pragmatic and conservative political thought of Britain.) The failure to reconcile bad theories with undeniable realities would prove to be an enduring theme in French culture. In the centuries ahead, it would surface numerous times, beginning with the French Revolution a generation hence, and always with devastating effect. It would reverberate outside France as well: One of Rousseau's lasting legacies may be found in the twisted utopianism of twentieth-century Communism.

On the night of August 2, lookouts at Fort William Henry spotted large campfires several miles to the north. The next morning, they watched as several hundred boats and canoes maneuvered down the lake toward its southern shore. This time, the French and Indians had brought cannons with them. An advance party took positions around the fort, cut off the road to Fort Edward, and fired the first musket shots at the defenders. The siege was on.

At three o'clock, Montcalm sent a messenger to Monro demanding an immediate surrender. Once again, a French commander used the presence of his Indian allies as a tool of terror. "I have it yet in my power to restrain the Indians . . . which will not be in my power . . . if you insist on defending your fort," wrote Montcalm.[23] He was apparently humiliated by the massacre at Oswego—but not so humiliated that he would refuse to put his new opponents at similar risk.

Monro replied that he would not give up. His situation was difficult but not impossible. His fort contained adequate ammunition and artillery. He also hoped for reinforcements from nearby Fort Edward and immediately sent messages pleading for relief. Yet the commander at Fort Edward refused to diminish his own defenses, which presented the only other obstacle between Montcalm and Albany. Fort William Henry was on its own. Monro would not know it for some time, because the enemy was intercepting his communications.

Over the next several days, the French gradually moved their cannons into position around the fort, launching shots over the ramparts and inching their weapons closer to the walls. On August 6, a French cannonball knocked down the fort's flagstaff—an act that both invigorated the attackers and disheartened the defenders. Meanwhile, the fort's own artillery was failing at an alarming rate. By August 7, the cannons had suffered such severe metal fatigue from heavy use that they had all exploded. As ammunition dwindled and the bombardment continued, Monro met with his officers. They agreed that they had only one option: surrender.

Terms were reached on August 9, and they seemed favorable: Monro and his soldiers would be allowed to march off to Fort Edward with their personal belongings and small arms under French escort. In exchange, they would agree not to fight for eighteen months. The wounded would stay behind under French care until they were able to travel to Fort Edward. The French would take possession of the fort and its provisions, and all French prisoners would be released. It was a very good and honorable deal for Monro and his troops—though Montcalm had little choice. His own supplies were running low, and he could not take on the added burden of feeding many prisoners.

Within hours of the formal capitulation, however, the French once again failed to control the bloodlust of their indigenous allies. The Indians had not been consulted about the surrender terms, and they still expected to bring home treasure and scalps as testaments to their personal bravery. Around three o'clock on the afternoon of August 9, shortly after the last of Monro's healthy troops had left the fort, a group of Indians attacked some seventy wounded and sick soldiers who had been left behind. Although the French intervened and saved some lives, an unknown number were lost.

After the killing inside the fort, the Indians turned their attention to the soldiers camped outside. There, they forced frightened captives to hand over arms and equipment, threatening violence against those who disobeyed. When night descended, Monro's men were probably as nervous about their fates as they had been at any point during the bombardment.

At dawn, just as the march to Fort Edward under French escort was set to begin, the Indians returned with renewed demands for booty. They started grabbing women and children from the back of the line, hoping to keep them as captives. They also set upon the wounded in a mad scramble for scalps. Within seconds, the camp descended into anarchy. Soldiers and civilians escaped into the forest, clung to each other in desperation, or begged French soldiers to intervene. According to several accounts, the French did nothing to stop the bloodbath. French officers merely advised the able-bodied to flee into the woods. In a piece of verse that failed to make him famous as a poet, survivor Captain Richard Saltonstall captured the sheer horror of the event:

> *See discompos'd the naked flying troops!*
> *Seek asylum in woods and miry swamps*
> *On bended knees implore the Gallic aid*
> *Remind them of their honor—but in vain!*[24]

At some point during the killing spree, Montcalm and other top officers tried to take control. But by freeing several of the hostages, they actually made matters worse: Because most Indians valued captives above scalps, and because they feared that Montcalm was going to deprive them of these prizes, they decided that scalps were better than nothing. When order was finally restored, as many as 185 soldiers were dead and 500 found themselves under the control of Indians. Once again, the slaughter distressed Montcalm, though his official report of the incident lacks the grisly details found in so many eyewitness accounts: "I cannot conceal from you that the capitulation has unfortunately suffered some infraction on the part of the Indians. But what would be an infraction in Europe cannot be so regarded in America."[25] Here perhaps was an early intimation of the moral and cultural relativism that would become the hallmark of French postmodernism in the twentieth century. Montcalm's aide Bougainville, who had predicted a massacre before their war party even left New France, was more candid: "Would you believe that this abominable action of the Indians at Fort William Henry had accomplices among those people who call themselves Frenchmen; that greed, and the certainty of getting all their plunder from the Indians at a low price are the primary causes of a horror for which England will not fail to reproach us for a long time?"[26]

The tragedy of Fort William Henry did not end when the killing stopped. Montcalm and other French officials made efforts to purchase prisoners from the Indians and repatriate them to New England, but some 200 never returned. Ironically, many of the victims had been infected with smallpox and the Indians who hoarded their scalps became the unwitting carriers of a deadly disease that would ravage their tribes.

The good news, at least for the American colonists, was that Montcalm did not advance beyond Fort William Henry. Most of his Indian allies were eager to return home with their loot and trophies and had simply quit his command following the massacre. Moreover, Montcalm's provisions were in short supply. Finally, thousands of militiamen from New England had been mobilized. Although too late to save Fort William Henry, they would have thwarted any march Montcalm might have made on Fort Edward.

The fall of Fort William Henry—the central event of James Fenimore Cooper's novel *The Last of the Mohicans* (1826)—was perhaps the military high-water mark of New France. In its wake, the French suffered a string of defeats in North America. In 1758, Louisbourg fell. The following year, the British captured Quebec in an epic battle that saw Montcalm die on the Plains of Abraham. Montreal capitulated in 1760. From a practical standpoint, New France was finished.

The formal end came in 1763, at the Treaty of Paris. France signed away territory in Europe as well as the bulk of its overseas empire in India and the Caribbean. Canada became a part of the British Empire, and Louisiana passed into the hands of Spain.[27] (France would reclaim it for a short time almost forty years later.) All that was left of the huge territory once controlled by France was a pair of small islands off the coast of Newfoundland called St. Pierre and Miquelon. Two centuries later, these tiny bastions of France's faded grandeur would spark a new controversy between the French and the Americans during the Second World War.

In Voltaire's *Candide*, the French and Indian War is derided as a struggle over "a few acres of snow." France, of course, had lost far more.

The dispossession of so much territory meant that France was no longer a power of the first order and that Britain was now the world's supreme colonial and maritime force. Despite Voltaire's best rhetorical efforts, the French could not pretend to ignore their defeat for long. The indignity of such an embarrassing rout would haunt them for generations and further embitter them against those who had inflicted it upon them. In the decades ahead, there would be feverish plans, driven by envy and greed, to regain their lost North American empire. Before they materialized, however, the French would be presented with an unexpected opportunity to deliver a blow to their hated rivals across the Channel. It would require them to suffer all manner of silly and subversive talk about freedom and democracy—but such was the price of revenge.

TWO

REVOLTING ALLY

We do not desire that a new republic shall arise . . . [and] become
the exclusive mistress of this immense continent.
—Count de Vergennes, French foreign minister [1]

A DARK FEAR CROSSED Benjamin Franklin's mind as a horseman blazed into his courtyard on the outskirts of Paris late in the morning of December 4, 1777. "Sir," blurted Franklin before the rider could say anything, "is Philadelphia taken?"

"Yes, sir," came the reply.

In that brief moment, all must have seemed lost to Franklin: The capital of his young country occupied by the enemy and the dreams of a new nation dashed less than a year and a half after declaring its independence. "But sir," added the rider, "I have greater news than that. General Burgoyne and his whole army are prisoners of war!"[2]

This was a great development indeed—just the sort of news that Franklin had become desperate to hear. Since arriving as a diplomat in France almost a year earlier, Franklin had engaged all of his considerable talents of persuasion trying to convince his hosts to take up arms for the American republic. Indeed, the canny French foreign minister, Charles Gravier de Vergennes, had been intrigued by the idea for some time. Here was a chance to deliver a smashing blow to Britain, a nation Vergennes thoroughly despised. "She is an enemy at once grasping, ambitious, unjust, and perfidious," he once wrote.

"The invariable and most cherished purpose in her politics has been, if not the destruction of France at least her overthrow, her humiliation, and her ruin."[3]

To be sure, Vergennes had no special affection for Franklin or the democratic values he represented, and neither did the French court. The idea of colonial rebellion dismayed King Louis XVI because of its potential to undermine royal authority everywhere, including France. His Majesty also failed to understand why so many Parisians swooned over the charming American and his rustic habit of wearing a fur cap on chilly days. The powder-headed Louis was so annoyed by the American ambassador's popularity among aristocratic ladies that he once gave a duchess a small portrait of Franklin—affixed to the bottom of a chamber pot.

As his country's top foreign policy official, Vergennes had no time to indulge the prankish humor of a twenty-something monarch. He remained focused on finding ways to stymie the British—and if that meant temporarily aiding an upstart little republic, then so be it. For now, however, direct military intervention was out of the question until he saw hard proof that the Americans were a good bet for success. Before the battle of Saratoga, that evidence was lacking, and Vergennes had studiously avoided the celebrated Monsieur Franklin. The resounding rebel triumph at Saratoga in the autumn of 1777, however, changed everything. It marked the true turning point of the American Revolution—and provided the French with an opportunity to catapult themselves back into the power struggles of the New World.

These years also gave birth to the enduring myth of Franco-American solidarity—a sentimental view grounded in the memory of French military assistance during the Revolutionary War and symbolized by the idealistic participation of the Marquis de Lafayette. When U.S. general John J. Pershing arrived in France during the First World War, he was said to have declared, "Lafayette, we are here!"— as if the United States were finally repaying a long-overdue debt. (The statement is apocryphal.) And while French aid was a tremendous help to the rebellious colonists, especially at Yorktown, much of it was also grudging, sporadic, and undercut by the incompetence and vanity of French commanders.

In the summer of 1777, British general John Burgoyne had set out from Canada with 8,000 troops along the same path Montcalm had followed twenty years earlier on his way to Fort William Henry. The ambitious Burgoyne—nicknamed "General Swagger" by Horace Walpole—envisioned a grand and decisive stroke against the Americans. Before the year was out, he intended to seize control of the Hudson River, split the colonies in two, and thereby deliver a potentially fatal blow to the rebellion. But as he moved south through Fort Ticonderoga (formerly Fort Carillon) and Fort Edward, his force met with stiff guerrilla resistance. Local militias destroyed bridges, blocked roads, and harassed his men. By late summer, Burgoyne's supply lines to Canada were almost completely severed, forcing his men to halt about three dozen miles north of Albany. In a pair of pitched battles on September 19 and October 7, the Americans under General Horatio Gates whipped their Old World foes. When Burgoyne surrendered on October 17, more than 5,700 British soldiers, including seven generals, laid down their arms. It was a crushing defeat for Britain and a decisive victory for the cause of American independence.

When Burgoyne started south that summer, it was still possible to believe in a decisive British victory and that the colonists had spilled their blood at Lexington, Concord, and Bunker Hill for naught. After Saratoga, however, the Americans seemed likely to achieve much if not all that they desired. At a minimum, this meant home rule for the colonies, an outcome the Continental Congress almost gladly would have accepted just two years earlier. Yet battlefield success had prompted the Americans to increase their demands. Full independence was now within reach, and the colonists had no intention of letting it slip away—although achieving it would require help from an unlikely source across the ocean.

After the Treaty of Paris formally ended the final French and Indian War in 1763, France had felt diminished and humiliated.

Almost all of its overseas empire had been taken away, and nowhere was the loss more painful than in North America. Like a wounded animal, France had retreated into a corner. And rather than accepting the reality of its decline—something the French would have tremendous difficulty doing over the next two centuries—it grew eager to lash out against the country responsible for its misery: Great Britain. Unfortunately for France, its traditional rival had emerged from the war more powerful than ever before.

Not to be deterred, France coldly and methodically plotted its revenge. First, it dispatched a number of special agents to gather intelligence on the British colonies in North America. One of them, a naval officer named Pontleroy, studied the economy, took soundings in ports and rivers, and drafted military plans for attacking Boston, New York, and Philadelphia. Throughout the late 1760s and early 1770s, he and other French operatives reported on the growing colonial discontent with British tax policy and their lack of representation in Parliament. Although fissures were apparent everywhere, they did not ensure a rupture with Britain. Pontleroy cautioned his superiors in Paris that British and American interests might just as likely reconverge in a war to seize France's last remaining territories in the Western Hemisphere. Yet he also understood that since the fall of New France, the Americans felt less dependent on British military protection. Herein, thought Pontleroy, lay France's grand opportunity.

It was a time of great uncertainty in North America. Although most colonists wished to remain subjects of the British crown, many had developed a deep resentment of Parliament for forcing unpopular and burdensome taxes on them, such as the infamous Stamp Act of 1765 and the Townshend Acts of 1767. Bad feelings grew worse when the colonial sloop *Liberty* was seized by the British and confiscated for smuggling in 1768. The ship's owner, John Hancock, became a hero and joined Samuel Adams, the brew-making political agitator, in fomenting widespread resistance to British rule. Two years later came the Boston Massacre, sparked by British troops trying to enforce customs duties. In 1773, Adams and a local silversmith named

Paul Revere staged the Boston Tea Party to protest yet another tax. Rather than seeking reconciliation, however, the British met these incidents with ever more coercion. In London, figures such as the great conservative statesman Edmund Burke warned of a widening rift and advocated home rule for the colonies. "Liberty is a good to be improved, not an evil to be lessened," he wrote.[4] But his wise counsel fell on deaf ears.

In 1774, nineteen-year-old Louis XVI ascended the throne after his grandfather succumbed to smallpox. One of the young monarch's first acts was to appoint Charles Gravier de Vergennes his minister of foreign affairs. In an aristocracy of inherited privilege, the portly Vergennes was not an obvious choice, coming as he did from a family of minor nobles. Yet he was a skillful and loyal diplomat who believed that God had endowed his country with a special importance. A classic French chauvinist, Vergennes exhibited the unresolved tension between rational statecraft and arrogant national pride that has bedeviled French leaders for centuries. "France," he once wrote, "has the right to influence all great affairs. Her king, comparable to a supreme judge, is entitled to regard his throne as a tribunal set up by Providence to make respected the rights and properties of sovereigns."[5] His loyalty to the king was compromised only by his devotion to a bourgeois woman he had met while he had been posted to Constantinople. Fearing that the court would not permit his marriage to someone of lower social standing, Vergennes had kept the relationship secret, even as he fathered two children. Ultimately, however, he broke down and begged for the king's approval, which was reluctantly granted.

A workhorse, Vergennes spent long hours at his desk reading reports and writing to his subordinates in foreign capitals. While some of his contemporaries considered him bland—one dubbed him "a mere clerk with his feet under the table"—he was in truth a methodical thinker who arrived at his decisions after careful deliberation.[6] He always kept his goals in clear sight, even as he hid them from both friends and adversaries. After France cast its lot with the

Americans, Vergennes issued cynical instructions to his deputy in Philadelphia on how to deal with his naive colonial hosts: "You will show them that we are making war only for them, that it is only because of them that we are in it, that consequently the engagements we have undertaken with them are absolute and permanent, that our causes are now common causes never to be separated."[7] It was a revealing statement that would guide the strategy of his successors in their dealings with the United States for the next two centuries. Thus was born the myth of France's eternal friendship with America—the brainchild of an overfed French toady.

The decision to aid the Americans was not an easy one for Vergennes or his king. Although they both knew that another war with Britain was inevitable—France was always preparing for its next conflict with Britain—they feared that it would begin before their country was ready. Louis XVI felt particularly uncomfortable encouraging a popular revolt against a fellow monarch, even one he despised.

Yet Britain's problems in North America had become too tempting not to exploit. In 1775, Vergennes sent the Americans a secret emissary who suggested that France might welcome their independence—without making any firm commitments. Privately, Vergennes explained his rationale for supporting American independence: "First, it will diminish the power of England, and increase in proportion that of France. Second, it will cause irreparable loss to English trade, while it will considerably extend ours. Third, it presents to us as very probable the recovery of a part of the possessions which the English have taken from us in America."[8] He had no sympathy for the intellectual, moral, or legal arguments for independence. Liberty, equality, and fraternity were of no interest to him. This would be an exercise in geopolitical maneuvering and little else. It was already bad enough that the ideas of the Americans, if applied generally, contradicted the very legitimacy of the French monarchy.

By the spring of 1776, Vergennes had prevailed upon his reluctant but pliable king to provide covert aid to the colonists. In May—two months before the signing of the Declaration of Independence and long before news of the event reached Europe—France began a program of clandestine assistance. It was not yet ready to give its full public support for colonial independence, but it was willing to give the rebels a few discreet nudges in that direction.

However resolved Americans may have been to forge their own destiny, direct military aid from France was desperately needed. In 1776, the thirteen colonies were populated by farmers, not factory workers, and the Americans would need more than pitchforks and plows to fend off their British masters. Much of the help came from a French agent, Pierre-Augustin Caron de Beaumarchais, better known as the playwright who authored *The Barber of Seville* and *The Marriage of Figaro*. He created a phony business concern called Roderigue Hortalez and Company, which would channel large quantities of arms and ammunition to North America. The majority of this materiel was obsolete and of little value to the modernized French military, but the resourceful Americans would make good use of it at Saratoga and elsewhere.

Although grateful for this support, the Americans wanted more from France: full diplomatic recognition. And they might have gotten it shortly after the signing of the Declaration of Independence if New York City had not fallen to the redcoats. To be sure, the year had concluded with Washington crossing the Delaware River and winning minor engagements at Trenton and Princeton. These victories were good for American morale, but they certainly were not the tide-shifting triumphs Vergennes wished to see. Indeed, France would commit itself only after the Americans had come close to achieving de facto independence on their own. Unfortunately, the succeeding months brought more disappointments, as the British defeated Washington at Brandywine and seized Philadelphia. But then came the surprise at Saratoga, and suddenly everything was different.

Benjamin Franklin saw the effect right away. No sooner had word of the victory arrived in Paris than Vergennes asked him to draft a proposal for a Franco-American alliance. Yet the French foreign min-

ister remained cautious. For if Britain now offered appealing concessions to the Americans, there might be a rapprochement with the
colonies and a priceless opportunity for France would disappear.
Vergennes had to act fast—something that did not come to him
naturally.

At the same time, Franklin recognized that he was being presented
with a chance to secure American independence. Already an accomplished author, printer, and scientist, he would more than prove his
mettle as a diplomat in his dealings with the crafty Vergennes. One of
his first steps was to welcome contacts with representatives of George
III of Great Britain and to make no effort at concealing them from
the French. Britain was ready to accept just about anything short of
full independence for the colonies, including tax relief and home
rule. "The two greatest countries in Europe were fairly running a race
for the favor of America," said Edward Gibbon, the great historian of
the Roman Empire (and a member of Parliament).[9] British intelligence, meanwhile, had sent an agent to Paris to meet with Franklin.
Although this man outlined his government's position, he had no
authority to negotiate, and Franklin insisted on dealing only with cre-
dentialed emissaries—and even then, only to discuss how Britain
might recognize American sovereignty.

As Franklin had anticipated, his conversations with the British
made Vergennes exceedingly nervous. "The question which we have
to solve," wrote the French minister, "is to know whether it is more
expedient to have war against England and America united, or with
America for us against England."[10] Vergennes knew that he had to act:
"What ought to have persuaded [France] and in reality has persuaded
her to join with America, is that great enfeeblement of England,
brought about by the removal of a third of her empire."[11]

On January 8, 1778, Vergennes notified Franklin that Louis XVI
was willing to form an alliance. A month later, on February 6, the two
diplomats signed their names to a pair of pacts that would shape
Franco-American relations for more than two decades. The first was a
commercial treaty extending privileges to American shipping. By

itself, this was tantamount to official recognition of colonial independence and it was clear grounds for war between Britain and France. When hostilities did erupt, the second pact—a treaty of defensive alliance—would take effect. It called for the two countries to fight together until American liberty was secure, to guarantee one another's territory in the New World, and to make no peace with Britain without the consent of the other. This final provision was important to both parties for different reasons: The Americans did not want the French to forsake them, and the French did not want the colonists to repair ties to their mother country. It would prove extremely difficult to enforce.

As Franklin and Vergennes bargained in Paris, Washington and his soldiers shivered through a frigid winter at Valley Forge. When spring arrived, many Americans grew restless at the slow pace of the negotiations. Indeed, there was more than a residual distrust of France, as many Americans still remembered the ravages of the French and Indian Wars. Yet most understood that French help was now vital to their survival as a nation. "When our house is burning," wrote one commentator, "we do not inquire too curiously into the moral antecedents of those who hand the water-buckets."[12] Meanwhile, the French began a cynical revision of their negative and self-serving opinion of Washington, the soldier they had publicly branded a vile assassin for his role in sparking the final French and Indian War. As one French visitor to Valley Forge commented, "All suspicions must now disappear before the name, the virtues, and the glory of George Washington: The murderer of Jumonville could never have become a great man."[13]

Washington himself applauded the French alliance even as he kept French motives in clear view: "France appears to have acted with politic generosity towards us, and to have timed her declaration in our favor most admirably for her own interest and abasing her ancient rival."[14] On May 4, Congress ratified the two treaties. By June, France and Britain were at war, and the Franco-American partnership was complete.

At the time, most observers shared Washington's view that the alliance was less a bond of friendship than a convergence of interest decorated with the language of amity. French motivation to aid the colonists did not spring from the liberal salons of Paris, which were strongly supportive of American ideals, but from the cold calculations of the foreign office. In short, each country desired something that only the other could help it acquire. "Perhaps one principle, self interest, may account for all," wrote Elbridge Gerry, a signer of the Declaration of Independence who would play a pivotal role in Franco-American relations two decades later.[15]

There was at least one Frenchman, however, whose concern for America seemed motivated by something other than raw self-interest. The Marquis de Lafayette came from a storied military family that could trace its ancestry back almost a thousand years and whose men had a reputation for dying young in battle. Lafayette's own father had been killed by British forces at the age of twenty-five during the Seven Years' War, when Lafayette was not yet two. The youngster subsequently inherited an enormous fortune and grew up as one of the richest men in France. In 1775, at the age of eighteen, he became enamored of the American cause and petitioned his king for permission to fight alongside the rebels. This was refused, as Louis could ill afford to have such a prominent French nobleman declare his allegiance so openly. But Lafayette was made of stern stuff. He disobeyed his monarch and sailed for America in the spring of 1777. After spending nearly two months at sea—much of it seasick—the young aristocrat made landfall in South Carolina and then traveled to Philadelphia. Impressed by his social rank and touched by his apparent devotion to American independence, Congress overlooked his inexperience and made him a major general. In France, he was declared a fugitive.

Just shy of his twentieth birthday, Lafayette presented himself to Washington. "I came to learn and not to teach," he declared, displaying a humility that immediately endeared him to the commander in chief.[16] The marquis was actually one of several Europeans who crossed the Atlantic and achieved lasting fame for service to the American cause. The others included the Polish officers Thaddeus Kosciusko and Casimir Pulaski as well as the Prussian drill instructor Baron von Steuben. Yet Lafayette outshone them all and became one of Washington's favorite subordinates. The childless general looked upon the young Frenchman as something of a surrogate son and Lafayette, who had never known his own father, returned the affection and went on to distinguish himself as an able and courageous commander. A few weeks after meeting Washington, he took a bullet in the leg at Brandywine. The following spring, he was widely praised for coordinating a difficult retreat at Barren Hill.

In truth, it is not altogether clear how well Lafayette actually understood the principles he was fighting for. Like many Frenchmen, he had grown up despising the British, his father's killers, and yearning for military glory. Many of his pronouncements on behalf of American liberty would come later in life, after he had matured and had time to reflect. Yet he became an enduring symbol of Franco-American ties, and his friendship to the United States obscured the machinations of Vergennes. A cynic might wonder whether Vergennes had planned it that way: For more than two centuries, whenever tensions arose between the United States and France, the French rarely missed an opportunity to invoke the memory of Lafayette as a way of shielding their true motives. It has proved an exceptionally effective ploy. In France, Lafayette's grave is said to be American soil—a symbolic gesture that cost the French nothing but reaped an enormous windfall of American goodwill in the twentieth century.

A year after arriving in America, Lafayette's reputation soared so high that Congress appointed him commander of an army that was chosen to invade Canada, a mission Lafayette fervently supported. Washington, however, doubted that a campaign in the north would improve the prospects of independence. He also worried that America might defeat Britain only to have France reclaim Quebec. "I am heartily disposed to entertain the most favorable sentiments of our new ally," Washington said of the French. "But it is a maxim founded on the universal experience of mankind, that no nation can be trusted farther than it is bound by its interests."[17]

Washington simply could not afford to spend his hours preoccupied with the possibility of French scheming. He had a war to win, and he understood that French assistance was critical to winning it. There would be no invasion of Canada, but there was much else to be done.

The British reacted to the Franco-American alliance by consolidating their military positions. They pulled out of the capital, Philadelphia, in order to concentrate their forces in New York. As they marched across New Jersey, Washington struck at their rear. The two armies clashed at Monmouth, where a confused battle took place on June 28, a day so hot that many men died from heat exhaustion. Although the Americans prevailed, the redcoats managed to slip away during the night. Five days later, they reached the safety of New York City.

By July 11, a French fleet had arrived on the scene under the command of Charles-Hector d'Estaing, a headstrong and pompous aristocrat who claimed the last king of the Visigoths as an ancestor. Had d'Estaing turned up in American waters just a little earlier, he might have thwarted the British retreat to New York. But it had taken him a full eighty-five days to cross the ocean, a long time even by the standards of the day. D'Estaing was no gritty veteran of naval operations; in truth, his knowledge of seafaring was rather poor. He had joined the army at the age of nine and had become an admiral only because of the unusual (and questionable) French practice of permitting officers of high rank to switch branches of military service and still retain large commands. On his way to America, he had wasted valuable time by insisting that his ships chase merchant vessels and hold training exercises. Thus, Washington lost a chance to deliver a potentially fatal blow to the British more than three years before Yorktown. D'Estaing's tardiness gave the Americans their first lesson in French military aid: It came with no guarantees of French military competence.

Their second lesson came soon enough, when d'Estaing was presented with another excellent opportunity to crush the British, whose ships were now bottled up in New York harbor. Although the French men-of-war were unable to enter the harbor because their deep hulls could not make it past a sandbar at its entrance, d'Estaing might have removed his heaviest guns and placed them on Sandy Hook, an island with a commanding view of the harbor. If d'Estaing had acted with dispatch, he and the Americans might have laid siege to the British and starved them out of New York. Unfortunately, the British noticed their vulnerability before the inexperienced d'Estaing saw his chance—and so they seized Sandy Hook for themselves and dug in. Over time, their position in New York only grew stronger.

With New York now securely in enemy hands, Washington and d'Estaing turned their attention to Newport, Rhode Island. Although several thousand British soldiers protected the city's harbor, Washington hoped for a victory even greater than Saratoga—"the finishing blow to British pretensions of sovereignty over this country," as he put it.[18] With so many redcoats pinned down in New York, Washington sent reinforcements to Providence, where General John Sullivan had raised a large militia. By the first part of August, Sullivan had about 10,000 men under his command, and the French fleet was planning to unload an additional 4,000 troops nearby. Lafayette was given command of his own detachment.

The Franco-American force planned a coordinated attack on Newport for August 10, though it was clear from the start that they would face serious problems working together. The aristocratic d'Estaing did not believe that a social inferior such as Sullivan, whose parents had been indentured servants from Ireland, had any right to issue him orders. The two men subsequently spent as much time bickering with each other as they did organizing their efforts. Lafayette tried to intervene, but at first his presence only complicated matters. Because there was still an order out for his arrest, d'Estaing did not know how to receive him. The admiral expressed "political anxiety about receiving a French officer who had violated the king's orders not to leave for America."[19] Only after a round of vacillation did d'Estaing decide that his country's new treaty obligations nullified Lafayette's criminal status.

Even then, Lafayette's mediation failed. A professional military man and social snob, d'Estaing regarded the Americans as untrustworthy provincials: "I was forced to show an austere firmness to make the allies understand that while their troops were good for a defensive, they had no qualities necessary for attack."[20] When the Americans attacked a weakness in the British defenses without first consulting d'Estaing, the admiral and his staff were furious. "The French officers sounded like women disputing precedence in a country dance," said one of Sullivan's colonels, "instead of men engaged in pursuing the common interest of two great nations."[21] It was the first occurrence of a problem that would be repeated many times in the twentieth century.

The assault on Newport might well have succeeded if the British fleet had remained in New York harbor. On the afternoon of August 9, however, a French lookout spotted the enemy ships approaching. D'Estaing had not anticipated this possibility. "The surprise was complete," he admitted.[22] Even so, the admiral could have denied them an engagement and continued supporting the attack on Newport by seeking refuge in Narragansett Bay, where the British navy would have had a difficult time challenging him. Instead, he chose to sail out to meet the British with his soldiers still onboard. For two days, the fleets probed each other, seeking advantage. Few shots had been fired when a violent storm rolled in with tremendous force, damaging and scattering the ships of both countries.

As the British sailed for the repair docks of New York, Sullivan decided that his attack had been delayed long enough. Assuming that d'Estaing would soon be landing his soldiers, he struck at Newport on August 14. But the French admiral had other plans. Anxious to patch up his own ships, d'Estaing made for Boston without putting any troops ashore. When the French quit Newport, so did many of Sullivan's militiamen, who had expected to take part in a victory made possible by support from the sea. Sullivan was in fact so weakened by the French abandonment and the subsequent defections of his own soldiers that British forces inside Newport were able to stage a successful counterattack. D'Estaing's ignominious exit had turned what should have been a glorious success into a shocking defeat. Meanwhile, the absence of the French fleet allowed the British to transport additional troops to the area. Only poor winds kept them from arriving in time to trap the Americans and make the disaster complete.

Lafayette had warned d'Estaing that his departure would not sit well with the Americans. Sullivan was furious with the French: "I confess that I do most cordially resent the conduct of the Count, or rather the conduct of his officers, who have it seems, compelled him to go to Boston and leave us on an island without any certain means of retreat."[23] Another American commander, John Laurens, complained in a letter to Washington: "The honor of the French Nation, the honor of the Admiral, the safety of the fleet, and a regard for the new alliance required a different conduct."[24]

Word of the French behavior at Newport—as well as Sullivan's unvarnished views on the subject—reached Boston before the French. There was even talk of closing the port to d'Estaing. It remained open, but local shipwrights at first refused to work on the fleet. French sailors brave enough to go ashore were met with angry mobs. In one bloody melee, two French officers were wounded, one of them mortally. The alliance that had been born six months earlier was now in full crisis as d'Estaing considered sailing back to France to urge his king to forsake the undeserving Americans.

Then Washington intervened. Eyeing the big picture, he refused to let the recriminations of a single unfortunate campaign imperil a vital alliance. "Prudence dictates that we should put the best face upon the matter, and to the world attribute the removal to Boston to necessity," he said. "The reasons are too obvious to need explaining."[25] Feeling contrite, the Massachusetts legislature voted to raise a statue to the dead Frenchman. Aware of the French susceptibility to flattery, Washington orchestrated a letter-writing campaign among his top officers, who sent appreciative missives effusively praising the admiral's bravery at Newport. Even Sullivan was compelled to apologize. D'Estaing played along with the fiction, though relations remained far from harmonious. He flatly turned down an American suggestion that he operate out of Boston, and Washington denied a French request to have American troops deployed there to protect the fleet. In early November, d'Estaing petulantly sailed off with his warships to the Caribbean without bothering to tell Washington where he was headed or when their forces might meet again.

After the debacle at Newport, Washington realized that French intervention would not bring the war to a rapid conclusion. Indeed, seven months would pass before he heard anything from the French admiral, who was busy in the West Indies trading shots with the British in pursuit of goals that had little to do with advancing American independence. Although d'Estaing did manage to capture the islands of St. Vincent and Grenada, his failure to take St. Lucia with a superior force was so bungled that one historian has labeled it the "Bunker Hill of the Caribbean."[26]

It was starting to look as though the war would last another year without the French making their presence felt, when, in September, d'Estaing suddenly appeared on the outskirts of Savannah, Georgia, which the British had captured the previous fall. The combined forces of the French under d'Estaing and the Americans under General Benjamin Lincoln greatly outnumbered the British inside the city. Odds of a victory seemed excellent. But d'Estaing, fearing the foul weather of autumn and perhaps recalling the debacle at Newport, ordered an assault before preparations were complete. The attack went poorly. A French bombardment inflicted more damage on the buildings of Savannah than on British entrenchments. A ground assault cost the allies 800 casualties while inflicting only 150 on the enemy. One of the dead was Casimir Pulaski, the dashing young cavalry officer from Poland. D'Estaing himself was wounded. His deputy ordered the retreat.

The injured and defeated admiral set sail for France. Having achieved nothing in two seasons of war, his role in the conflict was over. In 1794, he would become the victim of an altogether different revolution when he perished upon the Jacobin scaffolds of Paris.

As the siege of Savannah floundered, the American sea captain John Paul Jones was busy terrifying British shipping off the British Isles. Based in France, the tempestuous sailor known for the wild look in his eyes was already a scourge of the London press for his exploits, which included the capture of the H.M.S. *Drake*. In August of 1779, he set sail aboard the *Bonhomme Richard*, a ship he had named after Ben Franklin's *Poor Richard's Almanac*. A small squadron of supporting vessels joined him. One of these was the *Alliance*, captained by Pierre Landais, a French naval officer who had accompanied Bougainville in his travels around the world some years earlier. There had been hope in America that Landais might become a seaborne Lafayette. A more apt analogy would be Benedict Arnold. Whereas Lafayette gladly took orders from Washington, the bad-tempered Landais frequently disobeyed directives from the *Bonhomme Richard*. During one contentious meeting in Jones's cabin, the two men nearly came to blows. When Landais challenged Jones to a duel, Jones said he would gladly fight once their voyage was complete and they were back on land. After returning to the *Alliance*, Landais and his ship vanished for two weeks, only to be sighted once more on September 22, 1779—one day before Jones would fight one of the most famous naval battles in American history. It would have been better for Jones and the American navy if Landais had remained missing.

On the afternoon of September 23, Jones spotted a convoy of British merchant vessels guarded by the vaunted H.M.S. *Serapis*. This deadly warship featured copper sheathing below its waterline—the latest in British naval technology—as well as fifty guns. In short, it was faster and more powerful than the *Bonhomme Richard*. Despite these disadvantages, the intrepid Jones made straight for the *Serapis* and ordered Landais to join him. But the French captain ignored the command. As dusk fell, Jones knew he would have to face the British frigate on his own.

For four hours off Flamborough Head in the North Sea, the two ships clashed. Launching broadside after broadside at close range, they inflicted terrible damage on each other. Cannonballs were fired with such force that they crashed through the ship walls and burst out the other side. Sailors slipped on decks covered with blood. As night fell, the *Bonhomme Richard* was taking on water faster than its crew could pump it out, and the ship began to sink slowly. "Do you call for Quarters?" barked British captain Richard Pearson. Upon hearing this invitation to surrender, John Paul Jones shouted back his immortal reply: "I have not yet begun to fight!"[27]

As the fierce battle continued, Landais maneuvered his ship into range. But instead of attacking the British vessel, he opened fire on the *Bonhomme Richard*. The first salvo killed two American sailors and forced many away from their stations. Subsequent French volleys proved even more lethal, and a chief petty officer was among those killed. Although Landais would claim that he was trying to attack the *Serapis*, he would later confide privately to one of his colonels that his real goal had been to sink the *Bonhomme Richard* first and then overpower the exhausted men of the *Serapis* with a boarding party of fresh marines. He believed that this would make him—not Jones—the hero of the fight off Flamborough Head.

Yet Landais decided to pull away from both ships. Perhaps waiting for the *Bonhomme Richard* to go down before pouncing on the hobbled *Serapis*, he again held back as the naval duel entered its final stage. Jones, for his part, refused to give up, even though nearly half his crew was dead or wounded and his own sinking ship was doomed. The *Bonhomme Richard* did in fact sink, but not before Pearson asked his relentless American foe for quarter. The victorious Jones moved his flag and his men onto the captured *Serapis* and sailed to a neutral Dutch port. It was one of the most astonishing and dramatic naval victories in American history—and one almost ruined by the French.

Landais would go on to lose his command and spend much of his time trying to get Jones to honor his promise of a duel. Although the American preferred to battle his naval enemies at close quarters, he was not an expert swordsman and may have feared that Landais, an experienced fencer, would carve him up. When Jones suggested that a court-martial settle their differences, Landais refused and went on hating Jones for years. As late as 1787, Landais approached Jones in New York City and, so he claimed, spat in the face of his American rival. Jones admitted encountering Landais but denied that such a grievous insult had been committed. Landais responded with a letter to the newspapers: "I do hereby certify, to the public, that I really, and in fact, spit all the spittle I could spare out of my mouth then, out of contempt, in the face of John Paul."[28] A witness later corroborated Jones's version of the story, and the two antagonists never met again.

Notwithstanding the *Bonhomme Richard*'s inspiring victory over the *Serapis*, the following year held further disappointments for the Americans. In May 1780, the redcoats captured Charleston—and within three months, all of South Carolina fell into their grasp. Hoping the hero of Saratoga might turn things around, Congress dispatched General Horatio Gates to the Carolinas. But in August, Lord Cornwallis beat him soundly at Camden. The following month, Washington's most able subordinate, Benedict Arnold, defected to the enemy.

As the Americans encountered setback after setback on land, the French fleet spent the year away from American waters, blocked in at Brest by the British. With the war's progress apparently halted, Vergennes began to consider a negotiated settlement that might have granted sovereignty to some but not all of the thirteen colonies. "A sacrifice is among the possibilities," he wrote of a peace agreement, "and if it becomes unavoidable, it is necessary to be resigned." He pointed to the example of the Belgian provinces in their struggle against Spain: "Only seven preserved their independence. . . . We should make the Americans realize that the war cannot be eternal, and there is a time at which one must stop."[29] In February 1781, Vergennes proposed a truce based on the principle of *uti possidetis*, which meant that territory would go to whoever controlled it at the time of armistice. Had all the parties agreed to such a peace at the moment Vergennes suggested it, New York City as well as most of the Carolinas and Georgia would have remained part of the British Empire.

Acceptance of this French proposal would have altered the whole course of U.S. history. The map of North America might have become a patchwork of feeble republics and European colonies instead of a strong and united country. Ironically, such an outcome would have spelled disaster for France in the twentieth century, when its very survival depended on a powerful United States. Of course, it was impossible for Vergennes to anticipate such far-off and unknowable events. He was simply a desperate man trying to cut his losses.

Three years earlier, the rebels had stood on the verge of total victory. Now, after the French intervention, the positive momentum of Saratoga had stalled at Newport and Savannah—and the possibility of American independence seemed remote. In the spring of 1781, Washington braced himself for further disappointment: "Instead of having the prospect of a glorious offensive campaign before us," he wrote, "we have a bewildered and gloomy defensive one—unless we should receive a powerful aid of ships, land troops, and money from our generous allies; and these, at present, are too contingent to build upon."[30]

It was at this moment of deepest despair that the French fleet managed to escape from Brest under the command of Admiral François-Joseph-Paul de Grasse. In the months that followed, American and French commanders would coordinate their efforts with a seamlessness that stood in sharp contrast to what had come before. Although Washington was eager to attack New York, the problems of 1778 ultimately convinced both forces to focus on Virginia, where Cornwallis was stationed with 8,000 enemy troops.

The siege of Yorktown began on September 28, when a superior force of American soldiers under Washington and a French force under General Rochambeau began their attack on the cornered British. From the sea, de Grasse's navy hemmed them in at Cape

Charles. There were several skirmishes and even some heroics on the part of a twenty-four-year-old colonel named Alexander Hamilton. Yet the fighting was relatively light. From the start, Cornwallis understood his dire predicament. He surrendered his force after a three-week siege. On October 19, as the redcoats set down their arms, a British band played "The World Turned Upside Down."

"Oh, God!" exclaimed Lord North back in England when he heard the news. "It is all over!" Washington, however, did not share the sentiment. Yorktown was an enormous victory, but the British still occupied several major cities, and their combined forces remained larger than Washington's. Eager to continue his momentum, the American commander-in-chief asked de Grasse to join him in attacking Charleston. But the Frenchman refused, explaining that he was overdue in the West Indies and could not possibly participate in a new offensive. Having anticipated this response, Washington countered with a more modest request. Would the admiral at least consent to transport American soldiers to Wilmington, another city held by the British?

Initially agreeing to the proposal, de Grasse later reneged. The French loaded their troops onto their ships and sailed for the Caribbean once more. They met with disaster in the spring, when the British navy routed them in the Battle of the Saints, fought among a group of rocky islets between the islands of Dominica and Guadaloupe. It was one of the worst defeats in French naval history (which admittedly was none too glorious). De Grasse himself was captured and hauled off to England. When he returned to France after a few months, he insisted on a court-martial to restore his honor. It would prove only partly successful: Although acquitted, most continued to blame him for what had happened. De Grasse was never given another command—and probably died wishing that he had chosen to fight with Washington at Charleston.

In truth, the French were no longer needed after Yorktown. Lord North had been correct: It was all over. After six years of war, Britain had wearied of the conflict, and support for American independence had grown in London. Only the contentious peacemaking remained. Unfortunately, the French would prove to be even less reliable at the negotiating table than they had been on the battlefield.

In the spring of 1782, the British opened talks with Franklin in Paris. They were complicated by the fact that Vergennes finally had achieved his personal goal of drawing Spain into war with Britain in 1779. In a set of intricate negotiations culminating in a secret pact, the Spaniards had agreed to enter the fray only after the French promised to make war alongside Spain until the British gave up Gibraltar. But because the treaty obligations of 1778 forbade the Americans from negotiating a separate peace with Britain, this French commitment seemed to tie the prospect of American independence to the fate of a dry rock at the mouth of the Mediterranean Sea.

In reality, French support for American independence had been conditional from the start. Vergennes worried that the Americans might build a great nation whose interests eventually would clash with those of France. Although he wanted the colonies to separate themselves from Britain, he also wished to contain their future growth. Like a chess player thinking several moves ahead, Vergennes plotted to surround the young nation with rivals. Spain would perform an important function in this regard. It had acquired Louisiana at the end of the final French and Indian War, but the boundaries of the unsettled Mississippi region remained a matter of dispute. Many Americans were already showing an interest in moving westward, but France wanted to confine them to the strip of land between the Atlantic Ocean and the Appalachian Mountains. Vergennes also hoped that Britain would maintain a presence in North America. His instructions to Conrad-Alexandre Gérard, France's first minister to the United States, had put the matter plainly: "The King feels that the possession of these three countries [Canada, Nova Scotia, and Florida], or at least that of Canada by England, would be a serviceable principle for keeping the Americans uneasy and cautious."[31] In pursuit of these goals, Gérard discouraged expansionism through normal diplomatic contacts with members of Congress in Philadelphia. He also bribed Americans to write newspaper articles backing moderate territorial claims.

After Yorktown, the British agreed to grant independence to the colonies. Yet there were still many points to negotiate, from access to the fisheries of Newfoundland to compensation for loyalists who had lost property during the conflict. An even more important item was to determine the western boundaries of the United States. In this delicate matter the French were more interested in helping their frustrated Spanish allies—who still pined for Gibraltar after three years of unsuccessful siege—than the Americans. With the French treasury running short of funds, Vergennes felt pressure to end the war with Britain on whatever tolerable terms might be achieved quickly. With an eye on European politics, the foreign minister decided to support aggressive claims for Spain in North America, including possession of all territory west of the Alleghenies and exclusive rights to the Mississippi River.

Alarmed when he first learned of this French plan from one of Vergennes's aides, Franklin's fellow diplomat John Jay became doubly concerned when his contact secretly left Paris for London. It seemed that the French were holding their own negotiations with the British, in violation of the 1778 compact. Nothing good could come of this, Jay reasoned, so he sent his own emissary to the British government. On November 30, 1782, the United States and Britain reached a preliminary peace agreement whose terms were favorable to the Americans: On the matter of the western territories, Britain ignored Spanish aspirations and recognized American claims all the way to the Mississippi River as well as in the Great Lakes region.

The deal looked far different from the one Vergennes had envisioned. "You will notice that the English buy peace more than they make it," he sneered after learning of the agreement. "Their concessions, in fact as much as to the boundaries as to the fisheries and loyalists, exceed all that I should have thought possible."[32] The French foreign minister, however, was in no position to veto the treaty. He did, however, manage to complain about it. "I am at a loss," he wrote in a letter to Franklin, "to explain your conduct and that of your colleagues on this occasion. You have concluded your preliminary articles without any communication between us. . . . You are about to hold out a certain hope of peace of America without even informing yourself on the state of the negotiation on our part."[33]

The formal treaty was signed on September 3, 1783—and almost at once, France and the United States began to drift apart. The logic of their alliance had not been clear before Saratoga, and it began to lose coherence even as the ink dried on the peace treaty. In June 1783, an aide to Washington, James McHenry, penned an obituary for the partnership: Because France "took up the American cause as instrumental to her political views in Europe," he wrote, and because Americans had gained their independence, "the alliance is therefore completed and terminated without leaving behind it any political principle or true permanent connection."[34]

In the years that followed, many in France expected that American gratitude would lead to strong commercial ties. Thomas Paine, a longtime friend of France, once predicted that trade would keep relations tight so long as "eating is the custom in Europe."[35] But Franco-American commerce did not meet these expectations. The Chevalier de la Luzerne, the new French minister in Philadelphia, complained of French merchants in the United States as "a Parcell of little Rascals, petits conquins, and Adventurers who have sold the worst Merchandises, for great Prices."[36] French protectionism was another major problem: In the West Indies, France refused to open its ports to American goods. By end of the 1780s, the United States was trading more with Britain than it had before independence.

American gratitude did not disappear entirely, however. Most Americans sincerely appreciated the role the French had played in the war. Without France, there would have been no dramatic finale at Yorktown in 1781—and the former colonists knew it. Throughout the 1780s, expressions of goodwill toward the French were common even as political relations deteriorated and economic ones failed to develop. In the 1790s, however, relations between the two countries came under severe pressure during the Citizen Genet episode and eventually broke down altogether over the XYZ Affair and the undeclared naval war of 1798–1800.

The experience of French intervention taught a final lesson. In 1775, Congressman John Adams of Massachusetts had warned about the dangers of an alliance with France: "We should be little better than puppets, danced on the wires of the cabinets of Europe."[37] After six years of troubled cooperation, skepticism about European politics remained. Only this time the sentiment was based not on mere speculation, but on bitter experience.

THREE

THE FIRST FOREIGN SUBVERSIVE

You certainly never felt the terrorism excited by Genet.
—John Adams, in a letter to Thomas Jefferson [1]

THE BOOM OF distant cannon fire echoed through the cobblestone streets of Philadelphia on May 2, 1793. From his house in the heart of what was then the national capital, President George Washington must have listened to the noise with apprehension. Less than two weeks earlier, he had issued the Neutrality Proclamation, in which the United States pointedly refused to take sides in the war France had declared on England a few months earlier. It was designed to protect the young nation from the wars of Europe—but here were its awful sounds, right on the doorstep of Independence Hall.

As thousands of people rushed to the wharves to discover the source of the shots, they saw two ships entering the harbor. The first was the *Grange*, an English vessel—though high on its mast the British flag waved upside down, just below the flag of France. The *Grange* had been captured at sea. Behind it sailed the victorious thirty-six-gun French frigate *Embuscade*.

Some hours later, Secretary of State Thomas Jefferson paid an emergency visit to Washington to deliver a formal protest from Britain's minister to the United States, George Hammond. The French, Hammond claimed, had taken the *Grange* in U.S. territorial waters rather than on the high seas. He insisted that the *Grange* be returned to its rightful British owners.

Hoping to avoid a diplomatic incident, Washington instructed Jefferson to assure Hammond that his administration would conduct a full investigation. The United States, he said, "will not see with indifference its territory or jurisdiction violated."[2]

Ironically, the *Embuscade* had just completed a diplomatic mission of its own. A few weeks earlier, it had dropped off the new French minister to the United States, Edmond-Charles Genet, in Charleston, South Carolina.[3] Almost immediately, Genet had begun to cause trouble. Instead of hurrying to Philadelphia, where he could present his credentials to the American government and answer questions about the *Embuscade*, Genet had remained in South Carolina to arm privateers and encourage U.S. citizens to join French expeditions against British shipping.

Over the next several months, France's new minister would seize every available opportunity to undermine U.S. neutrality. These subversive acts came at a particularly vulnerable moment. Washington wanted the United States to trade with the nations of Europe, not fight them. He worried that Genet's determined effort to launch aggressive naval operations against Britain from American soil might lure his young country into an unwanted war. As was often the case during Washington's presidency, few precedents existed, and virtually every decision carried the potential to create lasting models of conduct. The new government was trying to define exactly what its neutrality would mean in practice, and every decision mattered. Yet Genet seemed determined to thwart each one. He was well on his way to becoming America's first foreign subversive.

Unlike previous ministers from France, Genet did not come from the court of a king. In the late 1780s, the Old Regime had begun to collapse under the combined weight of economic failure, food shortages, corruption, and sustained criticism from the intellectual class—the Enlightenment *philosophes*. Unable to pay off the large debts accumulated during the Seven Years' War and America's War of Independence, Louis XVI had conspired to squeeze the aristocrats, the one class that enjoyed tax exemptions. In an effort to reassert their authority, they forced the king to convene the Estates General, an ancient body consisting of the clergy (the First Estate), the nobility (the Second Estate), and everyone else (the Third Estate). Soon neither they nor the king could control the spontaneous rise of the National Assembly, dominated by middle-class lawyers and bureaucrats from the Third Estate. Before long, the lower classes added their own anarchic energy to the mix, and the French Revolution was born.

On July 14, 1789, a Paris mob stormed the Bastille, a medieval fortress used as a state prison. It had become a symbol of Bourbon tyranny, even though its walls confined only seven inmates on the day it was overwhelmed. (None was a political prisoner, and two were insane.) In the chaotic months that followed, peasants ransacked châteaus across the countryside and the king was kept under virtual house arrest. At one point, a horde of angry commoners marched on Versailles; the royal family was saved only through the intervention of Lafayette and his National Guard. Meanwhile, the National Assembly stripped the king of his authority and initiated a series of radical upheavals. The tax and tariff systems, the government ministries, the titles and privileges of the nobility, the regional law codes—all were swept away. The church was made a servant of the state, its lands confiscated, its religious orders suppressed, and its clergymen ordered to swear loyalty oaths to the state. In its place arose a bizarre state-sponsored deistic rite, the cult of the Supreme Being. Even the traditional calendar was brushed aside for a revolutionary one based on ten-hour days, ten-day weeks, and thirty-day months whose names were derived from the rhythms of nature: Frimaire, the month of hoarfrost, Thermidor, the month of heat, and so on. The beginning of the French Revolution was marked as Year One.

In June 1791, the king tried to flee the country disguised as a valet, but he was caught, and what little credibility he had retained with the public vanished. So, too, went any semblance of public order as France plummeted into anarchy. During the September Massacres—

a horrific prelude to the infamous Terror—armed bands butchered more than twelve hundred prisoners in their cells. Many were priests who had resisted the government's antireligious fervor. Three months later, King Louis XVI was put on trial.

At first, many Americans supported the revolution in France. They saw it as analogous to their own fight for national independence and believed the United States had a moral obligation to support the French masses demanding "liberty, equality, and fraternity." Thomas Jefferson, who had spent four years in Paris as the American minister in the 1780s, was particularly enthusiastic. "Here is but the first chapter in the history of European liberty," he declared. Even as the revolution's radicalism became more apparent, Jefferson continued to defend it: "Was ever such a prize won with so little innocent blood?"[4] In 1788—a year before the rupture—Washington himself had been cautiously optimistic: "If managed with extreme prudence, [events in France] may produce a gradual and tacit Revolution much in favor of the subjects."[5]

By the time of Genet's arrival, however, Washington had become more pessimistic: "The affairs of [France] seem to me to be in the highest paroxysm of disorder . . . because those in whose hands the [government] is entrusted are ready to tear each other to pieces, and will, more than probably, prove the worst foes the country has."[6] The president's closest political allies shared his skepticism. Early on, Vice President John Adams had predicted "great and lasting calamities." As the revolution's extremist tendencies became apparent, Adams expressed more doubts: "I do not know what to make of a republic of thirty million atheists."[7] Alexander Hamilton called the revolution "a disgusting spectacle" whose goal was "to undermine the venerable pillars that support the edifice of civilized society."[8] Genet's behavior over the course of several months would do much to bring American opinion in line with the views of Washington, Adams, and Hamilton. In time, even Jefferson's enthusiasm would wane.

When Genet disembarked in Charleston, he was only thirty years old. He had been born at Versailles in 1763, the year France forfeited the bulk of its overseas empire. His father was a civil servant who had collected data on British naval strength during the Seven Years' War and later kept a close watch on developments in America during the War of Independence. The boy was an only child, who "grew up the spoiled and cosseted darling of his family," according to one historian.[9] He was also something of a prodigy. By the time he was twelve, he could read several languages, including English, Italian, Latin, and Swedish.

This combination of family connections and natural ability led to Genet's appointment as a court translator at the age of eighteen. In 1788, he was sent to the French embassy in St. Petersburg. Like so many of his countrymen, however, Genet succumbed to the spell of the Revolution. He became intoxicated with its antiroyal spirit and grew to despise monarchs everywhere, from the Russian one with whom he was expected to interact to the French one he was supposed to represent. In 1792, Catherine the Great called his presence "not only superfluous but even intolerable" and expelled him.[10]

Back in France, Genet aligned himself with a political faction of Jacobins known as the Girondins. Among the various revolutionary groups, the Girondins were considered moderates, although they subscribed to the very immoderate program of overthrowing monarchs everywhere. Their slogan was "War with all kings and peace with all peoples." Members of the group addressed each other as "Citizen," much as the Bolsheviks would later call each other "Comrade." They were glad to enlist a promising young man with diplomatic experience.

In 1792, the Girondins attained supremacy in Paris. In November, they appointed Genet minister to the United States, though winter weather delayed his departure until the following February. In the meantime, Louis XVI was tried, convicted, and sent to the guillotine. Many Girondins had opposed the execution, but they were not able to prevent it. The violence of the Revolution was spiraling out of control and betraying many of its original principles. Whatever misgivings Genet might have had about the death of the king, he had no qualms about trying to subvert a country whose successful revolution had remained true to its ideals.

When Genet stepped off the *Embuscade* at Charleston on April 8, 1793, he had been at sea for seven weeks. It was a peculiar place to disembark: Charleston was hundreds of miles from Philadelphia, and diplomatic protocol required that Genet present himself at once to the national government in the capital. Although the Frenchman would maintain that high winds had blown him south, more likely it had been the pull of politics. Despite the military alliance of the American revolutionary period, relations between the United States and France had soured significantly in the 1780s and early 1790s— and growing alarm over the direction of the French Revolution was only partly to blame. Much of the friction was economic. Each country harbored grievances about commercial favors. In the meantime, Britain had become America's most important trading partner.

Genet hardly could have wished for a better reception than the one he received in Charleston. His arrival was greeted with an outburst of enthusiasm and excitement that lasted for more than a week. A string of parties was thrown in his honor, where he hobnobbed with the governor, senators, and other worthies. The handsome and eloquent Genet, who spoke excellent English, dazzled audiences across the city.

But Genet had more on his mind than a vigorous social life. One of his first goals was to recruit a small fleet of privateers to harass English shipping in North America. Many people considered privateers little more than pirate ships, but in the eighteenth century they were recognized as legitimate instruments of state. The privateers themselves were individually owned and operated ships commissioned by countries at war to prey upon the vessels of their adversaries. France made particularly extensive use of them because of its traditional weakness as a naval power. In practice, privateers targeted commercial rather than military seacraft. They also earned an unsavory reputation for routine violations of the rules of engagement and the frequent failure to distinguish between friendly and hostile crafts. Captured ships were brought into port, where special courts determined whether the seizures (or "prizes") were legal, meaning they could be sold, along with their cargoes. While in Charleston, Genet commissioned four privateers and named them the *Republican*, the *Anti-George*, the *Sans-Culotte*, and, in a gesture of modesty, the *Citizen Genet*. Soon, these newly minted French privateers were busy capturing British ships and escorting them back to Charleston.

Genet prepared for ground warfare as well. Because Spain had become an ally of Britain, Genet hatched a plan to mobilize infantry against the Spanish-controlled territories of Florida and Louisiana. The French consul in Charleston, a man named Michel-Ange Mangourit, organized American volunteers to fight for France in Florida. In Louisiana, Genet planned to recruit Revolutionary War hero George Rogers Clark to raise a militia against New Orleans. In the back of his mind was the audacious prospect of resurrecting New France.

In all, Genet spent eleven days in Charleston attending parties, commissioning privateers, and recruiting mercenaries. Many Americans favored France in its war against England and supported its machinations against Spain. They did not, however, constitute anything like a national majority, and they certainly did not represent the views of the Washington administration, which was determined to avoid getting drawn into the contentious world of European politics.

After ordering the *Embuscade* to Philadelphia, Genet set out on a slow-moving overland journey northward that normally required two or three weeks. In Genet's case, it took more than a month. His aim was to marshal support for the French cause among the American public. And indeed, as he slowly rumbled through the Carolinas and Virginia, he was met in places with some of the same fervor he experienced in Charleston.

A myth has sprung up that Genet encountered a deep well of French sympathy at every village and hamlet along his path. "His journey to Philadelphia was one long ovation," writes one historian.[11] The truth, however, is somewhat different, as newspaper records from

the period reveal. Although many towns received Genet with cour-
tesy and even enthusiasm, the adulation was far from universal. As
John Steele of North Carolina wrote of Genet to Secretary of the
Treasury Alexander Hamilton, "Permit me to say that he has a good
person, fine ruddy complexion, quite active, and seems always in a
bustle, more like a busy man than a man of business."[12] Moreover, the
welcome seemed to cool the farther north he went. Receptions in
Alexandria and Georgetown were particularly subdued, and those in
Baltimore were even more tepid. Genet blamed this on local merchants who traded with Britain—as if their opinions were not valid.
Despite this waning interest, Genet came away from his journey with
the overwhelming impression that the vast majority of the American
people were fervent French loyalists. This mistaken belief would cost
him dearly.

When Washington first learned of France's declaration of war on
England, just before Genet's arrival in Charleston, he immediately
cut short a vacation at Mount Vernon and rushed to Philadelphia to
consult with the four members of his cabinet. All supported neutrality, though there was some disagreement on how to achieve it, especially between Hamilton and Jefferson. In general, Hamilton wanted
a closer relationship with the British, while Jefferson favored the
French. After intense deliberation, Washington issued a statement on
April 22 declaring that the United States would "adopt and pursue a
conduct friendly and impartial towards the belligerent powers."
Moreover, any American providing illegal assistance to the warring
countries would be prosecuted. Upon Jefferson's insistence, the word
neutrality did not actually appear in the document, yet history has
remembered the decree as the Neutrality Proclamation.

Washington's doctrine experienced its first major challenge on the
day the *Embuscade* escorted the *Grange* into Philadelphia. The
Charleston privateers and Genet's operations against Spain were also
significant threats, but word of them had not yet reached the capital.
Having looked into the circumstances surrounding the capture of the
Grange, Attorney General Edmund Randolph determined that the

Embuscade had in fact seized the British ship within U.S. territorial waters—and therefore the *Grange* should be released immediately from French custody. On May 18, Genet obeyed Randolph's order. It would be the first and last time that he ever capitulated to American protests about French neutrality violations. (Jefferson later noted with chagrin that although Genet complied with the order, he never actually apologized for the incident.)

On May 16, Genet at last arrived in Philadelphia. On the following day, a large crowd turned out to celebrate. Genet estimated its size at 6,000, but this was almost certainly an exaggeration. Jefferson pegged the number at 1,000 and Hamilton at no more than 600. Whatever the case, Genet became even more convinced of America's affection for France and its policies. In his address to the crowd, Genet said that although he did not expect the United States to enter the war, he hoped French citizens would be treated "as brothers in danger and distress."[13]

It was a shrewd distinction. In military terms, the United States had almost nothing to offer France as a war ally. There was little point in seeking aid from a navy that did not exist or an army that had been drastically downsized since the Revolutionary War. In the early 1790s, the American nation could barely protect its own shores from invasion, let alone project force into the West Indies or across the Atlantic. "We know that under present circumstances we have a right to call upon you for the guarantee of our [Caribbean] islands. But we do not desire it!" said Genet in his meeting with Washington on May 18. In addition, the French minister promised "to lay open our country and its colonies to you for every purpose of utility, without your participating in the burden of maintaining and defending them."[14]

Genet "offers everything, and asks nothing," declared an obliging Jefferson after the meeting.[15] In truth, Genet had demanded all that the United States could give. Militarily, this meant safe harbor in American ports for French privateers. Economically, it meant provisioning France's Caribbean colonies, which the British navy might cut off from Europe. In calling on Americans to do everything in their power to assist one belligerent (France) against another (Britain), Genet was asking for a complete suspension of the president's neutrality doctrine. The French minister considered Washington's proclamation invalid under the terms of the 1778 treaty that allowed French warships and privateers to bring their seizures into American ports and obtain supplies. In reality, however, the treaty stipulated only potential privileges, not guaranteed rights. Despite Genet's insistence, the United States was under no requirement to accommodate French privateers. When Jefferson informed Genet that the Washington administration would not allow France to outfit privateers in American ports or let French consuls determine the fate of seizures, the minister objected in the harshest of terms.

This prompted Jefferson to reiterate the American position. In a June 5 letter, the secretary of state demanded that the defiant Genet comply with U.S. neutrality. French privateers able to sail, he added, should leave American ports immediately. "It is the *right* of every nation," Jefferson explained, "to prohibit acts of sovereignty from being exercised by any other nation within its [territorial] limits; and the *duty* of a neutral nation to prohibit such as would injure one of the warring powers."[16] To speak of neutral duties rather than merely neutral rights was something of an innovation. By doing so, the United States assured foreign powers that it was not merely dodging a conflict but also accepting the responsibility, as a neutral, of preventing activity within its jurisdiction that would harm any belligerent.

Yet Genet remained obstinate. As he quarreled with Jefferson, his privateers continued to wreak havoc. The *Sans-Culotte* alone captured eight ships within six weeks of its commission, and more French privateers were taking to the waters all the time. In an October letter to his government, Genet reported arming fourteen privateers that had seized more than eighty ships. "They fill the English merchant vessels with terror and have condemned more than three thousand sailors to idleness," he boasted. Although this claim of immobilizing thousands of sailors was probably another example of his boasting, there is little doubt that his activities put a serious dent in British shipping.[17]

Genet's relationship with the Washington administration deteriorated rapidly. Upon learning that American authorities had seized a French privateer in New York harbor, Genet sent an insulting letter to Jefferson. He mocked Jefferson's "extremely ingenious" interpretation of the 1778 treaty. "Let us not lower ourselves to the level of ancient politics by diplomatic subtleties," he sneered.[18] Hamilton labeled Genet's letter the "most offensive paper perhaps that was ever offered by a foreign minister to a friendly power with which he resided."[19]

The unrepentant Genet was no doubt frustrated by his failure to secure a commitment from the United States to aid the French war effort. He was also having difficulties securing an advance payment on the debt the United States owed France following the American Revolution. Although he claimed France needed the money to protect its islands in the West Indies, he actually intended to divert much of it toward the military campaigns he was organizing against Spanish Florida and Louisiana.

On June 11, the Washington administration officially denied Genet payment because London might have interpreted such a move as a violation of neutrality. Yet the French minister continued to plot against Spain from within the United States. George Rogers Clark had informed him that a force of 400 men would be enough to evict the Spaniards from the northern part of the Louisiana territory. With 800 men and the help of two or three frigates, Clark believed he could descend upon New Orleans and remove the Spaniards from the city. Throughout the month of June, the irrepressible Genet worked to arm Clark's soldiers in Kentucky and prepared an expedition to move on New Orleans from the sea.

Genet also thought that he would prevail in his contest against Washington. All those soirées apparently had gone to his head. His letters home boasted of how his enormous popularity with the American public would influence government officials. "I live in the midst of continual parties. Old man Washington is jealous of my success, and of the enthusiasm with which the whole town flocks to my house," he wrote.[20] He was convinced that in time the American people would turn against their aging president and rally around the charming young man from Versailles.

Meanwhile, the *Embuscade* continued to attack British shipping off the coast of the United States. In May, it captured a British merchant vessel, the *Little Sarah*, near Philadelphia. After taking immediate ownership of the craft, the French renamed it the *Little Democrat* and added ten guns to its arsenal. In plain defiance of the neutrality decree, it was being armed as a privateer. When Jefferson learned of this development in early July, he asked Genet to detain the *Little Democrat* for several days until the president returned from a short trip to Mount Vernon. Genet refused, but added that the ship would not be ready to sail "for some time."[21] He also issued a threat. "Let me beseech you," he told Jefferson, "not to permit any attempt to put men on board of her. She is filled with high-spirited patriots, and they will unquestionably resist."[22]

When Washington returned, he found papers on his desk marked "instant attention." The matter was indeed grave. Hamilton and the secretary of war, Henry Knox, both believed that failure to prevent the *Little Democrat* from leaving Philadelphia would give Britain cause to declare war against the United States. The packet also included a letter from a Pennsylvania official who had heard of Genet threatening to "appeal from the president to the people."[23] This enraged Washington: "Is the minister of the French republic to set the acts of this government at defiance, *with impunity,* and then threaten the executive with an appeal to the people? What must the world think of such conduct, and of the government of the United States for submitting to it?"[24]

In the end, the president declined to use force against the *Little Democrat.* The vessel had managed to slip down the river and away from any batteries that might have been erected against it. Moreover, a fleet of fifteen French warships was expected in the area at any time. If they were to encounter a party of Americans fighting their way onto the *Little Democrat,* the result might be disastrous. Within a few days, however, the question became moot as the *Little Democrat* made for open waters—where it became one of Genet's most successful privateers. The French minister eventually intended to send it to New Orleans, where it would guard the entrance of the Mississippi as Clark and his Kentuckians approached the city from land.

Despite Genet's best efforts to ruin Anglo-American relations, the British minister, Hammond, was convinced that the United States had done all it could to detain the *Little Democrat*. Washington and his cabinet began to discuss whether Genet's presence in Philadelphia would continue to be tolerated. Hamilton believed the French minister was applying to the United States the Girondinist principle of subverting foreign governments, with Washington playing the part of a monarch who must be overthrown. The secretary of the Treasury advocated suspending Genet immediately and asking the French government to send a replacement. The more diplomatic Jefferson preferred sending a firm but tactful letter of complaint. After much deliberation, Washington opted for Jefferson's approach and the secretary of state drafted an 8,000-word document, which the cabinet reviewed and edited. Despite its length, the thrust of it may be found in a single passage: "When the government forbids their citizens to arm and engage in war, [Genet] undertakes to arm and engage them. When they forbid vessels to be fitted in their ports for cruising with the nations with whom they are at peace, he commissions them to fight and cruise. When they forbid an unceded jurisdiction to be exercised with their territory by foreign agents, he undertakes to uphold that exercise, and to avow it openly."[25]

The letter was sent to France late in August, but Genet was not informed of its contents until September 15—when the boat carrying it to Europe was too far away for him to order its capture. No one felt the French minister was beneath sabotaging correspondence intended for his superiors in Paris.

When Genet finally heard the news, he was furious and wrote an impertinent letter that might have driven Washington to suspend the minister on the spot. Yet months would go by before the president actually saw it: Yellow fever had struck in Philadelphia, causing the federal government to evacuate and suspend many administrative functions. The Americans conducted virtually no diplomacy until December. In all, four thousand people out of a population of 55,000 died.

But this natural disaster paled in comparison to the man-made one then devastating France, where the Girondins had lost their grip on power to more radicalized, left-wing Jacobins. The Committee of Public Safety, dominated by Robespierre, imposed price controls and enacted even more severe crackdowns on the Church. In September, this new government announced that it would rule by "terror" and began rounding up people it regarded as enemies of the state. In less than a year, at least 300,000 people would be arrested. Official records indicate that 17,000 were executed, though the death toll would be considerably higher if it included those who perished in prison.

So far from home, Genet did not learn of these developments as they unfolded. He spent much of the fall complaining about Washington. In letters to France, Genet accused the president of displaying medallion portraits of the French royal family in his office—a detail he had neglected to mention when reporting to France shortly after his first (and only) meeting with Washington in May. The French minister also kept busy plotting his latest intrigues against Florida and Louisiana, with military campaigns expected in the spring. George Clark was preparing to move down the Mississippi, and forces were gathering in Georgia for an attack on St. Augustine. In December, Congress reconvened, and Genet tried to generate support among American lawmakers for moving against Spain in these territories, but nobody was interested. Soon, local authorities in Georgia, Kentucky, and Tennessee started cracking down on the French efforts in Florida and Louisiana. The American people were standing behind "old man Washington" and his commitment to neutrality.

In January, word arrived that a new minister would replace Genet. Jacobin leaders were only too delighted to welcome a Girondin back into their clutches. Shrewdly sensing that the guillotine awaited him,

Genet begged Washington to grant him safe haven in the United States. Unexpectedly, it was Hamilton, Genet's greatest adversary in the cabinet, who encouraged the president to let him stay. Washington took this advice—he did not want to sign the man's death warrant and become an accomplice to the Reign of Terror. His act of generosity transformed America's first foreign subversive into its first recipient of political asylum.[26]

Genet's replacement, Jean Fauchet, arrived on February 21, 1794. He immediately terminated his predecessor's Florida and Louisiana adventures and repeated the French demand for Genet's return. But it was too late. Genet left Philadelphia, married the daughter of New York governor DeWitt Clinton, and became a U.S. citizen. For the next four decades, he lived quietly as a farmer even as he continued to rage at both the minister who would have taken his life as well as the president who had spared it. In 1795, when offered the opportunity to toast relations between France and the United States, he responded with venom: "May the perfidious efforts of Robespierre and of Washington to smother the fire of liberty have answered no other object but that of concentrating and increasing its strength."[27]

When Genet died in obscurity in 1834, few noted his passing. Yet he left behind an important legacy, confirming the United States in its long-term strategy of neutrality toward Europe. It is impossible not to detect the influence of Genet in Washington's Farewell Address of 1796: "Against the insidious wiles of foreign influence (I conjure you to believe me, fellow citizens) the jealousy of a free people ought to be *constantly* awake, since history and experience prove that foreign influence is one of the baneful foes of republican government."[28]

FOUR

FIRST IN WAR

An American is the born enemy of all the peoples of Europe.
—*Pierre Adet, French minister to the United States* [1]

ON NEW YEAR'S DAY in 1796, the revolutionary government of France presented George Washington with a gift: a copy of its new tricolor flag. At the formal ceremony in Philadelphia, French minister Pierre Adet spoke with enthusiasm about his country's "sacred ties" to the United States and its desire to improve relations with the American people, "her most faithful allies." The American flag, he informed Washington, was on display in the hall of France's National Convention. It was Adet's hope that the French flag would receive a similar honor in the House of Representatives. Washington was about to disappoint him.

"My best wishes are irresistibly excited whensoever, in any country, I see an oppressed nation unfurl the banners of freedom," said Washington. "The [French] colors will be deposited with the archives of the United States." [2]

This sly put-down enraged Adet. If Washington so loved the banners of freedom, then why was he packing the French flag into storage? Did he not believe that France was a land of liberty? Adet told Secretary of State Timothy Pickering that his government would view such treatment "as a mark of contempt." In a report to Paris, he complained that the French flag "will be hidden away in an attic and destined to become the fodder of the rodents and insects that live there."[3]

Washington was about to enter the final year of his presidency. So close to retirement, he could look back on his long career of service to his country with a deep sense of accomplishment. As a general, he had led his ragtag army in a David-and-Goliath struggle against the most powerful fighting force in the world and prevailed. As a statesman, Washington had overseen the writing and adoption of the Constitution and had then served as a wise and able president. As far back as the 1770s, people had taken to calling him "the father of his country." In the famous words of fellow soldier Henry Lee, Washington was "first in war, first in peace, and first in the hearts of his countrymen." Even the British, his former foes, began to sing the praises of the Virginia planter. Byron would write that he had "the all-cloudless glory . . . To free his country."

The French, on the other hand, had developed a distinctly jaundiced view of him. Forty years before, Washington had been demonized as the "assassin" of Jumonville's Glen. Twenty years later, the French had found it necessary to revise this opinion when they determined that it was in their national interest to promote American independence and—more important—seal Britain's colonial defeat. In the 1790s, however, Washington's reputation among the French deteriorated once again, as he charted a course of neutrality between France and Britain, stood up to Genet's subversion and defiance, and refused to celebrate the bloodbath of the French Revolution.

By the end of his presidency, Washington believed that the Revolutionary government in France was waging a propaganda war against him. "[My] opinions are to be knocked down and [my] character reduced as low as they are capable of sinking it, even by reporting falsehoods," he complained.[4] He was particularly upset to discover that French agents had been busy circulating old documents, forged by the British a generation earlier, that purported to reveal Washington's secret love of monarchy.

Adet's response to Washington's Farewell Address is typical of the French animosity: "You will have noticed the lies it contains, the insolent tone that governs it, the immorality that characterizes it." The president, added Adet, was guilty of "representing interest as the only counsel which governments ought to follow in the course of their negotiations, putting aside honor and glory."

This is rich stuff, coming from a French diplomat. On one level, of course, it is a gross misreading of the Farewell Address, which is primarily devoted to Washington's ideas on how Americans might forge a national character that sustains republican self-government. Hadn't the French just shown themselves to be spectacular failures at a similar project in their own country? Yet Adet's interpretation of the Farewell Address was not merely wrong, it was deeply hypocritical. In fact, the best that might be said of French behavior toward Americans during the eighteenth century is that it was guided by a perception of "interest." Frontier massacres and mercenary flotillas surely had little to do with advancing French "honor and glory." France's intervention during the American Revolution had been guided exclusively by the principles of national interest. So were Citizen Genet's machinations in 1793, as much as they may have backfired.

A major problem was that France and the United States held fundamentally different expectations of each other. France wanted to pull the United States into the wars of Europe as an ally and simply could not tolerate a policy of neutrality, even as most Americans wanted to separate themselves from European politics and violence. But for these conflicting outlooks, the two countries might have overcome the unpleasantness of the Genet episode.

The real turning point in French opinion of America's first president—and therefore in Franco-American relations generally—involved another controversial document signed by Washington. In 1795, Adet denounced Washington as "a wretch" for putting his name to the Jay Treaty, which Chief Justice John Jay had negotiated with Britain. "The President has just signed the dishonor of his old age and the shame of the United States," said Adet.[5]

The Jay Treaty was not a very advantageous agreement for the United States, though it was perhaps a necessary one. More than a decade after Yorktown, the British continued to post troops in the Great Lakes region, even though they had promised to remove them. They also harassed American shipping and encouraged Indian violence against settlers. As the two countries inched toward open conflict over these and other matters, Washington sent Jay to London for talks. There, he obtained a single yet crucial concession when the British agreed to withdraw their soldiers permanently from American soil. Beyond that, however, many Americans considered the treaty a disappointment. It granted the British commercial privileges but obtained nothing significant in return.

Nothing significant, that is, except a substantial peace. In large part because of the treaty, the Americans and British would not face each other in battle for nearly a generation. Indeed, a war with its mother country in the 1790s would have been ruinous for the young republic, which was then struggling to achieve financial stability and create the conditions for long-term growth. And while many believed the treaty conceded too much, Washington fully understood the consequences of failure and convinced a divided Senate to ratify the pact in the summer of 1795. Without a figure of Washington's stature leading the way, it is likely the Jay Treaty would have died and war broken out.

Paris greeted the news with indignation. The French still harbored hopes of hauling the Americans into the war they had declared on Britain in 1793, even though Genet had discovered how difficult that would be. In French eyes, the accord amounted to a U.S.-British alliance. One item in particular angered them. Under the terms of the treaty, British ships could board American merchant vessels bound for France and seize their cargoes as enemy contraband, as long as the owners were compensated. This provision had the sanction of international law, as Britain could hardly be expected to tolerate France using American vessels to supply itself. But while it neither violated any previous agreement nor contradicted Washington's neutrality decree, it clearly hurt French interests. After its formal adoption, the French announced that they would treat neutral powers as they permitted England to treat them. In short, French attacks on American shipping would assume a new intensity.

The French government considered more drastic options as well. "Is it [in] our interest," asked France's foreign minister, Charles Delacroix, "to declare war against the United States or else is it more in line with our politics to oblige this power to break with England?"[6] In the end, the French chose to wage political warfare against the U.S. government by trying to influence the result of the 1796 presidential election. The central figure in this scheme was none other than Pierre Adet, who had arrived in Philadelphia as French minister in 1795, just as Congress was debating the Jay Treaty. Unlike Genet, he waited only two days before presenting his credentials. Although first impressions of him were favorable, these would change. Adet's instructions from Paris—to enforce commercial treaties, preserve the rights of French privateers, and collect debt payments and loans— actually differed little from those given to Genet. Almost immediately, he began protesting the Jay Treaty as a violation of previous Franco-American accords.

Although the treaty broke no agreements, Adet and his government believed that France deserved more favorable treatment from the United States. Like Genet, Adet thought that most Americans remained forever thankful for French intervention during the War of Independence and that Washington had betrayed them. Yet it was also clear that he regarded ordinary Americans who admired Washington with contempt. "You may feel somewhat astonished that the people of America, to whom is attributed a larger measure of enlightenment and knowledge than they really possess, could be deceived for such a long time by the mere shadow of a great man," he wrote to his superiors in Paris.[7]

Washington, for his part, still hoped to salvage relations with France. In the summer of 1796, he decided to replace his ineffective minister in Paris, future president James Monroe, with Charles Cotesworth Pinckney. The decision would have important repercussions later on, but for the time being relations between the two governments continued to worsen. Then the French government declared that it would seize American cargo bound for Britain—a move that clearly violated its treaties with the United States. Soon, there would be hundreds of incidents involving French cruisers capturing American ships. Secretary of State Pickering would document many of them, including examples of outrageous French behavior.

On Christmas Day in 1796, a French privateer ordered the American merchant ship *Commerce* to come to a stop. Although the *Commerce* obeyed the command, the privateer fired on it anyway, injuring four men. In another incident, the crew of an armed French brig tortured the captain of the *Cincinnatus* with thumbscrews, trying to force him to admit that his cargo was British contraband. When the captain refused, most of his personal property and the ship's provisions were stolen.[8] "We can account for such conduct," Pickering wrote, "only on the principle of plunder; and were not the privateers acting under the protection of the Commissioners of the French Government, they would be pronounced pirates." The secretary of state then made a grim prediction: "These proceedings are rapidly rendering the name of Frenchmen as detestable as once it was dear to Americans and if suffered by their Government to be continued, total alienation will be inevitable."[9]

The decision to meddle in the 1796 presidential election only aggravated matters. "We must raise up the [American] people and at the same time conceal the lever by which we do so," said Delacroix, who suggested ordering Adet "to use all the means in his power in the United States to bring about a successful revolution and Washington's replacement."[10] Delacroix wanted the United States to abandon the Jay Treaty and realign itself with France. But this could only be done, he reasoned, if someone outside Washington's Federalist circle was elected president. It would be the first time an agent of a foreign government plotted to exploit America's democratic vulnerabilities by manipulating voters in a presidential election. This cynical strategy of interference flew in the face of France's public rhetoric about its revolutionary kinship with the United States and demonstrated once again that its true concerns were based on narrow self-interest rather than shared republican ideals.

In both 1788 and 1792, Washington had been elected by unanimous consent. Had he run for a third term in 1796, he almost certainly would have triumphed. In his Farewell Address, however, Washington announced his intention to retire from politics. This meant that the 1796 election would be the first contested presidential race in American history. For the French, the election of Vice President John Adams was to be prevented at all costs. Although Adams had not been an active participant in Washington's administration—he once called the vice presidency "the most insignificant office that ever the invention of man contrived or his imagination conceived"—it was widely believed that he would continue the foreign policy of his hated predecessor.[11] This the French could not stomach.

From their standpoint, a better alternative was Thomas Jefferson, Washington's secretary of state through 1793. Although Jefferson was a true American patriot who had supported the Neutrality Proclamation, he was also correctly perceived as being much friendlier to French interests than Adams. The vice president, after all, had mourned the beheading of Louis XVI and believed (correctly) that such a terrible act would lead to more violence: "Mankind will in time discover that unbridled majorities are as tyrannical and cruel as unlimited despots." Jefferson's reaction was much more sanguine: "Monarchy and aristocracy must be annihilated, and the rights of the people firmly established."[12]

At a time when presidential candidates refrained from campaigning openly and instead sent forth surrogates to speak on their behalf, Adet's political activities drew a great deal of attention. In the fall, the French minister toured New England and encouraged Jefferson's supporters there. Upon returning to Philadelphia, he issued a series of manifestos. Because it was not customary for foreign diplomats to address the public, Adet came up with the ploy of writing formal letters to Pickering and leaking copies to the press. His first announced that the United States and France were hurtling toward war and that only the election of Jefferson would save both countries from a terrible conflict.

It was an astonishing threat. By appealing directly to the American public à la Genet, Adet infuriated Washington and his supporters. Yet he continued to pursue his strategy throughout the autumn. In a November 15 letter, he announced the suspension of his ministerial functions. It was as if he were recalling himself as ambassador. France, he said, was "justly offended at the conduct" of the American government over the Jay Treaty. He went on to echo Genet in emphasizing that his dispute was not with the public but with their elected representatives. "The American people are not to regard the suspension of [my] functions as a rupture between France and the United States, but as a mark of just discontent, which is to last until the Government of the United States returns to its sentiments," he wrote.[13]

There is evidence that Adet's efforts proved persuasive to some. In Pennsylvania, antiwar Quakers flocked to Jefferson. Yet the French minister ultimately hurt his cause more than he helped it. Just as Genet had sparked a backlash three years earlier, many Americans saw Adet as an unwelcome intruder in the business of their democracy. This was true even among Jefferson's supporters. James Madison, a Jefferson loyalist, condemned Adet's interference for affecting "all the evil with which it is pregnant."[14] The fateful moment came on December 7, when the Electoral College convened. In one of the closest votes in U.S. history, Adams defeated Jefferson, seventy-one to sixty-eight.

On March 4, 1797, John Adams was sworn in as America's second president. Within days of assuming his duties, the chief executive learned of the latest rupture in Franco-American relations: The French government had refused to receive Charles Pinckney, the man Washington had sent to France to replace Monroe, and instead had ordered him to leave the country or be arrested. Adams and his cabinet understood what this meant: War with France was suddenly a distinct possibility.

John Adams came into the presidency knowing more about France than perhaps any high-ranking French official knew about the

United States. His experience during the Treaty of Paris negotiations, plus two previous missions to France, had taught him a great deal about French customs and French thought—which is not to say that he approved of either. He had read the works of many of the great French *philosophes* and was not shy about expressing his low opinion of them. The theory of the noble savage especially irked him. "Reading your work," he wrote to Rousseau, "one has the desire to walk on all fours."[15]

The sixty-year-old gentleman lawyer from Braintree, Massachusetts, knew that the French problem would loom large during his administration. In the months between his election and inauguration, American opinions toward France had hardened. "The conduct of France toward the United States," said Washington shortly before leaving office, "is, according to my ideas of it, outrageous beyond conception."[16]

Word of Pinckney's treatment in Paris appeared to confirm the worst. To complicate matters, France announced that French warships would join the privateers in capturing American vessels transporting British goods. Furthermore, any American ship that did not carry a specially formatted list of crew and passengers—something very few did—would be deemed a legitimate seizure.

Although many of his advisors demanded retaliation, Adams was no warmonger. France, he wrote, "is at war with us, but we are not at war with her."[17] In a speech to Congress on May 16, 1797, Adams explained his position and laid out a plan of action. He began with a critique of France's recent behavior. By rejecting Pinckney, he said, the French had decided to "treat us neither as allies nor as friends, nor as a sovereign state." He condemned French attempts to "produce divisions" between Americans and their elected representatives. "We are not a degraded people, humiliated under a colonial spirit of fear and a sense of inferiority, fitted to be the miserable instruments of foreign influence, and regardless of national honor, character, and interest." Although the French had "inflicted a wound in the American breast," Adams suggested "a fresh attempt at negotiation."[18] Finally, he proposed building a navy and assembling an army, in what might be called an early American version of the peace-through-strength doctrine.

A few days later, Adams announced a new three-person mission to France. It would include Pinckney, who was still in Europe; John Marshall, a Virginia judge who would go on to become the most influential Supreme Court justice in American history; and Massachusetts politician Elbridge Gerry, who would achieve a different kind of fame some years later when his adventures in congressional redistricting inspired the invention of the word *gerrymander*. Adams's instructions to the three diplomats were simple: Return the United States and France to a state of peace, using the carrot of a new commercial treaty giving France rights similar to those enjoyed by Britain under the Jay Treaty. They were warned, however, not to do anything that might undermine U.S. neutrality such as agreeing to a loan for cash-strapped France.

There was some hope that the new French foreign minister, Charles-Maurice de Talleyrand-Périgord, might prove to be conciliatory. But Talleyrand was no pushover. Subtle, smart, and cagey, he would become one of the most durable statesmen in European history, with a career that lasted into the 1830s. The scion of an important family, he suffered from clubfoot—an ailment that rendered him unfit for a traditional military calling. It was said that a nurse had dropped him as a child; more likely, the handicap was the result of a congenital disorder. Whatever the cause, Talleyrand spent his life walking with a limp. Despite his inveterate womanizing, he entered the seminary and began a rapid rise in the ranks of the church hierarchy. Elevated to the rank of bishop, he used his office to support many of the radical reforms of the French Revolution. When the Terror began, however, he fled to America, where he spent two years in exile as a purchasing agent for European land speculators. He became a friend and admirer of Alexander Hamilton, but never quite forgave Washington for refusing to meet with him. (Washington had received a negative report about Talleyrand's character from Gouverneur Morris.) On the whole, the privileged Frenchman found America a curious place and wondered at the need for a man of Hamilton's stature to "work all night in order to support his family."[19] When the Terror ended, Talleyrand returned to France, presented himself as an expert on North America, and was picked to succeed Delacroix as foreign minister in 1797.

Talleyrand had been on the job for less than three months when he received the U.S. delegation at his home, in an informal meeting that lasted a mere fifteen minutes. With his drooping eyelids and carefully curled hair, he was a picture of aristocratic condescension. Although he promised to grant the Americans a formal reception soon, the short encounter was not what the Americans had hoped for, but it was an improvement over Pinckney's earlier mistreatment. Perhaps progress was at hand.

On the night of October 18, however, one of Talleyrand's agents, Jean-Conrad Hottinguer, approached the Americans and informed them of a problem. French officials, he said, had taken great offense at the speech Adams had delivered in May. It was now necessary to appease them before negotiations could begin. The delegation, he advised, must repudiate portions of Adams's speech, offer a loan to France, and pay a large bribe—a *douceur*, or "sweetener"—to Talleyrand.

Rather than working hard like Hamilton, the exceedingly venal Talleyrand planned to amass a fortune by extracting "sweeteners" from diplomats who wished to do business with him, and he succeeded marvelously. One of his biographers estimates that between 1797 and 1804, Talleyrand received more than 30 million francs in bribes from foreign governments. "Talleyrand, when he is not conspiring, is bargaining," said the Viscount of Chateaubriand.[20] Bargaining for bribes, that is. The Frenchman's behavior recalls the observation of his countryman, the novelist Honoré de Balzac: "Behind every great fortune there is a crime."

Both Marshall and Pinckney wanted to reject Talleyrand's proposal, not only because a loan to France would have compromised

American neutrality, but because they refused to pay any bribes as a prerequisite to negotiations. (They were quite willing to consider bribes later on, after a treaty had been concluded.) Gerry, however, thought it would be a mistake to cut off their negotiations so prematurely. The three did agree that Hottinguer should write down the specifics of his proposal. The size of the bribe shocked them: $250,000.

Two days later, Hottinguer returned with a colleague, Pierre Bellamy, who repeated Talleyrand's demands and assured the Americans that once these were met, a treaty would be possible. The bribe was the key to the deal. "I will not disguise from you," Bellamy said, "you must pay money, you must pay a great deal of money."[21] When the meeting continued the next morning, Bellamy announced that perhaps a direct loan to France was not necessary after all. Instead, he proposed a scheme whereby the United States would purchase Dutch florins at an inflated price and allow the French government to reap a $6 million profit.

Once more, Pinckney and Marshall wanted to halt the talks then and there, while Gerry argued that letting them continue might lead the French to soften their position. They agreed to a counterproposal. If the French promised to stop their attacks on American shipping, one of them would travel back to the United States to confer about a loan. But they refused to renounce their president's speech.

As the talks proceeded, a young general named Napoleon Bonaparte concluded a brilliant military campaign in Italy that boosted French arrogance and consequently weakened any incentive Talleyrand may have had to deal fairly with the Americans. At one meeting, Hottinguer tried to intimidate them into acquiescence, warning them of the "power and violence of France." The Americans replied that if France went to war, the United States would defend itself. "You do not speak to the point," insisted Hottinguer. "It is money, it is expected that you will offer money," he said. "We have given an answer to that demand," countered the Americans. "No you have not," replied Hottinguer. "What is your answer?" At this, Pinckney snapped: "It is no, no, not a sixpence!"[22]

Negotiations appeared to have hit a wall. Talleyrand threatened that his government would announce more hostile actions against the United States if the delegation did not agree to something within a week. Then Lucien Hauteval, yet another of Talleyrand's agents, informed the Americans that if a bribe were paid, two of them would be allowed to stay in Paris while a third returned to the United States to secure a loan. The Americans asked whether French attacks on American shipping would stop in the meantime. No, was the answer. Then what, they wondered, was the purpose of paying a bribe? In reply, Hottinguer and Bellamy threatened not only a war, but also personal violence against Pinckney, Marshall, and Gerry. "We experience a haughtiness which is unexampled in the history and practice of nations," wrote Pinckney to a friend.[23]

On November 1, the Americans decided to terminate negotiations with Talleyrand's henchmen. They sent the foreign minister a note, signed by all three, demanding formal recognition of their status as diplomats. Although Talleyrand chose not to respond, he did not ignore them completely. Intermediaries continued to apply pressure, often at social functions or under the guise of personal business.

The most novel approach may have been that of Madame de Villette, an attractive widow who was rumored to have been Voltaire's mistress years earlier—and who ran a hotel in which Marshall and Gerry took rooms. During their stay, she became their frequent companion, sitting with them for hours each day and organizing parties on their behalf. Marshall and Gerry accompanied their hostess to her country estate several times, and on each occasion Madame de Villette made sure to invite a fourth person, always a woman. Marshall in particular seems to have been attracted to his landlady. Indeed, their relationship was "sufficiently unusual to raise the question of whether Marshall and the Marquise de Villette were more than friends," writes Marshall biographer Jean Smith.[24] It seems that Marshall's wife, back in the United States, may have harbored her own suspicions. What is not in dispute, however, is that this comely hotel proprietress spent much of her time urging the American delegation to provide a loan to the French government. Was she a paid *femme fatale* operating at Talleyrand's behest? The evidence remains unclear.

By January, the Americans had lost patience with their lack of progress. The situation grew worse when the French government announced that henceforth all French ports would be closed to neutral shipping. "There is not the least hope of an accommodation with this government," wrote Pinckney. "We sue in vain to be heard."[25] Yet they stayed. In March, Talleyrand actually began to meet with them personally, though still in an unofficial capacity. In April, when negotiations remained deadlocked, the delegation ruptured. Pinckney and Marshall concluded that further talks were pointless and made plans to leave. To their dismay, Gerry insisted on remaining in Paris. He was convinced that war would erupt if the United States did not have at least one representative in France. But events across the ocean soon would render his continued presence in Paris irrelevant.

Back in the United States, Americans eagerly awaited news from Paris about the success or failure of the diplomatic mission. Rumors were rampant. "Are our commissioners guillotined, or what else is the occasion of their silence?" wondered George Washington from his retirement at Mount Vernon on March 4, 1798.[26] That very night in Philadelphia—exactly one year since the inauguration of Adams— Secretary of State Pickering received a package from Paris. It had been sent in January and included five dispatches. Four of them were written in code and would take days to decipher. The fifth, however, could be read right away. Realizing at once that a crisis was at hand, Pickering rushed to the president's house, three blocks away. There, Adams learned that his diplomatic mission had failed.

The magnitude of the problem became apparent over the next few weeks, as the other dispatches were decrypted, shown to Congress, and then made available to the public. Talleyrand's outrageous and insulting demands for apologies, loans, and bribes stunned Americans, even those who previously had sympathized with France. The event is known to history as the XYZ Affair because the dispatches referred to Hottinguer, Bellamy, and Hauteval, respectively, as "X,"

"Y," and "Z." It did much to wash away the goodwill that had existed since the American Revolution.

Anti-French sentiment swept the country. The slogan "Millions for defense, but not one cent for tribute" tripped off American tongues everywhere. Although initially attributed to Pinckney, who denied saying it, the statement took on such a life that it was later inscribed on a tablet in his native Charleston.[27] In this flag-waving atmosphere, Joseph Hopkinson authored the song "Hail Columbia," which would become the country's unofficial national anthem.

> Firm, united let us be.
> Rallying 'round our liberty.
> As a band of brothers joined,
> Peace and safety we shall find.

When "Hail Columbia" made its debut on a theater stage in April, the singer Gilbert Fox was called back to sing it three more times. The First Lady, Abigail Adams, was an enthusiastic member of the audience that night. "The theater," she commented, "has been called the pulse of the people."[28]

Responding to the growing public outrage, Congress authorized the capture of armed French ships, suspended commercial relations, and voided all treaties with France. Adams received the defense appropriations he had requested a year earlier—these included the creation of a new Department of the Navy, distinct from the Department of War, as well as a new army, to be commanded by the sixty-six-year-old former president, Washington. "I will never send another minister to France," declared Adams, "without assurances that he will be received, respected, and honored as the representative of a great, free, powerful, and independent nation."[29]

On July 6, 1798, Captain Stephen Decatur sailed out of Philadelphia aboard the U.S.S. *Delaware*, a merchant vessel that had been converted into a sloop of war. (In future years, his son, also named Stephen, would achieve lasting fame as the veteran warrior who declared, "Our country! In her intercourse with foreign nations may she always be in the right; but our country, right or wrong!") Decatur knew that French privateers preyed off the New Jersey coast. He also knew that his own ship was not likely to chase down a fast schooner, so he used the *Delaware* as bait, making it behave like a commercial craft. A French privateer, the *Croyable*, soon spotted the *Delaware* and made for it—only to discover that its intended quarry carried twenty-four guns and a crew of 180 men. At one-third the *Delaware*'s size, the *Croyable* did not stand a chance. Its captain surrendered, thinking he had stumbled upon a British man-of-war. When he discovered that his foes were Americans, he protested that France was not at war with the United States. Decatur replied that France certainly had been acting the part for some time and that finally the United States was going to respond. It was the first victory for the newly constituted U.S. Navy.[30]

Many other clashes would follow in a struggle that became known as the Quasi-War—so named because neither the United States nor France ever issued a formal declaration of war. Although such a declaration would not have been difficult for Adams to secure from Congress, the president did not want to be seen as the aggressor. He also held out hope that peace might still be possible. Yet hostilities raged across the Atlantic. Four months after its engagement with the *Delaware* in the waters off New Jersey, the *Croyable*—now in American hands and renamed the U.S.S. *Retaliation*—would find itself massively outgunned and forced to surrender in the Caribbean to a pair of French frigates, the *Insurgente* and *Volontaire*. A war by any other name can be just as deadly, as Abigail Adams made clear in one of her characteristically insightful observations: "Why, when we have the thing, should we boggle at the name?"[31]

By the end of 1798, the United States had fourteen men-of-war at sea, including the frigate U.S.S. *Constitution*, nicknamed "Old Ironsides."[32] In all, some 200 American merchant vessels had obtained privateering rights. While the U.S. Navy defended American and British vessels in the Caribbean, the U.S. government arranged for the British Royal Navy to protect American shipping in the Atlantic Ocean.

The first major naval duel of the Quasi-War took place on February 9, 1799, off the West Indian island of Nevis (Alexander Hamilton's birthplace). It began when the *Constellation* spotted the *Insurgente*, the ship that had captured the *Retaliation* two months earlier. Aboard the *Constellation*, Captain Thomas Truxton was determined to avenge that loss. At about 3:15 P.M., as the *Constellation* pulled to within fifty yards of the enemy, its fourteen starboard guns ripped into the hull of the *Insurgente*. The two ships exchanged blasts for less than an hour before the French ship surrendered. It was an exhilarating victory. "I would not have you think me bloody minded, yet I must confess the most gratifying sight my eyes ever beheld was seventy French pirates (you know I have just cause to call them such) wallowing in their gore, twenty-nine of whom were killed and forty-one wounded," declared Lieutenant John Rodgers.[33] Only two members of the *Constellation*'s crew had died—one of them when an officer ran him through with a sword for cowardice.

During the war, the new U.S. Navy performed exceptionally well. Although it never had more than around sixteen ships, it had managed to capture an impressive eighty-six French vessels. As French attacks became less common, insurance rates for American commercial shipping dropped sharply. Even more noteworthy was the fact that the American Navy lost only one ship, the *Retaliation*. The war signaled to France—and the rest of the world, including Britain—that the United States was growing into a major force on the seas.

On the eighteenth of Brumaire in year VIII of the French Revolution—or November 9, 1799, by ordinary reckoning—Napoleon Bonaparte seized power in a coup d'état. Both he and Talleyrand, who had been one of his supporters and who was now his foreign minister, agreed that the present naval war with the United States served no significant national purpose. Napoleon was especially eager to resolve matters with the Americans so that he might coax them into a conflict with Britain. He was also sensitive to the issue of neutrality, which he believed might hold the key to breaking British maritime power. Honoring the rights of neutral powers such as the United States might open the seas to a more robust commerce than the British navy was allowing. It might also lead to a revival of the French empire in the New World—a project that Napoleon was already starting to think about.

Talleyrand informed the U.S. minister at The Hague, William Vans Murray, that he would receive American diplomats if Adams would send them.[34] Adams then appointed Murray and two others as ministers to France. By the spring of 1800, negotiations were underway in Paris. The talks wore on for months, with the United States initially demanding that France pay $20 million in reparations for its attacks on American shipping. France countered with its old claim about treaty obligations. On September 30, 1800, they reached a compromise: The United States agreed to assume the burden of compensating its own citizens, while France agreed to release the Americans from their treaties.

The compact did little to help Adams politically. In 1800, supporters of his rival Thomas Jefferson were more determined than ever to elect their man. Adams's party, meanwhile, was fatally divided. One faction, led by former Treasury secretary Alexander Hamilton, believed that the president should have extracted more from the French. In the end, Hamilton's biting criticisms helped to seal Adams's fate and deliver a narrow victory to the man from Monticello.

Yet Adams held no regrets. "I will defend my mission to France, as long as I have an eye to direct my hand, or a finger to hold my pen," he wrote in 1815. "They were the most disinterested and meritorious actions of my life. I reflect upon them with so much satisfaction, that I desire no other inscription over my gravestone than: 'Here lies John Adams, who took upon himself the responsibility of the peace with France in the year 1800.'"[35]

John Adams was the first war president in American history, and a remarkably able one. His foremost goal had been to achieve peace with a stubborn adversary, which he managed to do by showing toughness when necessary and making sure a limited war did not explode into a wider one. Had Adams sent his own conniving Talleyrand to Paris, the United States and France might very well have suffered through a long and costly conflict. The peace of 1800 also made possible one of the greater accomplishments of his successor and rival: the Louisiana Purchase.

FIVE

THE LONG SHADOW OF NAPOLEON

We stand completely corrected of the error that either the government or the
nation of France has any remains of friendship for us. On the contrary, it
appears evident, that an unfriendly spirit prevails in the most important
individuals of the government, toward us.
—*Thomas Jefferson* [1]

EW MEN IN history have combined the ambition, audac-
ity, and skill of Napoleon Bonaparte, and fewer still have
marshaled these qualities in the service of a more awful
lust for power. Over the course of fifteen years, his wars cost Europe
at least six million lives. His insatiable drive for conquest destroyed
whole villages and turned hundreds of thousands of peaceful civilians
into desperate refugees. The ruthless soldiers of his *Grande Armée*
raped and pillaged their way across a continent. Troops who surrendered to French forces may have expected mercy, but thousands met
with execution upon his direct orders. Even an impartial rendering of
his legacy must conclude that Napoleon was one of history's great
monsters. "What year of his military life has not consigned a million
human beings to death, to poverty and wretchedness?" asked Thomas
Jefferson. "What field in Europe may not raise a monument of the
murders, the burnings, the desolations, the famines, and miseries it
has witnessed from him?" [2]

The little tyrant from the sun-soaked Mediterranean island of Corsica delivered a shock of imperial glory to France, yet his adopted

country would become his ultimate victim. Hundreds of thousands of French soldiers died in his series of superfluous and bloody wars. In the wake of his defeat at Waterloo in 1815 and final exile on St. Helena, France continued a pattern of national decline that had started half a century earlier and from which it has never recovered. And yet, in France, Napoleon is the most celebrated figure in its long history— more honored than Charlemagne, Henry II, or even Joan of Arc. Two centuries later, during a diplomatic crisis with the United States over Iraq, French foreign minister Dominique de Villepin would describe his own fascination with Bonaparte and evoke a threadbare vision of national glory based on the dubious achievements of a long-dead dictator. Millions of the French continue to bask in the glow of his memory. Indeed, their belief in French cultural and political superiority is based as much on the fact that the Western world once trembled before their emperor as on the reputation of their cheese.

Napoleon's rapid rise to power began amid the violence and chaos of the French Revolution. A Jacobin and a general, he first came to national prominence in 1795, when he dispersed a Paris mob with cannon fire, killing about a hundred people with what he dismissed as a "whiff of grapeshot." After a distinguished military campaign in Italy, his reputation for bold action grew. In 1798, Napoleon embarked upon an adventure in Egypt that demonstrated two important characteristics that would shape his tense relations with the United States: a willingness to project French power across the sea and a readiness to forsake a cause when it no longer promised success. Following some early victories along the Nile, catastrophe struck when the British navy under Admiral Horatio Nelson destroyed the French fleet in Aboukir Bay. As more frustrations followed, Napoleon eventually abandoned his men, returned alone to France, and organized a coup that made him head of a military state in November 1799. France had executed its king only to give itself a dictator—a short man who would cast a long shadow on the world.

Americans had first felt Napoleon's unwelcome influence during the XYZ Affair, when the general finalized the Treaty of Campo Formio with Austria in October 1797. The provisions of that peace accord had nothing directly to do with the United States, but they ultimately proved so favorable to France that they heightened the arrogance of Foreign Minister Talleyrand as he chased after bribes from U.S. diplomats. Without Napoleon, the XYZ Affair might have unfolded much as it did, but there can be no doubt that his military successes helped create the conditions for the Quasi-War that erupted in 1798.

Napoleon also played a role in bringing that conflict to a conclusion. The naval war begun by the French government he had deposed was, for him, an unwanted distraction. Not only did it interfere with his aspirations in Europe, it also hampered another great desire: his dream of resurrecting New France in the New World. Yet Napoleon's grand designs for North America ultimately would fall apart. A military disaster in the Caribbean as well as the determined opposition of the United States would force him to abandon plans for what may have been his loftiest ambition, in the territory of Louisiana.

French claims on Louisiana stemmed from La Salle's journey through the region in the seventeenth century. During much of the eighteenth century, French settlers migrated to New Orleans and its environs. One large wave came from Acadia, in Canada, where the British had evicted them during the final French and Indian War. Just as these French-speaking "Cajuns" were arriving in large numbers, however, France ceded Louisiana to Spain in an effort to curry diplomatic favor. By modern lights, making a gift of such a vast region seems outrageously generous. Yet the transfer came at a time when the tiny sugar islands of the Caribbean were considered far greater treasures than immense tracts of uncharted wilderness in North America.

The French philosopher Montesquieu once said that Spain knew best how to possess a great empire with insignificance, a claim borne out by its inability to assimilate Louisiana. Despite four decades of Spanish rule, New Orleans tenaciously maintained its French character and culture. During the American Revolution, many Louisianans had hoped that France would reclaim the province. But it was not until the late 1780s that French interest in its old colony revived.

Whereas Spain considered Louisiana little more than a buffer between its more prosperous settlements to the south and the western advance of the United States, French officials began to think about the untapped commercial possibilities at the mouth of the Mississippi. As thousands of Americans moved to Ohio, Kentucky, and Tennessee, the economic importance of New Orleans would only grow. A French-controlled Louisiana also could supply agricultural products to the sugar and coffee plantations of Santo Domingo, whose exports were so profitable that it made more sense to import food and wood than to divert the island's precious acreage away from its cash crops. New Orleans and Port-au-Prince would serve as the twin headquarters for French ambitions in the Western Hemisphere.

Shortly before the onset of the French Revolution, close alliances between the noble families of France and Spain made it impossible for one to take aggressive action against the other. By 1793, however, the French nobility had been marginalized and Citizen Genet had arrived in the United States with plans to subvert Spanish rule in Louisiana. Although he failed, French interest in its former territory did not disappear. In 1795, the United States had secured navigation rights to the Mississippi River from Spain—a move that irritated the French because it demonstrated America's growing influence in the region and led to an explosion of commerce that France wanted for itself.[3] In the meantime, France began to consider the possibility of regaining Louisiana through negotiation rather than force. Paris made overtures to Madrid and a slow-moving dialogue began.

Just in case Spain proved less than accommodating at the transfer talks, France also continued to plan for the hostile takeover of Louisiana. In 1796, Pierre Adet—the man who had tried to deny John Adams the presidency—asked General Victor Collot to head an expedition to Louisiana. The general was known to be a skilled geographer, and Adet believed he would become a useful spy. American officials were informed of his journey but not of its actual purpose: to survey land France one day might choose to invade. Remembering Genet's mischief, Secretary of War James McHenry ordered federal agents to follow the Frenchman, though they could not prevent Collot from compiling notes on how to burn the fort at Pittsburgh or how to establish a military base at St. Louis. The Frenchman also drew maps of rivers and tributaries, wrote an economic profile of the region, and suggested to Adet that frontier settlers probably would align themselves with whichever power controlled New Orleans.[4]

Anxious to put his plans of conquest into action, Napoleon ordered his deputies to revive the moribund Louisiana negotiations with Spain. "The possession of Louisiana seemed to him especially favorable to the project he had formed of rendering France preponderant in America," said François Barbe-Marbois, the secretary of the French treasury.[5] There was also talk of attempting to persuade several western American states to secede and join a new French union—an unrealistic goal, perhaps, but one that animated French planning at the time.

Although neither the United States nor France had issued a formal declaration of war during the 1790s, the two countries did sign a declaration of peace—the Treaty of Mortefontaine—on September 30, 1800. Americans welcomed the end of the Quasi-War, but they had no idea what would happen the very next day. On October 1, Paris signed a secret pact with Spain—the Treaty of San Ildefonso—in which it swapped a few Italian principalities for all of Louisiana. Napoleon knew that the United States would view their retrocession as tremendously provocative, so the agreement with Spain was kept under wraps. France worried that the United States might pre-emptively seize New Orleans in an act of self-defense. When the American minister in Spain learned of the retrocession talks, his colleagues from Paris denied the existence of any agreement. It was a bald-faced lie.

As it turned out, complications in Italy would prevent the formal transfer of Louisiana to the French for two years—a providential delay for the Americans, who would use the period to turn a potential calamity into an extraordinary opportunity. In the meantime, Napoleon would learn that the biggest obstacle to his plans for

Louisiana resided not in Europe but in the office of the American president.

The French had been delighted when Thomas Jefferson defeated John Adams in the 1800 election. In the 1780s, Jefferson had succeeded Benjamin Franklin as ambassador to France. There, he fell in love with French culture, especially its architecture, its food, and its wine. Yet he also became a sharp critic of European society, which he saw as dangerously corrupt. The continent's capitals, he wrote in a typically disparaging remark, "are worth seeing, but not studying."[6] It has been said that Jefferson did not become fully American until after he experienced Europe.

Like most Americans, Jefferson initially had been supportive of the French Revolution, believing that the turmoil in France was a natural sequel to America's War of Independence and that it would be relatively bloodless. Late in life, however, he became so embarrassed by his earlier naïveté that he edited his letters to suggest that he had not been completely blindsided by the Terror or the other deadly aspects of revolutionary radicalism.[7]

If Jefferson was one part Francophile, he was an American patriot many times over. To be sure, as secretary of state during the Washington administration, Jefferson often supported a foreign policy that seemed to favor France. He frequently and famously clashed with Alexander Hamilton, who preferred Britain. In recounting those debates, it is possible to forget that the two men shared much more in common with each other than they did with their European rivals. Jefferson, after all, had penned that colossal irritant to France, Washington's Neutrality Proclamation. Almost a decade later, he would extend Washington's foreign-policy legacy even further. "It is proper that you should understand what I deem the essential principles of our government," he said in his 1801 inaugural address. Among these: "peace, commerce, and honest friendship, with all nations—entangling alliances with none."[8] Contrary to popular belief, the well-worn term "entangling alliances" is not from Washington's Farewell Address but from this speech of Jefferson's.

Within a month of assuming the presidency on March 4, 1801, Jefferson learned that European newspapers were brimming with speculation about France acquiring a large swath of North America. "There is considerable reason to apprehend that Spain cedes Louisiana and the Floridas to France," he wrote. "It is a policy very unwise to both, and very ominous to us." The highest-ranking French diplomat in the United States, Louis-André Pichon, tried to assure Jefferson that France's acquisition of Louisiana was "a thing entirely unlikely."[9] (Despite persistent American concerns, Florida never passed into Napoleon's hands, and the United States would purchase it from Spain in 1819.)

The problem for the United States and its president was clear. Some fifteen years earlier in Paris, Jefferson had predicted that American settlers would spread across the entire North American continent within forty years. It was certainly possible to believe this early version of Manifest Destiny so long as Louisiana remained a part of Spain, whose hollow empire was withering into irrelevance. France, however, presented a genuine danger. Not only was it a European power of the first order, but its warmongering leader also happened to be one of history's greatest military commanders. This was not the sort of neighbor the young nation wished to have on its frontier. The potential French occupation of New Orleans was even an impetus behind the Lewis and Clark expedition, which Jefferson hoped would discover an alternate route to the sea for American commerce—one that would circumvent French mischief.

For Jefferson, the rise of Napoleon confirmed the failure of the French Revolution. In his correspondence, Jefferson labeled the French emperor a "military usurper," "an unprincipled tyrant," "a great scoundrel," "a moral monster," and "the ruthless destroyer of ten millions of the human race, whose thirst of blood appeared unquenchable, the great oppressor of the right and liberties of the world." The leader of America's francophilic faction at last understood that revolutionary France was not a sister republic or a natural ally to the United States but a cruel despotism and a serious threat.

American diplomats were not able to verify the secret Franco-Spanish pact until the fall of 1801. But it hardly mattered. Jefferson was convinced of its existence, despite a steady stream of French lies denying it. The denials simply made him more suspicious of French motives. Why hide such an agreement from the world? Why keep America in the dark? Soon, worries began to mount as France and Britain concluded a peace in 1801. Although short-lived, it allowed France to focus on colonial projects. By November 1801, Napoleon had a general and a force in place, but lacking transportation they never left port.

Another expedition was consuming much of France's military resources. It was bound for the island of Santo Domingo (present-day Haiti and the Dominican Republic), where a decade of slave revolts and international intrigue had left François Dominique Toussaint L'Ouverture in control of the entire island and its productive plantations. A former slave, this remarkable man led armies of black soldiers in guerrilla warfare against several colonial masters. L'Ouverture, which means "the opening," was a nickname Toussaint earned for his ability to create gaps in enemy lines. (By another tradition, it referred to the gap between his two front teeth.) As the 1790s came to a close, this Bonaparte of Santo Domingo, as he liked to call himself, had triumphed over forces from Britain, France, and Spain. His victories had made Santo Domingo for all practical purposes an independent nation—the second in the Western Hemisphere.

The real Bonaparte, however, was determined to defeat Toussaint, reassert French control over its former colony, and reestablish the institution of slavery. Once accomplished, he would turn his rapacious gaze to Louisiana. Napoleon gave the command to his brother-in-law, General Victor Leclerc—an obvious sign of the importance he attached to the mission. In the fall of 1801, Leclerc set course for Santo Domingo with 20,000 veteran troops, the largest force that had ever sailed from France. They arrived in January and, in a brutal three-month campaign, vanquished the rebel army. After Toussaint's surrender, Leclerc invited him to dinner "to discuss important matters that cannot be explained by letter."[10] When the native leader arrived, however, he was captured and shipped to France, where he died the following year in a freezing prison cell in the French Alps.

Jefferson's government watched all of this with considerable nervousness. From Paris, U.S. envoy Robert Livingston reported that Leclerc would soon be heading for Louisiana. Although Napoleon may have intended for a portion of Leclerc's massive army to move on New Orleans eventually, he gave no such instructions.

Leclerc, however, did initiate an aggressive anti-American policy in Santo Domingo. Upon arriving in port, the treacherous Frenchman seized twenty American vessels and imprisoned several of their captains. One of the captured sailors was the naval hero John Rodgers, who had been aboard the *Constellation* when it defeated the *Insurgente* in the Quasi-War. Leclerc also accused American merchants of price gouging, confiscated their stores, and forced them to accept inflated currency as payment. Yet the general and his army would receive a fatal comeuppance: Yellow fever began to spread among the ranks.

In the early months of 1802, however, Leclerc was enjoying considerable success in Santo Domingo—and the Napoleonic menace loomed large in North America. A report in the French press described government plans to restore New France by absorbing the western part of the United States. Such rumors were treated with great seriousness and apprehension in American circles because the French government controlled the newspapers. Jefferson went so far as to warn the French minister that French occupation of New Orleans would mean war between their two countries. Then, on April 18, he penned one of the most astonishing letters of his life. "There is one spot on the globe, the possessor of which is our natural and habitual enemy," wrote Jefferson.

> It is New Orleans, through which the produce of three-eighths of our territory must pass to market, and from its fertility it will ere long yield more than half of our whole produce and contain more than half our inhabitants. France placing herself

in that door assumes to us the attitude of defiance. Spain might have retained it quietly for years. Her pacific dispositions, her feeble state, would induce her to increase our facilities there so that her possession of the place would be hardly felt by us, and it would not perhaps be very long before some circumstance might arise which might make the cession of it to us the price of something of more worth to her. Not so can it ever be in the hands of France. The impetuosity of her temper, the energy and restlessness of her character, placed in a point of eternal friction with us . . . render it impossible that France and the United States can continue long friends when they meet in so irritable a position. . . . The day that France takes possession of New Orleans fixes the sentence which is to restrain her forever within her low water mark. It seals the union of two countries who in conjunction can maintain exclusive possession of the ocean. From that moment we must marry ourselves to the British fleet and nation. . . . Every eye in the U.S. is now fixed on this affair of Louisiana. Perhaps nothing since the revolutionary war has produced more uneasy sensations through the body of the nation."

Jefferson addressed this document to Livingston and placed it in the hands of Pierre du Pont de Nemours, whose family would eventually become a household name to Americans. Du Pont had been living in the United States but was returning to his native France, where he would have audiences with Napoleon, Talleyrand, and other top officials. Jefferson gave him the letter unsealed so that he could convey its message directly to the highest authorities in France. The letter detailed almost every facet of Jefferson's policy toward Louisiana: recognition of the commercial importance of New Orleans, the hope that the United States might one day acquire the city through peaceful means, opposition to French imperialism, and the possible necessity of an Anglo-American alliance to contain French ambitions. The president believed that if the French understood both the intensity and clarity of the American commitment, they might reconsider their provocations. Secretary of State James Madison made the fundamental point to Pichon: "France cannot long preserve Louisiana against the United States."[12]

Amid such blunt talk, the Americans began to convey to the French that they would rather buy New Orleans than fight over it. But Napoleon had no intention of selling. Instead, he was planning a bold military expedition to occupy Louisiana. In a letter to the man responsible for organizing the operation, Admiral Denis Decrès, Napoleon disclosed his plans: "My intention, Citizen Minister, is that we take possession of Louisiana with the shortest possible delay, that this expedition be organized in the greatest secrecy, and that it have the appearance of being directed on St. Domingo."[13] Several months later, Napoleon set down his formal policy: "The intention of the First Consul [i.e., Napoleon] is to raise Louisiana to a degree of strength which will allow him in time of war to abandon it to its own resources without anxiety; so that enemies may be forced to the greatest sacrifices merely in attempting to attack it."[14]

Some 3,000 men were assigned to the expedition under the command of General Claude Victor. Although this was just a fraction of the troop strength that had been committed to the conquest of Santo Domingo, it was more than enough to secure New Orleans against any American force. Moreover, Victor would bring along some 5,000 muskets to pass out among Indians who would use them to attack American settlers, as well as 20,000 pounds of powder, 5,000 tomahawks, and other assorted weapons. Napoleon was eager to revive the wave of frontier massacres his nation had directed with such brutal effectiveness during the French and Indian Wars. The plan was to sail for New Orleans in the fall of 1802.

Before setting forth from Europe, however, the French wanted Spain to deliver the royal order ceding Louisiana, something that did not actually happen until October 25. There were further delays as the growing demand for reinforcements in Santo Domingo created provisioning shortages and transport problems. When it finally looked as though Victor was ready to sail in early 1803, freezing weather inter-vened—and the French found themselves icebound.

Then came two unexpected developments, both advantageous to the United States. The first was sparked by a decision made in New Orleans the previous November to close the city to American com-merce for reasons scholars still do not fully understand. Here was a complicated situation, with France technically owning Louisiana but Spanish officials still operating in the territory because of the holdup surrounding the formal transfer. Was it the work of a renegade bureau-crat? Were the Spaniards trying to create a headache for the French? Whatever the truth, the decision infuriated Americans, who were inclined to believe that France was somehow behind the unfriendly order. Soon, there were calls for New Orleans to be taken by force. Madison claimed that an army of militiamen "would march at a moment's warning" on the city. "This consideration ought not to be overlooked by France and would be alone sufficient if allowed its due weight to cure the frenzy which covets Louisiana,"[15] he said. Jefferson sent his own urgent note to Livingston in Paris: "We must know at once whether we can acquire N. Orleans or not. We are satisfied noth-ing else will secure us against a war at no distant period."[16]

If this display of American determination was not enough to dis-suade Napoleon from invading Louisiana, the bleak news from Santo Domingo almost certainly did the trick. On January 7, the French dic-tator learned that Leclerc had died, felled by yellow fever. Moreover, the main body of his troops also was gone, devastated by disease and the ongoing black resistance. Of the 34,000 French soldiers initially committed to Santo Domingo, there was barely a man left standing: A staggering 24,000 had perished, and 8,000 were seriously ill. Leclerc's successor, Donatien Rochambeau (whose father had fought at York-town), demanded 35,000 additional troops from Napoleon and prom-ised something akin to genocide. France must "destroy at least 30,000 negroes and negresses—the latter being more cruel than the men," he wrote. "These measures are frightful, but necessary."[17] The French had committed previous atrocities on the island, but nothing that approached this magnitude. Napoleon finally understood that he had planted his tiny foot into a quagmire. There would be no mass slaughter of Haitians. At a social event, Napoleon shrieked his frustration: "Damn sugar, damn coffee, damn colonies!"[18]

Years later, when Napoleon was in exile on St. Helena, he observed: "There is a moment in every battle in which the least maneuver is decisive and gives superiority, as one drop of water causes overflow."[19] In this case, it had been a sudden torrent of bad tidings. The United States almost certainly would have fought over New Orleans, and the experience of Santo Domingo—like Egypt before it—had taught the dictator how difficult it was to wage war in a distant land. And even if Napoleon had wanted to fight for Louisiana in the early months of 1803, he would have lacked the means. When the ice trapping Victor finally melted, a British blockade prevented his ships from reaching open water. France's war with Britain had resumed, and Napoleon knew a large distraction in Louisiana would not help him win it.

On April 9, Napoleon declared Louisiana to be entirely lost. The next day, Talleyrand summoned Livingston to his chambers. This time, there were no demands for bribes, just a straightforward proposal to sell all of Louisiana to the United States. Livingston, who was hard of hearing, must have wondered whether his ears were deceiving him. He was not sure how to reply at first. Although his instructions discussed only the possibility of obtaining the city of New Orleans and perhaps Florida, in less than three weeks he and his newly arrived colleague, James Monroe, hammered out a monumental deal with the French: For $15 million, the United States would acquire 828,000 square miles of land—a territory so immense and undefined that neither buyer nor seller knew its exact size. Although the deal was an undeniable bargain at pennies to the acre, Livingston and Monroe went outside their authority to make it. When news of the purchase reached the United States, however, there were few complaints. Jefferson was ecstatic. "This removes from us the greatest source of danger to our peace," he said.[20] It was the finest moment of his presidency.

It was certainly a low point in Napoleon's reign. Most of his biographers, many of them admiring, have given the Louisiana Purchase only the slightest attention. But Napoleon had not been snookered. With his vaulting ambitions for North America utterly dashed, he made about as good a deal as he could have gotten at the time. Had he waited any longer, France's inability to occupy New Orleans would have been exposed, and the selling price would have dropped precipitously—perhaps to nothing at all.

Meanwhile, the French colonial empire was collapsing. Later that year, Rochambeau would evacuate Santo Domingo, having no better luck quelling the island than Leclerc. For the second time in a quarter century, a country in the Western Hemisphere had thrown off the yoke of colonialism. Taking its name from the language of Santo Domingo's original Arawak inhabitants, the nation of Haiti was born. After the French retreat, one of Toussaint's compatriots, Jean-Jacques Dessalines, had himself crowned emperor and issued an unambiguous assessment of French colonial rule: "Accursed be the French name! We declare eternal hatred of France!"[21]

It hardly matters whether Napoleon ever learned of the Haitian's curse. His attention now refocused on European concerns, he gave no further heed to Santo Domingo. He did, however, occasionally reflect back on what had transpired in Louisiana and once made the revealing suggestion that he had cleverly planted the seeds for the future dismemberment of the United States. A sprawling country trying to settle such a vast territory, he said, "would separate the interests of the eastern and western states and would perhaps prepare the moment when they would separate into two powers."[22] On other occasions, he claimed that one of his motives in making the sale was to cripple Britain, harking back to France's old rationale for intervening in the American Revolution: "I have just given England a maritime rival that sooner or later will lay low her pride."[23] Another time, he offered a prophecy: "The Americans may be found too powerful for Europe in two or three centuries. But my foresight does not embrace such remote fears."[24]

Soon after the great transaction, Jefferson scribbled a note to a friend in France: "Your government has wisely removed what certainly endangered collision between us. I now see nothing which need ever interrupt the friendship between France and this country."[25] Unfortunately, there would be no blossoming friendship. In 1804, Napoleon crowned himself emperor. Within a few years, the French Empire and the American republic again would come dangerously close to war.

In 1805, two events set the stage for future tensions. On October 21, the British navy under Nelson demolished the French fleet at Trafalgar. Six weeks later, Napoleon smashed the Austrian and Russian armies at Austerlitz. Britain was now the ruler of the seas and France the master of continental Europe. Lacking the means to strike the other directly, the two rivals prosecuted their conflict through naval blockades and port closures.

The United States found itself trapped between both powers, as if in a vise. American ships attempting to trade with France gambled that they could elude the frigates of the mighty British navy. If captured, the sailors faced the additional risk of impressment because Britain, always needing to bully more men onto its warships, still refused to recognize the U.S. naturalization of British-born subjects. Moreover, American ships bound for Britain had to escape the clutches of French privateers. (Napoleon's "condemnation of vessels taken on the high seas by his privateers and carried involuntarily into his ports is justifiable by no law [and] is piracy," wrote Jefferson.)[26] The problem became so acute that one Philadelphia merchant placed a Frenchman with phony papers on some of his vessels so that if they were boarded, he might convince the French marauders that the ship was actually sailing for France.

The depredations became so great that Jefferson might have gone to war with either Britain or France. Yet the president understood the futility of declaring a war that his country could not wage. Seizing New Orleans with a horde of frontier militia was one thing; mounting a serious challenge to a major European power was quite another.

So Jefferson chose to pursue a policy of economic coercion, and Congress passed the Embargo Act of 1807, prohibiting the export of products from the United States. Jefferson hoped it would pressure the British and French to change their anti-American trade policies. But this radical initiative proved to be both unpopular at home and difficult to enforce. It was quickly branded the "dambargo." American sailors lost their jobs and merchants found ways to smuggle their goods out of the country. The restrictions did result in some food shortages and factory closings in Britain, but the effect was not enough to force London to lift its blockade. Napoleon, for his part, was delighted with Jefferson's decision because the British were far more dependent on trade with the United States—and therefore more vulnerable—than France was. The emperor then did a devious thing. On April 17, 1808, he ordered the seizure of all American ships arriving in French-controlled ports on the grounds that because the U.S. embargo was supposedly working, the ships must be British vessels in disguise. American merchants lost upward of $10 million, and Napoleon defended his banditry by claiming that he was merely helping Jefferson enforce his own policy.

After more than a year of the hated export ban, American patience ran out. Three days before Jefferson retired to Monticello and James Madison became America's fourth president, Congress repealed the Embargo Act. A new policy permitted exports to all but British and French ports. This weaker version, however, also failed to achieve its purpose. And so it, too, was replaced with something even less onerous: a law permitting exportation anywhere but with the threat that if either Britain or France repealed its trade restrictions, the president was authorized to impose an embargo on the other. Having failed with a stick, the United States tried a carrot.

Napoleon responded, though not in the way Madison would have liked. The president, in the words of historian Henry Adams, was about to get "hoodwinked."[27] In August 1810, the emperor had one of his deputies write a letter that appeared to revoke French policies on American trade. "His Majesty loves the Americans," said the note.[28] A close reading, however, revealed that there would be no revocation until Britain lifted its naval blockade on continental Europe. The emperor wanted to leave the matter, in his words, "a little obscure" to the Americans.[29] Although Madison fully understood the potential for duplicity, he honestly believed he had achieved a diplomatic break-through and imposed a new embargo on Britain. Unfortunately, Napoleon had no intention of altering French policy. On the very day of his supposed overture to the United States, he ordered the sale of several confiscated American ships. "I really pity Mr. Madison," commented William Short, a veteran U.S. diplomat. "He does not know the wheel within the wheel on which [the French] roll him and from which they will let him down whenever they have no further need for him."[30]

The case for war against France was now strong. The French had overtaken the British in their attacks on U.S. commerce: In the five years before 1812, France had captured 558 American ships, compared to 389 by the British. Napoleon had even imprisoned American sailors. According to the New York *Evening Post*, these men had been "robbed and manacled . . . and marched without shoes to their feet or clothing to their backs in the most inclement weather some hundreds of miles into the interior of France; lashed along highways like slaves, treated with every possible indignity, and then immured in the infer-nal dungeons of Arras or Verdun."[31]

The United States did indeed drift into war—but against Britain rather than France. Indeed, the War of 1812 sprang from many sources. Napoleon's wiles had prompted Madison to adopt policies antagonizing London. The Americans, it was assumed, were in league with the sinister Bonaparte. Moreover, many Americans hoped to invade British Canada and bring it into the union. British impress-ments and support for Indian warfare on the frontier added to the rancor. Finally, King George III went mad and Prime Minister Spencer Perceval was assassinated, resulting in a period of confusion and paralysis that caused Britain to neglect the diplomacy that prob-ably would have averted an open conflict. By the time the British gov-

ernment got back on its feet and took steps to satisfy the United
States, it was too late. (If a transatlantic cable had been operating in
the summer of 1812, the war probably would not have been fought.)
When the United States declared war on Britain, it came very close to
including France in the measure. Madison gave the idea serious
thought before finally rejecting it. By a narrow vote of eighteen to
fourteen, the Senate defeated a proposal that would have made
France a cobelligerent.

The War of 1812 ended in a frustrating draw. The American invasion of Canada failed and the British burned much of the District
of Columbia, including the Capitol and the White House. Yet the
Americans also won a number of important victories, such as
the decisive one in New Orleans under General Andrew Jackson.
Peace came with the Treaty of Ghent in 1814. Within a year of that
agreement, Napoleon met his fate at Waterloo and was removed from
the European stage for good. (He had briefly considered fleeing to the
United States.³²) Afterward, tensions between the United States and
both Britain and France eased considerably, though the restoration of
the Bourbon monarchy disappointed many Americans, who saw
France once again turning against the democratic ideals of 1789.

Napoleon spent his remaining years in exile on St. Helena, where
he cheated at card games and accused the British of trying to poison
him until his death, most likely from stomach cancer, in 1821. The
tyrant was gone but hardly forgotten: His legacy would continue to
project an enormous influence over both France and the United
States. Indeed, it did not take long for the French people, dissatisfied
with Napoleon's successors, to begin longing for the days when their
conquering armies had caused an entire continent to quiver in fear.
French imperial nostalgia gave birth to a Napoleonic cult that seized
the national imagination and has never let go. Famous writers com-
posed tributes to the dead emperor. Picture books celebrating his life
sold hundreds of thousands of copies and became the first introduc-
tion many children received to the history of their country. Countless
statues were erected in his honor. In 1840, the British allowed his

body to be moved from its grave on St. Helena to a magnificent tomb in Paris. Rather than reflecting seriously upon a legacy of despotism, death, and destruction, the French have chosen to revere their former dictator, if only for the temporary glory he brought to France. Instead of taking the difficult course and making peace with the past—as Germany and Japan have done since the Second World War—the French have chosen to elevate a murderous tyrant into their pantheon of national heroes. It should come as no surprise that many of the most monstrous dictators who came in his wake, from Hitler to Hussein, have admired and tried to emulate him—and their reverence owes as much to the way the French have enshrined their dwarfish hero as it does to the man himself.

The American response to Napoleon was much more pragmatic. The experience of the War of 1812 and the events leading up to it reminded Americans that European entanglements came with a heavy cost. In 1823, Madison's presidential successor, James Monroe, issued a statement that broadened the principles of both Washington's Farewell Address and Jefferson's first inaugural speech. Responding to Russian provocations in the Northwest and a renewed concern that other nations might meddle in Central and South America, Monroe announced a new national foreign-policy doctrine: "The American continents, by the free and independent condition which they have assumed and maintained, are henceforth not to be considered as subjects for future colonization by any European powers," he declared. "We should consider any attempt on their part to extend their system to any portion of this hemisphere as dangerous to our peace and safety." America would regard any country violating these conditions as having "an unfriendly disposition toward the United States."[33] Although France had few interests in the Western Hemisphere at this time, it is impossible to read these words—submitted to Congress by a man who sat at the bargaining table for the Louisiana Purchase— and not detect a residual fear of the Napoleonic menace. Indeed, while Britain roundly applauded Monroe's statement, France attacked it. "Mr. Monroe, who is not a sovereign, has assumed in his message the tone of a powerful monarch," said the French foreign minister. "[U.S.] independence was only recognized forty years ago; by what right then would the two Americas today be under its immediate sway from Hudson's Bay to Cape Horn?"[34] Yet France would not stage a provocative challenge to the decree until the American Civil War. Over time Monroe's words became accepted, and in the 1850s—two decades after their author's death—they took on their familiar name: the Monroe Doctrine.

The ghost of Napoleon continued to complicate relations between the United States and France well into the 1830s. Monroe had petitioned the French to reimburse American citizens for illegal ship seizures and burnings that had taken place under Napoleon. For a long while, the Bourbon regime resisted payment on the grounds that it would not be held responsible for the actions of an ousted despot. But this was a spurious argument, for France had paid much more than the $7 million the United States was demanding to settle similar claims with Britain and Germany. Negotiations dragged on for years and remained locked over France's insistent counterdemand that it be compensated for even older claims: namely, its aid to American colonists during the Revolutionary War.

Like his predecessors, President Andrew Jackson came into office believing that diplomacy would lead to an acceptable resolution with France. Yet the combative Old Hickory, a radical democrat who denounced aristocracy at every turn, was determined to conclude the compensation matter once and for all. Unsurprisingly, the French greeted Jackson's determination with more stalling tactics. At one point, their foreign minister even told the president's envoy that if the United States really believed Napoleon's actions were not legitimate, then it should return Louisiana to its previous owners. Jackson, however, had no patience for such nonsense. In 1829, he began to speak of a "possible collision" with France over the matter.[35] Jarred out of its complacency, the French government was soon offering concessions, though its initial proposal of $1 million fell far short of what Jackson was willing to accept. Skillful American diplomacy and a change of governments in France—the ultraroyalist Charles X was replaced by the more pragmatic Louis-Philippe—led to further progress. On July 4, 1831, Jackson had his deal. The United States would get $4.6 million to satisfy the spoliation claims. In addition, the United States would lower its tariffs on French wine and France would lower its duties on American cotton. Finally—and grudgingly—the United States agreed to give $270,000 to the Beaumarchais family, which demanded payment for assistance its ancestors had provided to the rebel colonies half a century earlier.

The controversy appeared to be over. But in February 1833, when the United States presented the first bill, France refused to pay. The foreign minister explained that his government had not appropriated the funds. Jackson was livid at the news, especially as the United States already had cut its tariffs on French wine. His new ambassador to France sent a none-too-subtle message by traveling across the Atlantic aboard the U.S.S. *Delaware*, a seventy-four-gun warship. The situation grew worse the next year, when France not only neglected to make the necessary appropriation but actually voted it down.

"I know them French," said Jackson, referring to his years in Louisiana. "They won't pay unless they're made to."[36] In his next message to Congress at the end of 1834, the president was candid: "It becomes my unpleasant duty to inform you that [the] pacific and highly gratifying picture of our foreign relations does not include those with France at this time."[37] He asked for a law authorizing reprisals upon French property and mentioned the possibility of "hostilities."[38] Jackson's saber-rattling rhetoric managed to get the attention of the French, who finally approved the payments in 1835. There was one provision: Before the United States could receive any cash, Jackson would have to "explain" his comments. France, in short, was demanding an apology.

Legend has it that Old Hickory replied with fist-clenched fury: "Apologize! I'd see the whole race roasting in hell first!"[39] He became even more incensed when a contact in Paris informed him that the French planned to wait him out and negotiate with his successor. "It is high time that this arrogance of France should be put down," Jackson declared.[40] Within a few months, the United States and France suspended diplomatic relations. "If the two countries be saved from war, it seems as if it could only be by a special interposition of Providence," worried former president John Quincy Adams.[41]

In the end, however, the French had no interest in fighting a war over etiquette, and Jackson made a gracious gesture that allowed France to save face and brought a rapid conclusion to the standoff. "The honor of my country shall never be stained by an apology from me for the statement of truth and the performance of duty," he declared in December 1835. But he also added that he meant no "menace or insult" to the French government.[42] The gambit worked. Passions died down, and France paid up.

Animosities between the United States and France then subsided until the 1860s—when France flaunted the Monroe Doctrine in a brash attempt to subvert democracy in the Americas.

SIX

THE NEXT NAPOLEON

I never admired the character of the first Napoleon; but I recognize his great genius. . . . The third Napoleon could have no claim to having done a good or just act.
—*Ulysses S. Grant* [1]

O N APRIL 10, 1865, the day after the Confederate surrender at Appomattox, General Ulysses S. Grant boarded a train for his headquarters outside Petersburg, Virginia. After nearly two days of aggravating derailments, he arrived at midnight and collapsed into bed. The next morning, he listened to Navy ships on the James River fire their guns in salute to him, wrote a letter to General Sherman, and attended to other paperwork. His chores done, he set down his pen and said to an aide: "On to Mexico." [2]

It was an incredible statement. The Civil War was not yet over—a large Confederate army remained active in North Carolina—and Grant was already thinking about a new campaign against a foreign foe.

In truth, the general was weary of all the fighting and dying. Thousands of men had perished under his command. During an assault he had ordered at Cold Harbor less than a year earlier, some 7,000 federal troops had fallen in just half an hour. Together, the North and South had inflicted nearly a million casualties on each other, including 620,000 deaths. This was more than all of America's other wars combined, through the twentieth century.

But an end to the rebellion did not mean an end to America's troubles. Two years before, France had toppled the republican government in Mexico City in flagrant violation of the Monroe Doctrine. "I, myself, regarded this as a direct act of war against the United States," wrote Grant in his memoirs.[3]

The French emperor Napoleon III—nephew of the dictator from Corsica—had installed a puppet monarch on the restored Mexican throne. Known as the "Grand Design," this plot aimed at the heart of American power and its geopolitical interests. Ultimate success not only would allow Napoleon III to fulfill his uncle's abandoned dream of a North American empire, it would announce France's triumphal return to *le nouveau monde* and act as a fulcrum for the rejuvenation of French imperialism. On a more sinister level, it would also serve to stop the spread of democracy in Latin America and limit U.S. influence in the Western Hemisphere. In its crucial elements, it was as rapacious as anything ever imagined by the first Bonaparte. In its reactionary design, the plot was both grand and destructive—a scheme befitting an extravagant and imaginative autocrat in an increasingly modern world.

Napoleon III was born in 1808, near the peak of his uncle's power, the son of King Louis Bonaparte of Holland and Princess Hortense, the daughter of Empress Josephine and her first husband, the Vicomte de Beauharnais. An adventurous and romantic man with a wide-ranging if less than powerful mind, Louis had spent his boyhood in exile. Savants had tutored him in the requisite academic subjects, and his mother instructed him in his destiny to rule.[4]

After his mother's death in 1840, Louis wasted little time in giving that destiny a vigorous nudge. Setting out from England with a small band of supporters, he landed on French soil near Boulogne, hoping to rally the garrison there to the Bonapartist cause of overthrowing King Louis-Philippe, who had grown increasingly unpopular for refusing to expand political rights. But his feeble plan failed disastrously. He was captured, tried, and sentenced to life imprisonment in the Château de Ham, a castle along the Somme where Joan of Arc had been held centuries before. There, within its damp walls, the young man would spend the better part of five years reading, reflecting, and, in what would become his *spécialité*, scheming.

On what subjects did his conniving mind fixate during these years of confinement? His royal jailer? Women? Truffles? Undoubtedly. But these did not obsess him nearly as much as the visionary prospect of constructing a canal across the tiny Central American nation of Nicaragua. Perhaps succumbing to the mental privations of incarceration, he became consumed with the wish to know all he could about that tropical republic and its plan to connect two great oceans. Soon the Nicaraguan government was sending piles of documents and related materials to the single-minded prisoner in the Château de Ham. His royal enthusiasm so impressed the Nicaraguans that they petitioned the French government for his release so that he could carry on the project in person. When France refused, Louis shaved off his beard and mustache, slipped into the clothes of a workman, and sauntered unnoticed through the front gate. Within a few days, he was back in England.

There, his passion undiminished, he published a revealing pamphlet: "Canal of Nicaragua; or, A Project to Connect the Atlantic and Pacific Oceans by Means of a Canal."[5] More than a mere engineering treatise, it presented a sweeping case for the profound political and economic transformation of the entire region. With the help of European powers, Louis argued, Nicaragua not only would become a prosperous state, it would be able, "by supporting Mexico, to put a stop to fresh encroachments from the North."[6]

In these few words, Louis Napoleon revealed his naked animus toward the United States. Although he sincerely wished to see Latin America flourish economically, his desire to check the growth of U.S. power was paramount. His *bête noire* was American expansion southward—and he had drawn the line in the sand at the Mexican border. He was certainly influenced by the widespread concern among many in France that the logic of Manifest Destiny would have the American colossus sweeping down all the way to the Straits of Magellan.

Journalist Clément Duvernois warned of "the prodigious development of the American power," believing that it was up to France to
"create a counterweight to the Republic of the United States."[7] These
worries only increased as American territorial expansion followed the
Mexican War. Throughout the 1850s, there were calls in the United
States for the further annexation of Mexico's northern states and
Cuba. One congressman suggested turning the Gulf of Mexico into a
"great American lake."[8] The people of the world's largest democracy
seemed confident and on the move—and the elites of monarchical
France recoiled in fear. This dread of American power, as well as
French desire to contain it, would become increasingly dominant
themes in Franco-American relations over the next hundred years.

The future emperor, however, had little time for his New World
dreams. The political tides in Europe were turning in his favor. In
1848, the dam burst, and France's Louis-Philippe was swept off his
throne in a wave of democratic revolts that deluged the continent.
Louis Napoleon was called out of exile and elected president by four
million votes, largely on the magic of his name. Then, in 1851, after
years of backroom intrigue, he betrayed the democratic ideals of
France's February Revolution and staged a coup d'état. Within a few
months, he proclaimed himself emperor. "No event to which the present century has given birth," said the *Boston Courier*, "has offered so
melancholy, mortifying, and disheartening a spectacle to the eyes of
the friends of liberal and constitutional government as the political
changes now taking place in France."[9] But the French public seemed
willing to embrace a figure who evoked past glories. Louis changed his
name to Napoleon III and embarked on an eighteen-year reign characterized by grand accomplishments and even grander delusions.[10]

As the 1850s progressed, Latin America returned to his thoughts.
French officials and citizens began to express concern over the instability of the Mexican republic and its brand-new constitution as well
as their suspicion that the United States would exploit the situation.
During an audience with the emperor in 1856, the Marquis de Radepont, a diplomat with experience in Mexico, outlined his "Design for

Mexican Regeneration."[11] Radepont, a thoroughgoing monarchist, warned the dictator that liberal elements were making dangerous headway in Mexico. Believing he understood the unarticulated will of Mexican royalists, the marquis proposed that a monarchy could unite the populace and thwart the inherently destabilizing forces of democracy. In short, the French emperor should conspire to place a European prince on the throne of Mexico—thus "opening for [him] the best future that was ever offered to any man."[12]

Once installed in Mexico, France's pawn would be free to lead a popular movement of national renewal. Any objections from the United States would wither before the sincerely expressed enthusiasm of the Mexican people for their new sovereign. Internal stability achieved, Mexico then would reach out to Brazil's emperor and form a monarchical axis against existing Latin American republics such as Argentina, Chile, and Peru. With the demon of democracy erased from the Latin American map, the New World would look to Rome for spiritual guidance—and to Paris for political direction. American dominance in the region would be decisively nullified. All that was needed, in Radepont's optimistic view, was a few hundred French troops and an unemployed prince willing to learn Spanish.

This presentation impressed Napoleon III. During his reign, France had expanded its influence around the globe. Saigon had been captured and a protectorate set up over Cambodia. There were expeditions to Peking and Syria as well as several exploratory probes into West Africa. Radepont gave independent weight and credibility to the emperor's Latin American dreams of two decades. But what roused the emperor more than anything else, perhaps, was Radepont's disturbing reminder that the Americans already had built a railroad across Panama. If France did not act with haste, the United States might dig its own canal and establish a veritable *imperio americano*.

In the late 1850s, Mexico plunged into violence as royalist and republican factions battled for supremacy. The economy crumbled. Amid all the lawlessness, combatants from both sides stole great quantities of European silver and other goods. When the fighting halted, the Mexican legislature voted to end all interest payments on debts and claims for two years. Here, at last, was a ready-made excuse for French intervention. Then, in 1861, the country most likely to oppose the move—the United States—became embroiled in its own civil war. Napoleon III could not have asked for more propitious circumstances.

Most people in France did not care whether the North or the South prevailed in the American Civil War. They just wanted it to end so that cotton shipments might resume. Napoleon III was sensitive to this concern because he hoped to avoid economic troubles that could lead to social unrest within France itself. Yet he also understood that Confederate success presented a remarkable opportunity for France to weaken the United States and seize power in Mexico.

Early on, the French minister to the United States, Henri Mercier, urged Napoleon III to extend formal recognition to the South. But the emperor would do so only in conjunction with Britain. He knew that recognition meant war—and acting alone threatened to isolate him in Europe and leave France vulnerable to countries without such extensive commitments overseas. In London, there was much sympathy for the South, but the British also demanded clear evidence that the American rebels could sustain their cause. What they wanted was a Confederate Saratoga. Napoleon III would have to wait.

Meanwhile, there were many things France could do to aid the Confederates. The first was granting it belligerent rights, a weakened form of diplomatic recognition that allowed Southern ships the same port privileges as federal ones. In practice, it meant that sea captains who preyed upon Union vessels could find safe harbor in France. Confederates also gained the ability to purchase French goods and secure loans. In Paris, emissaries from the Lincoln administration who protested this move met with derision. "The government at Washington is the last to have a right to complain of the recognition of a revolutionary government," sneered Napoleon III's foreign minister, Edouard Thouvenal. "It has made itself always conspicuous in recognizing revolutionary governments all over the world."[13] This was not quite true: The United States had put off recognizing the republican governments of Latin America for more than a decade following the outbreak of revolution. Such details hardly mattered to the French government, however. Napoleon III was working every angle. By the summer, both Britain and France had announced their respect for the South's wartime rights. They also issued proclamations of neutrality, which the French emperor would spend the ensuing months doing his best to transform into declarations of war.

One of the most important battles of the Civil War, therefore, would be fought not in the fields of Virginia or along the riverbanks of the Mississippi but in the diplomatic circles of Europe. Several months earlier, Secretary of State William Seward, a savvy New Yorker with a big nose and a bad haircut, had proposed that North and South reunite themselves by making common cause against a foreign enemy. Although President Abraham Lincoln rejected this idea, he gave Seward tremendous leeway in conducting foreign policy. This was possible in large part because the mission was so clear: keeping Britain and France from aligning themselves with the Confederacy.

Many in Napoleon III's circle believed that Lincoln and Seward were hopeless simpletons, unlike the cultured plantation owners of the slaveholding states, who formed the closest thing there was in America to an aristocracy of inherited privilege. In the summer of 1861, as the North was beginning to understand that Southern insurrection would last more than a few weeks, the emperor's cousin, Prince Napoleon, visited the White House during a tour of the United States. Seward arrived first to greet the imperial guest. The prince—mockingly nicknamed "Mr. Plod" by critics—was distinctly unimpressed: "Mr. Seward is a little old man, who looks very much like a schoolteacher; very intelligent, very shrewd, rather bad mannered, self-important and conceited," he scoffed. "He looked frankly dingy, was wearing a coat of undefined color, a piece of string for a necktie, and a large straw hat." The dapper Frenchman was even less impressed by Seward's boss. Lincoln, he said, "looks rather like a bootmaker." Their encounter did not go well. "After shaking hands with me, we both sat down. He hardly said a word, and then nothing but commonplaces. I gathered, however, that he was asking Mr. Seward whether my father was named Lucien or Jerome. After some ten minutes of that kind of thing I became bored and took my leave," said Mr. Plod. "What a difference between this sad representative of the great republic and its early founders! . . . He's a poor specimen of a president, and they tell me here that he is the commonest they have had thus far."[14]

Several months after this meeting, Lincoln and Seward weathered a crisis that came close to granting Napoleon III his wish for war. On November 8, the U.S.S. *San Jacinto* captured the *Trent*, a British steamer carrying a pair of Confederate diplomats from Havana to Europe. James Mason was assigned to London, and the French-speaking Louisianan John Slidell was bound for France. Both were arrested, despite the fact that the *Trent* flew the flag of a neutral country and was traveling between neutral ports. Although a clear violation of international law, the seizure proved enormously popular in the North, which was craving any sign of wartime success. Britain loudly demanded the release of Mason and Slidell—and France informed London once more that it would recognize Southern independence if Britain did the same. Reluctant to take such a dramatic step, the British gave the Americans a chance to back down. After several tense weeks, the United States released its prisoners, who promptly traveled to Europe and pressed for formal recognition of the Confederacy.

Both Mason and Slidell knew that without a demonstration of Southern military prowess in America all their efforts would be in vain. Fortunately for them, the Confederates were winning battles in the eastern theater. The North seemed unable to put down the rebellion. In March 1862, Union general George B. McClellan launched his Peninsula Campaign against Richmond—but was stopped four months later at the Seven Days' Battles. In Paris, federal envoy John Bigelow reported to Washington his belief that Napoleon III was ready to pounce: "It is clear that he has lost pretty much all of the little faith he had in our ability to reduce the South to obedience, and he is now hovering over us, like the carrion crow over the body of the sinking traveler, waiting until we are too weak to resist his predatory instincts."[15]

Napoleon III was already in the process of pouncing—in Mexico. The previous fall, as Americans fought among themselves, France, Britain, and Spain agreed that they would force Mexico to pay its foreign debts under threat of occupation. By January 1862, the three countries had landed thousands of troops at Veracruz on the Gulf coast.

Almost from the start, disagreements erupted on how to proceed. The French, who had their own ambitious plans for Mexico, pressed for an immediate incursion into the center of the country. But their compact with Britain and Spain stated clearly that no territory would be taken and no effort would be made to frustrate the Mexicans in choosing their own government. When it became obvious that Mexico lacked the money to pay its debts, London and Madrid made arrangements with the Juárez government and recalled their forces. Napoleon III, of course, had something else in mind. His troops remained on Mexican soil. As France prepared to launch its offensive, Napoleon III's commissioners assured the Mexican people that they had only Mexico's best interests in mind. The Mexicans were not so convinced, and they were determined to resist.

On May 5, 1862, a force of about 6,000 French troops assaulted a fortress defended by a smaller number of Mexicans in the city of Puebla. By nightfall, more than a thousand French soldiers lay dead or wounded in a bloody trench surrounding the battlements. Mexico's army was widely rated as one of the world's worst, but it had just defeated an imperial army that inspired fear wherever it marched. To the great shame of France, its soldiers were forced to retreat. Commemorated as *El Cinco de Mayo*—a national holiday in Mexico—the battle did not drive the French from the New World. Yet it demonstrated the resolve of the Mexican people to resist foreign tyranny. It also served as a harbinger of things to come.

Despite its humiliating defeat, France continued to taunt the Lincoln administration for failing to subdue the Confederates. Following McClellan's debacle outside Richmond, North and South clashed at Manassas for a second time, and once more the Union limped away. In September, as General Lee's forces streamed into Maryland searching for their Saratoga, Thouvenal predicted failure for the Union cause. "I think that the undertaking of conquering the South is almost superhuman," he said.[16] On October 2, he made an even bolder pronouncement: "I am confident that at this time there is not a reasonable statesman in Europe who believes you can succeed in carrying out your first conception [i.e., a reunion between North and South]."[17]

Thouvenal did not know that two weeks earlier, on September 17, federal soldiers had repulsed Lee's army at Antietam in the Civil War's bloodiest day of fighting. Tactically, the battle was a draw. But strategically, it was a triumph for the North, because it convincingly denied the Confederates the rousing victory they so badly needed. By the end of the month, Thouvenal had been dismissed from his post and replaced by Edouard Drouyn de Lhuys, a rotund man noted for his ability to say much and reveal little. Thouvenal's departure was unrelated to the Civil War, though it had an important consequence on Franco-American relations: Drouyn was much more favorably disposed to the North than his predecessor. He would ultimately moderate the emperor's more aggressive tendencies.

Yet it would take several months before his influence would be felt. By the end of October, Napoleon III was trying to rally the European powers in support of an armistice in America, a cease-fire that would have aided the South enormously and laid the foundation for the international community to recognize Confederate independence. The proposal was poorly timed. Following Antietam, Britain was more hesitant than ever to oppose the Union. In addition, Lincoln had used the victory to announce his Emancipation Proclamation, a document that highlighted the Civil War's moral dimension and attracted many Europeans to the Northern cause.

In November, Britain once again turned down French pleadings.

For nearly two years, the Lincoln administration had believed that Britain posed a greater threat to its interests, if only because it was far more dependent on American cotton exports and therefore susceptible to the South's "King Cotton" diplomacy. Unlike France, however, Britain had stockpiled cotton before the war and had found other sources in Egypt and India. It now looked as though only a stunning reversal of Union fortunes could compel London to intervene. By 1863, France had become the far more dangerous foreign power.

Nowhere was this more apparent than in Mexico, where Napoleon III was determined to avenge the catastrophe at Puebla and overthrow the republican government. He quickly reinforced his Mexican operation with 30,000 troops. They rolled over Puebla in March and captured Mexico City in June. All along, the French had lied to the United States about their intentions in Mexico, assuring the Lincoln administration that they aimed to do nothing more than collect their debts. "Truthfulness is not, as you know, an element in French diplomacy or manners," said William Lewis Dayton, the U.S. minister in Paris.[18] Yet the Americans were in no position to stop them. Lincoln had little choice but to stick to his doctrine of fighting "one war at a time." Even so, Seward circulated a document declaring that the United States would not tolerate "any person not of Mexican nationality" on the Mexican throne.[19]

Neither would the Mexicans. "The imperial [French] government has decided to humiliate Mexico and impose her will on it," said president-in-exile Benito Juárez, a Zapotec Indian. "I can assure you . . . the imperial government will not succeed in subjugating the Mexicans, and its armies will not have a single day of peace."[20]

Despite the threats of Seward and Juárez, Napoleon III did not waste a moment implementing the next phase of his "Grand Design." He continued his policy of deception, announcing at one point that "it is contrary to my interest, my principles, or my origin to impose any kind of government whatsoever on the Mexican people." He was in fact finalizing plans to send a handpicked lackey to sit on his Mexican throne.[21] He settled on the hapless Archduke Ferdinand Maximilian of Austria. A kindly, indecisive man whose only previous experience in governance was commanding his gardeners around his estate near Trieste, he was all of thirty-one when he and his wife, the ambitious Archduchess Carlotta, set sail for their imperial future.

Maximilian was, by all accounts, the perfect dupe—a man who would gladly take orders from those to whom he owed his crown. But to send such a lightweight into the violent world of nineteenth-century Mexican politics was a crime. "They will murder you," prophesied Carlotta's grandmother, the exiled former queen of France.[22] Throughout history, many Europeans had imposed their will on the Mexican people. But men like Hernán Cortés and his successors at least were smart, resourceful, and strong-minded. Maximilian was something else entirely. Believing that this pampered archduke would survive the brutal tumult of Mexican politics—as well as convince the proud Mexicans that their future lay in French hands—seemed an astonishing flight of fancy. But self-delusion was common currency in France. In 1863, French journalist Michel Chevalier wrote that the French invasion would "save from irreparable ruin not only Mexico but also the whole branch of Latin civilization. Without France, without her intelligence, her elevated sentiments, and her military power . . . Latin nations would be reduced to make out a very humble figure in the world, and would long since have been completely eclipsed."[23]

In May 1864, the royal couple arrived in Veracruz. As they passed through the city streets and noticed the unenthusiastic reception, did they experience doubts about their chances of success? Did they feel any unease about imposing France's will on a foreign land? The French, of course, harbored no such reservations. They were abundantly convinced of their ability to change the world—or at least rearrange it to serve their interests. As long as Maximilian paid off Mexico's debt, secured exclusive mineral rights for France in the northern half of the country, and conducted foreign policy under French guidance, everything would fall into place. Maximilian showed occasional signs of independence, such as when he denied Paris the mining rights it desired. But his clumsy efforts to find a third way between French imperialism and Mexican nationalism merely loosened his ties to his Gallic sponsors without endearing him to the people he hoped to rule.

Although Napoleon III may have been rubbing his hands in anticipation, the Latin republics were uniformly outraged at his plans for hemispheric domination. Seeing through French assurances, they informed Lincoln of their wish to embark immediately on a crusade with the United States to expel the invaders. But Lincoln urged caution. He feared a general European response that would result in even more unwanted incursions into the hemisphere. Still, the Latin sentiment of resistance only gained momentum. It was a "war of the crowns against the Liberty caps," said Peruvian president Ramón Castilla. Mexico's exiled foreign minister Franciso Zarco agreed: "In it is to be decided the antagonism which exists between despotism and liberty, between monarchy and republicanism; therefore, it is a continental question, an American question which no people in the New World can contemplate with indifference without being false to their destiny."[24] As the war of words expanded, the republican forces of Juárez gathered strength throughout Mexico. In contrast, Maximilian and his French generals were having more and more problems pacifying the country.

It was a volatile time, and many Americans began to wake up to the French threat south of the border. The *Atlantic Monthly* hollered in protest: "A dependency of France established at our door! The most restless, ambitious, and warlike nation in Europe our neighbor! Who shall tell what results, momentous and lasting, may follow in the train of such events?"[25] Wild rumors abounded: France was set to annex the northern regions of Mexico outright; France had plans to create an empire consisting of Mexico, the Confederacy, and the United States. Other schemes surfaced in which the South would invade Mexico and chase the French from the continent, placing Jefferson Davis on the Mexican throne.

Then, as the French were trying to establish themselves in Mexico City during the summer of 1863, the Union dealt a pair of deadly blows to the Confederacy at Gettysburg and Vicksburg. The South's final collapse seemed only a matter of time. Yet this change in fortune did nothing to stop Napoleon III from plotting further moves against the North. He tried to enlist Britain in a plan to break the Union naval blockade by sending a fleet of warships to the mouth of the Mississippi. He also permitted Confederate minister Slidell to obtain a large loan from a French bank in order to commission the construction of four cruisers and two ironclad rams in Bordeaux—a clear violation of French neutrality.

Yet even Napoleon III could now discern the South's dim prospects. Although he remained a sympathizer—the emperor was said to be "deeply grieved" when the U.S.S. *Kearsarge* sank the C.S.S. *Alabama* off the northern coast of France—he also knew the British were not going to side with him. So he began to turn his attention away from aiding the Confederates and toward securing U.S. recognition of Maximilian's government. Perhaps he could win a partial victory for French imperialism. But Seward toyed with the emperor masterfully, stating firmly that the United States would not recognize Mexico's phony government, while leaving the door open just enough to keep the French (and Maximilian) on their best behavior. When federal agents uncovered the Confederate naval construction, Paris feigned surprise and blocked the ships from falling into Southern hands.[26]

As the Civil War came to an end, both Lincoln and Seward were anxious for peace. Other Americans, however, wanted to fight the French. Senator James A. McDougall of California called for a declaration of war if France did not remove its troops from Mexico. The House passed a resolution announcing opposition to "any monarchical government erected on the ruin of any republican government in America under the auspices of any European power."[27] When Drouyn de Lhuys learned of this, he confronted Dayton with a stark question: "Do you bring us peace or bring us war?"[28] General Grant was particularly outspoken about his wish to invade Mexico as soon as the fighting stopped.

Less than three weeks after Appomattox, Grant set his plans in motion. He sent one of his most determined and capable warriors, General Philip Sheridan, to the border in Texas. A fiery little officer who had lied about his age to get into West Point, Sheridan was just the man to put on an impressive show of force along the Rio Grande. The matter was urgent enough that Grant ordered Sheridan to move on May 17, less than a week before the Grand Review, a two-day parade down Pennsylvania Avenue and in front of the White House. Every general was eager to participate in it. But Grant made a strong case for immediate action, recalled Sheridan: "He looked upon the invasion of Mexico by Maximilian as part of the rebellion itself, because of the encouragement that invasion had received from the Confederacy, and that our success in putting down secession would never be complete till the French and Austrian invaders were compelled to quit the territory of our sister republic."[29]

Although Grant and much of the public wanted war, Seward wished to see the interlopers leave Mexico of their own accord and Lincoln, now dead—assassinated a week after Appomattox—most likely would have agreed. "There has been war enough," the president had told Grant a year earlier. "During my second term there will be no more fighting."[30] Seward believed that Napoleon III would appreciate the simple fact that it would not take much for the United States to muster a massive force of battle-tested veterans. Indeed, Grant thought that a joint military effort in Mexico would not only rid North America of a corrosive presence but also help a sundered nation find reconciliation. Although Seward himself had proposed something along these lines four years earlier, he now believed that the solution lay in allowing the proud French an honorable exit. In the end, Seward at least secured their removal.

It surely did not hurt to have Sheridan on the border itching for a fight. When he discovered that Mexican royalists stationed across the river from Brownsville had purchased several Confederate cannons in the final months of the Civil War, the combative general insisted on their return. "These demands, backed up as they were by such a formidable show of force," wrote Sheridan, "created much agitation and demoralization among the Imperial troops, and measures looking to the abandonment of northern Mexico were forthwith adopted by those in authority—a policy that would have resulted in the speedy evacuation of the entire country by Maximilian." He was disappointed that his government did not take advantage of the situation, "contenting itself with a few pieces of the contraband artillery varnished over with Imperial apologies."[31] But the general continued to create problems for the monarchy as he blocked retreating Confederates from seeking safe haven in Mexico and provided munitions "by the most secret methods" to the republican forces of Juárez.[32]

Seward was not pleased with Grant's eagerness for war or Sheridan's displays along the Rio Grande. When the Mexican government complained about Sheridan in the fall, Seward ordered the general to observe American neutrality. But Sheridan kept on providing assistance to Juárez. "During the winter and spring of 1866 we continued covertly supplying arms and ammunitions to the Liberals—sending as many as 30,000 muskets from Baton Rouge alone," he wrote. "By mid-summer Juarez, having organized a pretty good sized army, was in possession of . . . nearly the whole of Mexico down to San Louis Potosi."[33]

The game was just about up for France. As the cost of the Mexican expedition mounted and as Maximilian proved unable to win over his subjects, Napoleon III began to reconsider his beloved scheme. In truth, he had many other things to worry about, such as the construction of grand boulevards and state-of-the-art sewers in Paris—as well as the troubling emergence of Bismarck's Prussia, dreaming of its own place in the sun.

Many in France, however, felt that their weakening position could be improved through chest-thumping threats. "If the Americans increase the difficulties of the Empire," wrote French journalist Emanuel Masseras, "the Empire in turn would have little trouble in reviving the [U.S.] Civil War. The thousands of refugees from the

South who have preferred exile to submission would welcome the occasion to return to their country with means to raise the Confederate flag."[34] This was a fantasy, but then fantasies had not stopped Napoleon III from mounting his invasion in the first place. Now that the emperor's "Grand Design" was unraveling before his eyes, it looked like the perfect time to cut and run. In January 1866, he sent a letter to Maximilian informing him of his decision to withdraw French troops. A few days later, he declared that France had done its service to civilization in Mexico. With Maximilian now secure on his throne, France was no longer needed.

Few were deceived. Napoleon III had convinced Maximilian to leave his tranquil garden, placed him on a foreign throne by force of arms, and promised him imperial splendor. Napoleon was now discarding his puppet at the moment of Maximilian's greatest vulnerability and when retreat looked most favorable to France. Even Maximilian saw the impossible situation he occupied. Yet, strangely, he steeled himself to a grim fate.

Meanwhile, his wife refused to abandon hope. Carlotta traveled to Paris in a pathetic attempt to convince the emperor to reconsider. But Napoleon III held firm. Within a few weeks, she fell into a state of insanity from which she never recovered. Back in Mexico, with his enemies closing around him, Maximilian rejected calls to abdicate and join the French troops in retreat. His decision to remain, noble in its way, would be one of his last.

On March 12, 1867, the last French soldier left Mexico. Maximilian's military situation deteriorated rapidly. He retreated to Querétaro, where republican forces surrounded and captured him. Despite pleas from the United States to spare him, the would-be ruler of France's second New World empire was executed by firing squad on June 19. "He was an amiable man," said republican general Porfirio Díaz, "and I believe he tried to do his best. He would probably have made an excellent ruler in his own country, but we, as Mexicans, would not have him thrust upon us at the point of French bayonets."[35]

In the end, Mexico's victory was a victory for the United States as well. For Americans, it vindicated both the Monroe Doctrine and the specific policy of Lincoln and Seward, who had not only kept Europe out of the Civil War but also skillfully encouraged the French to leave Mexico without resorting to war. It was a time of great optimism in U.S.–Latin American relations. Indeed, Seward would proclaim in Mexico City in 1869 that during the crisis "the United States became for the first time, in sincerity and earnestness, the friend and ally of every other republican state in America."[36]

French leaders are always claiming that their country helped make American independence possible. Yet they never acknowledge France's role in a brazen effort to dissolve the American union. Had Napoleon III succeeded in splitting the United States in two and establishing a monarchy in Mexico, he would have harmed Americans as much as Louis XVI had helped them nearly a century earlier. Because France failed, however, Ulysses S. Grant was able to accept his party's nomination for president in 1868 with words that an exhausted nation was glad to hear: "Let us have peace."

SEVEN

DECADENCE AND DEMOCRACY

Trivial Americans go to Paris when they die.
—Mark Twain[1]

ON AUGUST 9, 1870, William Seward embarked on a 44,000-mile tour around the world. Seventy years old and still suffering from stab wounds delivered by one of John Wilkes Booth's co-conspirators on the night of Lincoln's assassination, the former secretary of state hoped to escape from a New York winter and see a bit of the world. In Chicago, on the first leg of the journey, he met with the new president, Ulysses S. Grant, "who seemed," Seward wrote, "as much travel worn and a great deal more office worn than myself."[2] In Salt Lake City, he attended a Mormon church service and was cordially received by Brigham Young and nine of his sixteen wives. Then he crossed the Pacific, visited Japan, spent two months in China, traveled through India and the Middle East, and finally made his way up the Danube and into the heart of Europe.

A year after setting out, he arrived in Paris. Although Seward sat down with one of his former rivals, French foreign minister Edouard Drouyn de Lhuys, he would not be received at the French court—for France no longer had a court. Several months before, Napoleon III had fled the country as a Prussian army advanced on the capital. (Prussian soldiers were still in Paris during Seward's visit.) The deposed emperor was harmlessly living out his days in a final exile in Britain.

Although Napoleon III had done much for France—reforming its banking industry and overseeing the physical transformation of Paris—he had presided over a crooked despotism. With the emperor gone, French liberals hoped that liberty might be just around the corner, and that Seward's America might serve as a model for their own republic. But it was easy to have doubts. Since the heady days of 1789, when the French Revolution aimed to banish tyranny from the globe, France had enjoyed only a few short years of representative government; otherwise, it had been ruled by a sorry succession of autocrats. Prior to that, there had been more than a thousand years of kings, all the way back through Charlemagne and Clovis.

It is well to remember, in light of French admonitions to the contrary, that while France may be the older nation, America is the older democracy. For more than two centuries, even in the midst of civil war, the United States has enjoyed uninterrupted republican government, while France has known no fewer than five different republics as well as numerous periods of monarchy, dictatorship, and political chaos—many of them bloody. One reason is that modern French political history, unlike its American counterpart, has been dominated by the extremes on the left and right and has lacked a strong and effective liberal tradition.

Still, there have been a few liberals of note. In 1865, a small group of them met on a summer evening near Versailles as guests of the eminent legal scholar Edouard-René Lefebvre de Laboulaye. An ardent admirer of the United States, Laboulaye had penned several legal and political histories of the American republic, a country he believed France would do well to emulate. In light of recent U.S. history, Laboulaye proposed that a gold medal be commissioned and sent to Lincoln's widow. Inscribed upon it would be a few simple words: "Lincoln, an honest man; abolished slavery, saved the republic, and was assassinated on the 15th of April 1865."[3] Laboulaye further suggested a much larger gift—a monument that might help heal the wounds in Franco-American relations as well as inspire the United States and its people to support the cause of French liberalism. A young sculptor in attendance, Frédéric-Auguste Bartholdi, agreed to design a statue that would be unveiled at America's centennial twelve years hence. Yet the project would be largely forgotten until the Franco-Prussian War altered the course of French history and spurred a politically frustrated Bartholdi into action.

The conflict originated in a piece of Prussian chicanery. Prussian chancellor Otto von Bismarck conceived of the conflict as a way to achieve German unification by bringing the small German states into his orbit, and Napoleon III proved a willing dupe. By manipulating a trivial dispute over the succession to the Spanish throne, Bismarck conned the French monarch into declaring war on the Prussians. With the greatest dispatch, the Prussian army pounced on an ill-equipped and outclassed French force.

In the twentieth century, French cries for American help rarely fell on deaf ears. But in 1870, the memories of France's recent Mexican adventure were still fresh in American minds. When the House of Representatives heard of France's declaration of war, congressmen cheered for the Prussians. President Ulysses S. Grant vowed neutrality. The American people, he wrote, "remembered that while the Germans sympathized with the Union . . . the French people had manifested no sympathy for the Union but had negotiated a loan for the Rebels, and the French government had sent an expedition into Mexico which had been construed by the people as an act hostile to this country."[4] Some even felt that America should formally side with the Prussians.

Much of this anti-French sentiment came from the large and influential German-American community. Since the eighteenth century, the United States has absorbed many times more immigrants from Germany than France, and this demographic fact helped shape U.S. perceptions of both antagonists. Although the dangers of Prussian militarism were beginning to capture some attention, Germany was still seen as a land of great philosophers, scientists, and poets. And Prussia had the added advantage of having supported (along with most German Americans) the Union cause during the war. "I side with the Prussians," wrote Louisa May Alcott to her mother, "for they sympathized with us in our war. Hooray for old Pruss!"[5]

The Prussians soon captured Napoleon III at the battle of Sedan and forced him to abdicate. Upon learning this, a French mob compelled the establishment of the Third Republic. Almost immediately, the United States discarded its posture of neutrality and threw its support behind the new democracy. "While we adhere to our traditional neutrality in civil contests everywhere," said President Grant, "we cannot be indifferent to the spread of American political ideas in a great and civilized country."[6] In recognizing the world's newest republic, the U.S. minister to France, Elihu Washburne, said: "The government and the people of the United States . . . have learned with enthusiasm of the proclamation of the republic of France, accomplished without the shedding of one drop of blood."[7] The blood, unfortunately, was just about to flow.

In the chaos that ensued, the Prussian army poured into France. Paris was besieged, and in early 1871, after many harrowing months, it fell to the enemy. During this period, America sent aid to the suffering Parisians. With the collapse of the capital, elections were called. But when it became clear that the vast majority of deputies in the new National Assembly would be monarchists, republican Paris rose up and threw France into civil war. Paris again was besieged, this time by the forces of the National Assembly. In Paris, a revolutionary council, or Commune, was instituted. Representing the views of republicans as well as revolutionary elements, this new Jacobinism would incite fear in the hearts of many in France and across Europe. During the Commune's three months of existence in the spring of 1871, the capital was plunged into bedlam. Although the Commune set fire to countless buildings and executed the archbishop of Paris, the real bloodbath occurred when the forces of the National Assembly retook the city. In all, 38,000 people were arrested and 20,000 put to death. Another 7,500 were deported to New Caledonia, an island in the Pacific Ocean. The violence was worse than what had taken place in the bloodiest years of the French Revolution.

Just when Americans were beginning to sympathize with the new French republic, the excesses of the Commune brought out their latent disgust and exasperation. "No greater curse could fall upon a dissolute and wicked city like Paris than to abandon it to its own evil passions," declared the *Trenton Gazette*.[8] The *Wilmington Daily Commercial* would temper its anti-Parisian sentiment with optimism. "Gay, volatile, fickle Paris is dead, let us hope, with the destruction and devastation of the war. Since she no longer is the imperial city of Luxury, Wealth, and Pleasure, we may trust that from among her ruins will issue a purer and steadier, a higher and nobler life."[9]

A similar hope animated Bartholdi. In 1871, despondent over the German annexation of his beloved Alsace, he decided to take a journey to the United States. At the same time, a meeting with Laboulaye rekindled the earlier idea of a statue. Laboulaye felt that a visit would help the young artist gather valuable impressions of the land he was to honor as well as begin to build much-needed support for the project in the United States. In a letter to Laboulaye before setting off in May 1871, Bartholdi wrote: "I will try to glorify the Republic and Liberty over there, in the hope that someday I will find it over here."[10] In the United States, he met with many prominent Americans, including President Grant and the poet Henry Wadsworth Longfellow. He also found a spot on Bedloe's Island in New York harbor that he felt would be an ideal place for his great statue. Upon his return to France, other projects would intervene, including a statue of Lafayette for New York City in gratitude for the aid given Paris during the terrible siege. But the idea refused to die. Laboulaye established a French-American Union to coordinate fundraising. The bulk of the money came not from governments or the wealthy but from the general public of both nations.

When the statue was finally unveiled on July 4, 1886, Americans were genuinely grateful. But while their own democracy had never been stronger, France's new republic was a tenuous affair. In fact, the only reason that the country did not devolve back into monarchy was because the monarchists had split into quarreling factions. Many of the French were deeply reluctant to let the United States become any sort of role model.

In 1831, the aristocrat Alexis de Tocqueville had arrived in the United States on a mission to survey American prisons and penitentiaries for the French government. He returned the following year with a number of profound and original insights into the nature of democracy itself. Although clearly impressed by America's political and industrial achievements, he was less comfortable with the cultural and social deficiencies that he believed resulted from a doctrine of radical equality. He was particularly hard on American culture. America, he observed, had "no literature," because republics were more interested in the present than the past.[11] It remained culturally dependent on England. Perhaps this is one of the reasons his magisterial *Democracy in America* was largely ignored by the French, save for a few liberals, until the 1960s. Indeed, the French paid scant attention to American culture until the twentieth century. They admired a few American writers, such as James Fenimore Cooper and Longfellow. But they were seen as rare birds in a barren wilderness. Even Charles Baudelaire's famous "discovery" of Edgar Allan Poe was described by the French poet as the finding of a great genius in the midst of that "maelstrom of mediocrity," that "greedy world, hungry for material things."[12]

Many Americans agreed with this harsh assessment of their cultural deficiencies and looked to Europe for leadership in literature, philosophy, and art. Although they themselves possessed a rich and varied literary tradition that included writers such as Hawthorne, Melville, Emerson, Whitman, and Thoreau, they still felt a certain insecurity in the realm of civilization. Beginning in the late nineteenth century, Americans in growing numbers would begin to cross the Atlantic to seek it out.[13] After 1865, the American population in Europe—and especially France—increased dramatically. When the U.S. minister to Paris John Bigelow sent out invitations for an Independence Day fête in 1865, it was possible for him to invite nearly every American then living in Europe. By 1867, there were about 4,400 Americans residing in Paris. Half a century later, there were as many as 35,000.

They came for many reasons. First and foremost was the attainment of a certain polish or refinement that could not be acquired in Baltimore or Biloxi. Parents sent their young men (and occasionally their young women) to study art in the Parisian academies. For the American writer and aesthete Henry James, Paris provided a backdrop against which the mind and the senses could extend themselves into places they had never been. For James, the novelist of sensibility par excellence, the exotic charms of Paris were perfectly suited to the discovery of inspiration. Such would be the hope of countless American writers, from Washington Irving and James Fenimore Cooper in the nineteenth century to Edith Wharton, William Faulkner, and James Baldwin in the twentieth. Paris would become the ideal setting for cultural refugees from a rapidly industrializing America. But if James had found the French "admirable," other Americans found them downright detestable.[14] Writing about his "squandered" months in Paris before the Civil War, Henry Adams admitted to disapproving of "France in the lump." Writing about himself in the third person, Adams said, "He disliked the Empire and the Emperor particularly, but this was a trifle; he disliked most the French mind. To save himself the trouble of drawing up a long list of all that he disliked, he disapproved of the whole, once for all, and shut them figuratively out of his life. France was not serious, and he was not serious in going there."[15]

Financial difficulties and health problems had persuaded Mark Twain to take his family to Europe for five years in the 1890s. Why he chose to spend the majority of that time in Paris is unclear in light of the strongly negative (but humorous) impressions that gushed forth from his pen. "The race consists of human beings and the French," he wrote. "There is a Moral sense and many nations have it. Also there is an Immoral sense. The French have it." "Scratch a F[renchman] & you find a savage . . . a F[renchwoman] & you find a harlot." To him, the "French are the connecting link between man & the monkey"; they "have bestialities which are unknown in civilized lands." Reflecting on France's history, he noted its inhabitants' penchant for "burning and slaughtering people." France, he wrote, has "two chief traits—love of glory & massacre."

Weary of French claims of cultural superiority, Twain believed that the United States could actually boast the more impressive civilization. "I can't describe to you," he wrote a friend, "how poor & empty & offensive France is, compared to America."[16] In an 1895 essay, he asked:

> What would . . . France teach us? Railroading? No. France knows nothing valuable about railroading. Steamshipping? No. French steamboating is still of Fulton's date—1809. Postal Service? No. France is a back number there. Telegraphy? No, we taught her that ourselves. Journalism? No. Magazining? No, that is our own specialty. Government? No; Liberty, Equality, Fraternity, Nobility, Democracy, Adultery—the system is too variegated for our climate. Religion? No, not variegated enough for our climate. Morals? No, we cannot rob the poor to enrich ourselves.[17]

America, he noted, is a pioneer in those areas that lead to the development of personal freedom: laws, fundamental equality, women's rights, and technological progress. In other words, Americans should not allow the French to condescend to them and their country. Nevertheless, Twain refused to abandon all hope for the French. France, he believed, "is capable of being raised to quite a fair sort of civilization by the right sort of Am[erican] & Eng[lish] missionaries. [But] the Am[erican]s we have established there are not the right sort, for they ape & admire the natives."[18]

While Twain's fulminations can be attributed to a mile-wide misanthropic streak that finds expression throughout his work, there was more than a little truth to his critique. By the last decades of the nineteenth century, France had slid into a state of obvious moral decay. In the aftermath of France's shocking military debacle in 1870, the country may have yearned for revenge, but it clearly had lost confidence in itself. In the words of the German ambassador to Paris in 1886: "The wish that there may be one day a holy war is common to every Frenchman; but the demand for its speedy fulfillment is met with a shake of the head."[19] Instead the French turned to pleasure in order to forget. Paris became a frivolous whirlwind of cabarets, absinthe, prostitutes, and culinary excess. Moral codes were loosened; Parisian life was, for those who could afford it, one giant, degenerate soirée.

While some decried this sorry state of affairs, others reveled in it, creating a whole conception of life around the idea of decadence. In order to escape the dreary world of petty bourgeois concerns, the true decadent would attempt through the contemplation of beauty or the ingestion of narcotics to reach a rarefied state of sensation. Everything outside a morbidly self-absorbed subjectivity, except that which could provide pleasure, was soundly rejected. And already, the United States served as a convenient symbol of all that deserved condemnation. In the opinion of the protodecadent Charles Baudelaire, the United States was to blame for corrupting so much of the modern world. To him, America was "Gargantuan and yet naive . . . totally confident in her material, unpredictable, and almost monstrous growth . . . [with] a primitive faith in the omnipotence of industry . . . [and] almost no consideration whatsoever for spiritual things."[20] His words express the fascinated horror with which many of the French view America today.

Yet France has hardly been remiss in producing its own sordid cultural exports. Around the middle of the nineteenth century, France unleashed a powerful and volatile force into European culture—the idea of the avant-garde. Combining the romantic cult of the artist with a radical critique of existing and past traditions, the avant-garde ideal would not only transform the world of art but also exert a considerable influence on totalitarian political ideologies. Originating in the French Middle Ages, the term took on its modern meaning of a radical rupture with the past during the French Revolution. In subsequent decades, the term would filter through the hands of Charles Fourier and Saint-Simon, who both sought to create a utopian state in the radical tradition of Jean Calvin and his Jacobin heirs. From there, it would go on to infect the realm of aesthetics.

Just as the French revolutionaries had sought to overthrow the existing political order, so the new aesthetic vanguard sought to overthrow all existing rules, forms, and conventions in the realm of art. To be sure, the avant-garde impulse is responsible for many of the great artistic achievements of the modern era—Impressionism, Post-Impressionism, and Abstract Impressionism, as well as the many forms of literary modernism. But the successful exemplars of this new modern outlook—Monet, Manet, van Gogh, Cézanne, and Matisse, as well as Picasso, Eliot, de Kooning, Kafka, and Schönberg—were not essentially nihilistic. However innovative and novel their work might at first appear, they first mastered artistic traditions before breaking with them, and they always retained a keen sense of their relation to the past.

The other strand of the avant-garde was more destructive. Indeed, it would attempt to pulverize the entire edifice of Western art. The "newcomers," French poet Arthur Rimbaud had written, "are free to condemn the ancestors."[21] Rimbaud, the first of what historian Jacques Barzun calls the French Abolitionists, sought to bring about a clean slate in the realm of culture by the use of coarse language and disorienting rhetoric. An anarchist in politics and aesthetics, Rimbaud would pave the way for writers such as Alfred Jarry, who not only created one of the most offensive characters in literature in his play *Ubu Roi* (King Turd) but was equally obnoxious in real life. With a powdered face and a highly affected falsetto, Jarry would wander the streets of Paris, occasionally pulling a revolver from his pocket and firing blanks at terrified bystanders. The avant-garde imperative of shocking the bourgeoisie had reached its literal, twisted apotheosis.

From here, the path of this destructive impulse became clear. In the work of the twentieth-century Dadaist Marcel Duchamp, everyday objects ("ready-mades") were "nominated" as legitimate art beside authentic masterpieces. In the urinal that Duchamp exhibited under the name "Fountain," we see the tawdry culmination of much of what went wrong with modern art in the last century. Today, completely untethered from the moorings of tradition, much of contemporary art must be either eye-poppingly trivial or shockingly repulsive to be noticed.

It should therefore come as no surprise that Lenin used the term *avant-garde* to describe his vision of a revolutionary elite intent on wiping away all political and economic foundations of the state. The Italian Futurists' own destructive understanding of art and politics would help pave the way for Fascism.

Despite these mounting absurdities, most educated Americans continued to believe in the superiority of French high culture, and those who aspired to make or collect art went to Paris. Indeed, in the last decades of the century, France surpassed Britain as the center of the American aesthetic universe. Thousands of aspiring American artists descended on the French capital to learn the latest techniques and styles. The French had little interest in American art and generally ignored these interlopers. Unfortunately for the French, however, their taste in art was not infallible. Focusing their attention and praise almost exclusively on works deemed acceptable by the stuffy and pedestrian French Academy, not only did they overlook many first-rate American painters, they scoffed at some of their own countrymen who in time became recognized as great geniuses, including Camille Corot, Edgar Degas, Edouard Manet, Jean-François Millet, Claude Monet, and Pierre-Auguste Renoir. Instead, these painters were avidly collected by Americans, many of whom lacked the money to buy Old Masters or the latest darlings of French fashion. The Impressionists, wrote Renoir, "perhaps owe it to the Americans that we did not die of hunger."[22] In the twentieth century, the writer Gertrude Stein and her brother Leo were important early collectors of the next generation of modern art. At her apartment at 27 rue de Fleurs, there were more Cézannes than at the esteemed Musée du Luxembourg. Toward the end of the nineteenth century, the French would begin to regret that so many modern masterpieces would be "buried" in American homes and museums.[23]

By the twentieth century, however, American culture had gained a depth, breadth, and profundity that rivaled or surpassed that of France in the areas of literature and painting. Besides, many of the most cutting-edge European artists—Picasso, Strauss, Stravinsky, James Joyce—were not French. As a consequence, Americans began to lose their previous obsequiousness. Nowhere was this more noticeable than in the 1920s, when thousands of Americans—the celebrated "Lost Generation"—flocked to Paris to find themselves in the wake of the First World War. Ernest Hemingway, F. Scott Fitzgerald, John Dos Passos, E. E. Cummings, and Alexander Calder, among many others, all sought their artistic fortunes in the City of Clubs. Yet the great majority of that boisterous and thirsty bunch made the pilgrimage not to genuflect before the shrine of modern French culture but to take advantage of extremely favorable exchange rates.[24] A three-course meal could be had for the equivalent of two dimes, a prostitute for a quarter.

Although Paris teemed with intellectual and artistic activity of the highest order (much of it the product of foreigners), most Americans living in Paris remained oblivious. They generally kept to themselves and their pleasures. And while their novels sometimes featured European backdrops, more often than not they were set in the States. Fitzgerald penned *The Great Gatsby* (1925)—that quintessential portrait of lost American dreams—while on holiday in the French Riviera. Truth be told, he could hardly wait to get back to his American friends (and his drinking) in gay Paris. In a sense, much of modern American literature was created through the deliberate act of ignoring the French—at least those who were not bartenders or ladies of the evening.

On May 21, 1927, when Charles Lindbergh landed in Paris to thunderous applause (on both sides of the Atlantic), the Franco-American cultural exchange had arguably reached a new low of triviality. Where the French had historically paid scant attention to American culture, the rise of American economic, political, and cultural power would eventually force them to take notice. Unfortunately, French jealousy and resentment in the face of America's rising global prominence manifested itself in a tide of virulent anti-Americanism that began in the 1930s and beyond. To Americans, proud of their native culture as well as their important new role in the world, such French behavior would become hurtful, maddening, and all too familiar. It is one of the greatest of ironies that as both countries developed into modern, stable democracies, with France following America's lead, the level of cultural animosity between them would only grow.

Indeed, in these early years of the twentieth century—certainly the most tranquil of the entire Franco-American relationship—there were numerous exchanges of artwork meant to enshrine the growing friendship. In 1889, the American diplomatic colony in Paris had bestowed upon the city a small version of the Statue of Liberty. On the Fourth of July in 1900, the French capital was presented with a Lafayette statue, paid for by American schoolchildren with help from Congress. In 1902, French dignitaries unveiled a statue of the Revolutionary War hero Rochambeau in the park across from the White House. Four years later, the French returned the body of naval hero John Paul Jones to be interred with great fanfare in Annapolis, Maryland. After a commemorative ceremony in Plattsburgh, New York, in 1912 for the French explorer Champlain, the *New York Sun* wrote that "each celebration such as the present must serve a useful as well as a sentimental purpose, useful because it demonstrates the possibility of permanent international amity, sentimental because it recalls an ancient association in an honorable triumph."[25] The coming years would test this assessment severely.

EIGHT

GREAT WAR, POOR PEACE

The French program . . . was all outwardly so clever, so able, so perfect—
so monumentally stupid and short-sighted underneath.
—Ray Stannard Baker, press secretary to Woodrow Wilson [1]

WHEN GENERAL JOHN J. "BLACKJACK" PERSHING arrived in France on June 13, 1917, he possessed supreme confidence in the military campaign that lay ahead. He was considerably less certain, however, that he would be able to endure the tedious welcoming ceremony that had been arranged for him and his staff in the city of Boulogne. First the Americans were forced to stand at attention through interminable renditions of the "Star-Spangled Banner" and "La Marseillaise." When the music finally ended, a long line of dignitaries greeted the general's entourage. Next came a tour of a sixteenth-century harbor fort. The Americans were beginning to wonder if they would ever board the train for Paris. Yet their French handlers had carefully orchestrated each delay. They wanted Pershing and his men to enter the capital at the end of the day, when their appearance would cause the greatest stir.

Everything went as planned. At the mere sight of the Americans, crowds of excited Parisians cried, *"Vive l'Amérique!"* and waved Old Glory. Women broke through police lines to kiss the newly arrived soldiers. After so much stuffy protocol, these genuine demonstrations of joy touched the normally stoic Pershing. The mere presence of

Americans in uniform had an immediate and invigorating effect on the French, who had suffered through three years of grinding conflict. By then, the Great War—as it was already being called—had claimed some two million French casualties and national morale was reaching dangerous depths. Just a few weeks before Pershing's appearance, an entire division of mutinous troops had marched on the city, intending to overthrow the government. Only the frantic and courageous efforts of General Henri-Philippe Pétain—as well as the extraordinary news that the United States had declared war on Germany—had succeeded in thwarting them. "We must wait for the Americans!" Pétain had declared. Now the waiting was over. "I hope," Pétain said to Pershing as they escaped from the delirious throngs, "it is not too late."[2]

Over the course of the next year, thousands of fresh American soldiers poured into the trenches of Europe to fight alongside the hardscrabble veterans of Belgium, Britain, and France. By the autumn of 1918, more than 4 million Americans had been mobilized for war, and more than 120,000 of them were dead. But their sacrifice was decisive. Disciplined and well supplied, they helped push back the last desperate German offensives and played a critical role in persuading the Central Powers to sue for peace.

Victory did not come easily. General Pershing had fought a war within a war as the French and British repeatedly tried to absorb the American force into their own. At one tense meeting, French general Ferdinand Foch confronted Pershing over who would control the U.S. troops. "You are willing to risk our being driven back to the Loire?" he screamed. "I have thought this program over very deliberately," replied Pershing, "and will not be coerced."[3] Although willing to cooperate with Allied generals and even take orders from them, he would not have Americans serving as replacement fodder for the depleted armies of Europe.

For the Europeans, it had been a long and bitter struggle. Since August of 1914, Europe had engaged in an act of collective suicide. By the time the Great War was over—the guns finally falling silent at precisely 11:11 a.m. on the eleventh day of the eleventh month in 1918—nearly ten million men were dead. More than twice that number had been wounded, many permanently maimed.

In the course of a few short years, an entire generation had been cut to ribbons by machine guns or torn apart by the shrapnel of artillery barrages. The French lost a staggering 329,000 men in the first two months alone. What particularly shocked the European elite was that neither good breeding nor officer-school heroism had made any difference to the indiscriminate slaughter wrought by the new angels of death that terrorized the modern, mechanized battlefield.

After four years of devastation, Europe was transformed. Entire empires had fallen. The Ottomans and Habsburgs were no more. In Russia, a former lawyer named Lenin had seized power through a coup d'état, and the murderous specter of Bolshevism now haunted Eastern and Central Europe. Vast swaths of pastoral countryside had become fields of mud and broken trees. By late 1918, it was abundantly clear that Europe had reached a vital crossroad. Desperate for deliverance, many of its fractured peoples now shared a faith in another American—not a military man, but a former professor who believed he could rescue the continent and, indeed, the world from another cataclysm.

Although President Woodrow Wilson had abandoned the ivory tower for politics years earlier, many could still detect in his public manner the tenor of the exacting schoolteacher—part haughty scholar, part self-righteous minister. First elected in 1912, he won reelection four years later on the slogan "He kept us out of war." A few months into his second term, however, Wilson reneged on his pledge and became a wartime leader. Now, with the war finally over, he was preparing a bold and visionary plan to repair a broken collection of nation-states.

Yet the settlement that followed the First World War promised to be even more complicated than the thorny tangle of secret alliances that had caused its eruption. France lacked patience for anything but its own self-defeating agenda. Long absent from the victors' table at any meaningful peace negotiation, French leaders were eager to make up for lost time. As the Allied Powers began to discuss the specifics in the early months of 1919, the French worked tirelessly to derail Wilson's plans. In the process, France created the conditions for and unleashed many of the raw passions that would lead to an even more destructive war, one that would require another American rescue effort. Nor, despite what many assume, was World War II an unforeseen consequence of the failure of Versailles. To the contrary, a number of observers predicted this outcome at the time. The Versailles Treaty stands condemned as one of the worst, most shortsighted agreements in history—a tragic failure that had precisely the opposite effect from what was intended. Why? Because the French intentionally derailed and subverted it. Over the next two decades, Adolf Hitler would use this record of French intransigence and vengefulness to rally Germans to the Nationalist Socialist cause—and ultimately to war.

So committed was Wilson to his platform of peace and accountability that he did something no sitting American president had ever done: He traveled to Europe, where he could personally participate in the negotiations. When he landed on French soil on December 13, 1918, he met, like Pershing before him, a delirious French public.[4] Some two million war-weary Parisians—the largest crowd in the country's history—turned out to cheer him and throw flowers on his carriage as he moved through the streets of the jubilant city. (This genuine outpouring of gratitude would long influence American popular opinion, which imagined France as a fair virgin saved from German rapacity by the prowess of American arms.) Universally lauded as the man who had ended the war, "Wilson the Just," as he was known, was arguably more popular in France than in the United States. In such an atmosphere, there was every reason to believe that the United States and France would continue the era of good feelings that had existed between them for the past few decades. Even the Germans and Austrians viewed the earnest and sober-minded American as their best hope for a fair and honorable peace.

The French government, however, did not share in this sentiment. Whereas Pershing represented the raw American manpower that had turned the tide of battle, Wilson was seen as a meddler and opportunist who threatened to deny France its share in the spoils of victory. Although several of Wilson's advisors had warned against making the trip ("diplomatic Europe is enemy soil," cautioned one), the president failed altogether to anticipate the enormous challenge—and the trap—that lay ahead.

In the final days of 1918, the prestige and moral authority of the United States had never been greater. While the European powers had spent four full years locked in a bloody death grip, America had passed the first part of the war in its traditional neutrality. With few exceptions, Americans were proud of their political distance from the intrigues of the Old World. "Peace-loving citizens of this country," noted the *Chicago Herald*, "will now rise up and tender a hearty vote of thanks to Columbus for having discovered America."[5] In not rushing to war, they believed that they had avoided one of history's most catastrophic "foreign entanglements."

But the oceans no longer provided the same protection they had in the past. As Germany let loose unrestricted U-boat assaults on U.S. shipping, American isolationism suddenly seemed indefensible. An intercepted telegram from German foreign secretary Arthur Zimmermann described plans to recruit Mexico for an invasion of the American Southwest and revived old fears of foreign scheming in Napoleon III's former playground.

Americans were ready for war, and while many German Americans hoped for a German triumph, most citizens felt a closer cultural bond to Britain and France. Hundreds already had volunteered for service as ambulance drivers or members of the Lafayette Escadrille air squadron (named in honor of America's favorite Frenchman). On April 6, 1917, Congress declared war on Germany. In laying out his goals, Wilson urged the United States "to vindicate the principles of peace and justice" and create "a concert of peace and action as will henceforth assure the observance of these principles."[6]

With the war over, Wilson continued his idealistic program. Indeed, his generous and imaginative vision for postwar Europe was as responsible for Germany and Austria-Hungary's decision to lay down their arms as America's timely military intervention. The core of Wilson's program was contained in his famous Fourteen Points, issued as the war still raged on January 9, 1918. These guiding principles banned secret treaties and hidden diplomacy, called for a general reduction in armaments, mandated that Germany return the long-contested province of Alsace-Lorraine to France, favored self-determination and a redrawing of Europe's borders along ethno-nationalist lines, and envisioned the formation of an international organization called the League of Nations to adjudicate future disputes.

The tone of the Fourteen Points was hopeful, and several of them were aimed specifically at convincing Germans they would not have a brutal peace imposed on them by vengeful conquerors. Two items on Wilson's list held special appeal: freedom of the seas (neutralizing Britain's unrivaled dominance on the waves) and the removal of trade barriers (outlawing the economic reprisals that Germans feared). In making his proposal, Wilson spoke directly to the German people, telling them that he wanted no "alteration or modification of [German] institutions." Instead, Wilson sought to create a new trust and solidarity among the nations of Europe and to challenge the politics that had caused such a deadly war to break out in the first place. He pleaded for "justice to all peoples and nationalities, and their right to live on equal terms of liberty and safety with one another, whether they be strong or weak."[7] Although the United States had taken sides in the conflict, Wilson wanted no part in a victors' peace that took unfair advantage of the vanquished.

As its armies crumbled on the Western Front, Germany had jumped at the opportunity to make peace on Wilson's broad-minded terms. On October 5, 1918, the Germans opened peace negotiations with the Americans. Three days later, the Austrians joined them.[8] Yet the Central Powers were not alone in appreciating Wilson's Fourteen Points. The Allies liked them as well, though not as a set of guiding values. Rather, they viewed Wilson's proposal as a device for getting the Germans to quit fighting, thus making a bloody invasion of Germany unnecessary. Once that had occurred, Wilson's plan could be abandoned and the war could continue at the peace table. Because of this duplicity, the Peace of Paris failed to live up to its promise. The ink had barely dried on the Treaty of Versailles in 1919 when the recriminations began. The Germans felt betrayed and claimed that they had been strong-armed into signing a harsh settlement with a gratuitous war-guilt clause. They simply did not believe they held sole responsibility for lighting the powder keg. The Byzantine causes of the war, they thought, had been nurtured by a feverish jingoism throughout Europe. Even many members of the Allied delegations were upset at what they saw as the vindictive nature of the agreement.

Late in 1919, John Maynard Keynes published *The Economic Consequences of the Peace* to wide acclaim. The British economist had participated in the peace talks and was troubled by what they had produced. He inveighed against the Allies for their shortsighted attempts to impose a crushing burden on Germany. Predicting dire consequences, Keynes called Wilson "the greatest fraud on earth" for failing to follow through on his promises.[9]

How had things unraveled so terribly in just a few months? How had Wilson gone from a shining beacon of hope to a symbol of capitulation and weakness?

Whatever his own illusions about Europe, Wilson was not guilty of arriving unprepared. Months before, he had assembled 150 experts from various fields in an ad hoc organization called the Inquiry. Working out of the American Geographical Society building in New York, this proto–think tank ensured that the U.S. delegation was by far the best-informed of all the participating nations. "Had the Treaty of Paris been drafted solely by the American experts," wrote the British diplomat Harold Nicolson, "it would have been one of the wisest as well as most scientific documents ever devised."[10]

But American experts would not draft the Treaty of Versailles. In its final form, the treaty bore little resemblance to Wilson's original vision. During the course of the negotiations, the Allied powers abandoned Wilson's principles whenever it suited them. The greatest offender was France, America's wartime ally. Its leaders remained fixated on short-term advantage rather than the larger goal of European peace. To be sure, the French people had suffered enormously during the war. Most of the fighting had taken place on their soil, and many of France's most industrialized and economically productive regions now lay in ruins. Moreover, it was the second time that Germany had tried to conquer France in less than fifty years. Popular passions were understandably high. Still, it is the duty of statesmen to temper such passions for the sake of the national interest.

Sadly, French leaders failed to fulfill their duty. The French government refused to grasp that its national security might benefit more from a settlement in which adversaries were not humiliated but welcomed back into the European fold. The French seemed to have forgotten the great mercy that had been shown to them a century earlier during the Congress of Vienna, the last time such an international conference had been held. Then, the armies of Napoleon had been the clear aggressors in a terrible series of wars. Afterward, however, France was not only allowed a seat at the negotiating table but given an important role in the plan for postwar stability that became known as the Concert of Europe. The result was a century of relative peace. Just as Napoleon's departure had convinced Europe that France could be reformed, so Germany's transformation from an empire to a republic in the last days of the war should have led to better treatment.

France instead resolved to do everything in its power to cripple its larger and more populous neighbor. In its most ambitious form, the French plan included breaking Germany into its original disorganized components, creating an independent state in the Rhineland to act as a security buffer between France and Germany, seizing control of the coal-rich Saar region, granting large chunks of German territory to Poland, and mandating massive reparations that would not only pay for war damages but make Germany an economic vassal to

France. Where Wilson called for a peace based on trust and mutual interests, the French were intent on creating a settlement that would secure their own continental supremacy for decades to come.

The diplomatic ambush would take place in Paris. Although other venues had been considered, the French insisted that the peace talks occur in their capital. "[Paris] should be chosen," wrote the semiofficial newspaper *Temps*, "because of its sacrifices, its heroism, [and] its martyrdom."[11] The Palace of Versailles, just south of Paris, would be used for the official signing of the German treaty. It had obvious symbolic value as the place where the Germans had proclaimed their empire in 1871 after their victory in the Franco-Prussian War. The French could almost smell their revenge.

In Paris, the French government would enjoy home-field advantage and exert a powerful influence on the conference through the newspapers it tacitly controlled. "It will be difficult enough at best to make a just peace," wrote Wilson's aide Colonel Edward House, "and it will be almost impossible to do so while sitting in the atmosphere of a belligerent capital."[12] "I thought it would be better to hold it in a neutral place," wrote British prime minister David Lloyd George, "but the old man wept and protested so much that we gave way."[13]

That old man was Georges Clemenceau. Known as the "Tiger of France," the French prime minister was a cunning, resourceful aristocrat from the Vendée, who had cut a figure in French politics for more than forty years. Originally trained as a doctor, he had been drawn instead to the subtle give-and-take of political life, as well as the intellectual and cultural world of Paris. He had traveled widely and for several years lived in the United States, where he achieved fluency in English and developed a penchant for New York slang. In Connecticut, while teaching French and horseback riding at an all-girls school, he met and married an attractive but dim-witted student, Mary Plummer, and whisked her back to France. Soon, however, Clemenceau tired of the poor girl, whom he left with his parents as he escorted actresses about Paris. Their union did not endure, but Mary stayed on in France, where she dutifully and pathetically followed her ex-husband's political rise, even though she herself never learned French. "What a tragedy she ever married me," Clemenceau would say at her death.[14]

The prime minister was a lifelong republican who had come to political consciousness under the tutelage of his father, an admirer of the French Revolution and an opponent of Napoleon III. Like many French statesmen throughout history, Clemenceau was also an extreme chauvinist convinced of French superiority and intent on restoring French glory. From the American standpoint, Clemenceau was another in a long line of condescending and treacherous French leaders whose ranks included Napoleon III and his monstrous uncle as well as Talleyrand, Adet, Genet, and Vergennes. More interested in nakedly nationalistic goals than the common man, Clemenceau "loved France," said Lloyd George, "but hated all Frenchmen."[15] If so, he hated Germans even more. A month after the 1918 armistice, when food-relief administrator (and future president) Herbert Hoover described the starvation he had found in Germany, Clemenceau countered, "There are twenty million Germans too many."[16]

Such callousness had its origins in the French humiliation at the hands of the Prussians almost half a century earlier. The seventy-year-old Clemenceau remembered the roar of siege guns surrounding Paris in 1871. He had even been present in the Hall of Mirrors at Versailles when the German Empire was inaugurated. Indeed, Clemenceau may be considered the very embodiment of wounded French pride and egotism. In a widely reported remark, he was said to have requested that he be buried upright, facing Germany.[17]

In 1917, the fearless old man with the bushy white mustache had been chosen prime minister and had displayed great courage in the face of the relentless German war machine. When the French parliament considered abandoning the capital, Clemenceau facetiously agreed: "Yes, we are too far from the front."[18] As the war came to a conclusion, the pugnacious politician searched for another foe and found it in Wilson and his Fourteen Points.

During the Paris Peace Conference, Clemenceau's ascetic routine resembled that of a disciplined warrior. Most days he awoke at three o'clock in the morning to read. At seven, he ate a special homemade gruel. When his trainer and masseuse arrived, he exercised and fenced. Lunch consisted of boiled eggs and water. Dinner was milk and bread. Without other distractions, he remained ruthlessly focused on his quarry: the American president. He had nothing but contempt for Wilson. "God gave us His Ten Commandments," Clemenceau quipped, "and we broke them. Wilson gave us his Fourteen Points—we shall see."[19]

The French president proceeded with caution and cunning. At the outset, he cloaked his strategy as consensus opinion by cleverly agreeing in principle to Wilson's Fourteen Points. Then he set about undermining their intent and spirit. His plan was to stake out extreme preliminary negotiating positions and then achieve his objectives through "compromise."

On October 29, 1918, Clemenceau and Lloyd George met secretly with Colonel House and various U.S. representatives and agreed on a framework that became known as the Commentary. Although vague and nonbinding, it emphasized those elements that the Germans objected to most strongly in the Versailles treaty: the breakup of Austria-Hungary, the creation of a Polish corridor through Prussia, the loss of Germany's colonies, and war reparations. The Commentary also elevated the hitherto implied principle of German war guilt to a core concept and emphasized that a main objective of the treaty would be to provide "rewards" for the victors and "punishments" for the losers.[20]

It is true that Wilson had become noticeably more anti-German after a U-boat torpedoed an Irish civilian craft, the *Leinster*, on October 12, killing 450 people. But why had he agreed to support the Commentary? Perhaps it was his intention to promote goodwill in the same way that Clemenceau had tentatively agreed to the Fourteen Points. The next few months would tell which vision would prevail.

Begun in January, the Paris Peace Conference quickly reached agreement on several points, including the punishment of German war criminals. The larger question of how to contain Germany, however, would have to wait until after the winter recess, during which Wilson returned to the United States to generate congressional support for the League of Nations, a pet proposal that would increasingly become his overriding interest in the talks.

When Wilson returned to France, Clemenceau unleashed an aggressive push to get his platform approved. Having compromised earlier on small issues, he now waged an unrelenting battle to achieve his greater goals. With French troops occupying the strategically important Rhineland, the French general Foch argued vociferously for either a permanent French military presence in the area or the creation of an independent republic that would separate the two countries. To nudge the Rhinelanders in the direction of independence from Germany, the French army employed all manner of inducements. This hearts-and-minds campaign included economic concessions as well as French-sponsored festivals and fireworks.

France's allies were appalled at this dangerous tack, which violated Wilson's goal of ethnic self-determination. "We regarded it," said Lloyd George, "as definite and dishonorable betrayal of one of the fundamental principles for which the Allies had professed to fight." Carving up Germany, he wrote, "would cause endless friction and might provoke another war."[21] Seizing the Rhineland was dangerous and unwise. "The desires of the people were German in character," Wilson had said while in the United States. "Taking the territory away from Germany would simply give a cause for hatred and a determination for a renewal of the war throughout Germany that would always be equal to the bitterness felt by France against Germany over the lost provinces [Alsace and Lorraine]."[22] Sadly, he would be proven correct.

With Wilson's blessing, the French already had succeeded in creating a large and independent Polish state, with territory containing three million ethnic Germans, including the economically rich coal regions of Silesia and the Polish Corridor, a strip of land that cut off East Prussia from the rest of Germany. Twenty years later, these controversial annexations would serve as convenient justifications for Hitler's invasion of Poland.

The issue that caused the most rancor, however, was reparations. This initiative, which the French pursued with ruthless single-mindedness, threatened to destabilize Germany economically and politically. In Keynes' opinion, it was the most foolish part of the Treaty of Versailles. It simply made no sense, he argued, to try to bankrupt the Germans before robbing them blind—and then expect them to buy French goods with money they did not have. Indeed, in the terrible years after the war, reparations would aggravate the newly created Weimar Republic's postwar financial problems. Inflation became so rampant that a single cabbage cost as much as 50 million marks. It was one more calamity that contributed to the fateful decisions Germany would make in the 1930s.

After the winter recess, Wilson held his ground against the French on reparations, and the conference became deadlocked. Lloyd George, who had once backed reparations, became exasperated by the impasse and fearful that the settlement would destroy Germany. He expressed his new concerns in a prophetic statement that became known as the Fontainebleau Memorandum. "You may strip Germany of her colonies, reduce her navy to that of a fifth-rate power," he said, "all the same . . . if she feels she has been unjustly treated in the peace of 1919 she will find means of extracting retribution from her conquerors."[23]

The French, however, remained tenacious in their pursuit of German humiliation. Their aggressive aims began to infuriate the British and the Americans. "We spend an hour reasoning with Clemenceau, getting him around to an agreement," said Wilson, "and find when we go back to the original question Clemenceau stands just where he did at the beginning."[24] At one point, Clemenceau ridiculously accused Wilson of being "pro-German" and of "seeking to destroy France."[25] The rattled and weary president would later characterize the French stalling as "damnable."[26] General Pershing, still commanding American soldiers in an army of occupation, put the matter plainly: "Our men have the sporting instinct. They don't believe in hitting a man when he is down."[27]

Wilson also had been enraged by the constant and vicious attacks that the government-controlled French press was directing toward him and his program. "What the most terrible and insidious war has not been able to accomplish, the division of our alliance," wrote the pseudonymous "Pertinax" in *L'Echo de Paris*, "has been obtained by four months of [Wilson's] diplomacy."[28] In the meantime, with each new report of political chaos in Eastern Europe and the threat of Bolshevism in Germany, pressure grew on the Allies to reach an agreement. Hoover also remained exasperated with the French. "The French by obstruction of every financial measure that we can propose, to the feeding of Germany in the attempt to compel us to loan money to Germany for this purpose, have defeated every step so far for getting them the food which we have been promising for three months," he wrote the president on February 4, 1919.[29]

On April 3, the drained and demoralized president suffered a sudden and violent bout of coughing. He ran a fever and was confined to his bed. Known for his delicate health, Wilson probably had suffered a stroke—pushed over the edge by the strain of the French onslaught. Wilson's fragile condition seemed to please the French prime minister. "He is worse today," Clemenceau said cheerfully to Lloyd George. "Do you know his doctor? Couldn't you get round him and bribe him?"[30]

As the president lay in his sickbed, the negotiations continued in an adjoining chamber. Predictably, attempts were made to exploit the situation. But Wilson stood firm, refusing to budge and replying "No!" as each French proposal was sent to him.[31]

"I have been doing a lot of thinking," said Wilson in his dark room, "thinking what would be the outcome on the world if these French politicians were given a free hand and allowed to have their way and secure all that they claim France is entitled to. My opinion is that if they had their way the world would go to pieces in a very short while."[32] Finally the stubborn president decided enough was enough. On April 7, he ordered the *George Washington* to steam for France and retrieve him. It was a bold attempt to force Clemenceau's hand and reach a settlement.

The announcement broke the impasse, but not in Wilson's favor. In truth, Wilson was no negotiator, and his illness only made things worse. In the past, his greatest accomplishments had come from consensus achieved through calm discussions with fair and like-minded men. In Paris, however, he was out of his element and no match for his conniving French adversaries. Their aggressive style simply undid him.

In the flurry of activity to try to secure a peace before his ship arrived, Wilson capitulated, making the fateful compromises that would betray his previous ideals. Like the Germans, he was defeated in a war of attrition. He had become so confident in the League of Nations and its potential for solving all the problems that might be caused by the treaty that he caved on reparations and Rhineland control in order to secure French (and British) support for his beloved League.

Wilson mistakenly believed that America would influence future conflicts through the economic leverage it wielded as a result of the enormous war debt Europe owed it. To be sure, Clemenceau surrendered on a few points, such as the creation of a Rhenish republic. But because the French negotiators had purposely charted such extreme initial positions rather than the reasonable ones described in Wilson's Fourteen Points, their "concessions" still allowed them to achieve much of what they wanted. With an agreement on reparations, a clear war-guilt clause, French control over the Saar's coal fields for fifteen years, and Allied military control of the Rhineland for the same period of time, the spirit of Wilson's Fourteen Points was no more. Hoover predicted that the agreement would "pull down the whole continent" and that it "contained the seeds of another war."[33]

Ironically, the United States would refuse to enter the League. The Senate remained unconvinced that American participation in such a cumbersome and poorly defined organization was in the best interests of the country. Without American participation or any true guiding principles, the League would prove powerless to act as conditions for an even greater war began to grow in the 1930s.

Even in his moment of triumph, however, Clemenceau continued to claw for further advantages. In the Rhineland, plotters supported by the French army proclaimed an independent republic. Only strongly worded objections from the Allies succeeded in forcing the French army to back down. There was also a French plan to sever the left bank of the Rhine economically from Germany. In yet another scheme, France tried to spread disunity by asking each German state to sign the treaty separately. Although these efforts failed, they managed to alienate the Germans even further and demonstrated the tenacity of France in its reckless quest for mastery in Europe.

In June 1919, the Germans were summoned to Paris and handed the treaty in a humiliating ceremony orchestrated by Clemenceau. It was an indignity they would not soon forget. Not allowed to negotiate, they were given two weeks to decide whether to sign at the point of a bayonet. The Germans were astonished. "The [German] people," wrote an American diplomat in Berlin, "had been led to believe that Germany had been unluckily beaten after a fine and clean fight . . . but that happily President Wilson could be appealed to, and would arrange a compromise peace satisfactory to Germany."[34] When they realized that they were giving up 13 percent of their population and 10 percent of their territory, they blamed the Americans for not protecting their interests from the greedy and vengeful French.

Yet the Germans had no real choice. On June 28, 1919, two obscure officials sent from the Fatherland scrawled their names on the discreditable document, and the treaty participants went their separate ways. In the end, Wilson himself seems to have grasped the fundamental injustices of what had happened. "If I were a German," he commented after reading the completed treaty, "I think I should never sign it."[35] Seeing Wilson off at the train station, Clemenceau is reported to have said, "I feel as though I were losing one of the best friends I ever had."[36] The myth of the historical friendship between America and France was alive and well—and shamelessly sustained by Clemenceau for his cynical purposes.[37]

As Wilson steamed for home, it was already clear that he had been, as Keynes would later say, "bamboozled."[38] In a letter drenched in rage, William Bullitt, a member of the American delegation, told the president: "I am sorry that you did not fight our fight to the finish and that you had so little faith in the millions of men, like myself, in every nation, who had faith in you. . . . Our government has consented now to deliver the suffering peoples of the world to new oppressions, subjections, and dismemberments—a new century of war."[39]

In a few years, an ex-corporal from the German army would begin to make a name for himself in the beer halls of Munich, denouncing the "peace of shame" and reminding Germans not only of Allied treachery but also Weimar's complicity in signing such a tainted document.[40] In his autobiography, *Mein Kampf*, Adolf Hitler railed against "this instrument of boundless extortion and abject humiliation" that has led to an "unprecedented pillaging of our people."[41] He also shrewdly perceived that continued Allied stubbornness in carrying out the letter of the Versailles *Diktat*, as the Germans now referred to it, was "a precondition of the success of our movement in the future."[42]

When Hitler became German chancellor in 1933, one of Germany's foremost foreign-policy goals would be to erase the disgraceful legacy of Versailles. In September 1939, as the German army sliced through Poland, Foreign Minister Joachim von Ribbentrop declared in triumph, "The Führer has done nothing but remedy the most serious consequences which this most unreasonable of all dictates in history imposed upon a nation and, in fact, upon the whole of Europe."[43] Within a few months of Ribbentrop uttering these words, France would reap the bitter harvest of Germany's all-consuming hunger for vengeance—and so would the rest of the world.

NINE

FRENCH RESISTANCE

Next to the weather . . . [the French] have caused me more trouble
in this war than any single factor.
—Dwight Eisenhower [1]

JUST AFTER THREE in the morning on November 8, 1942, two British cutters carrying a battalion of American soldiers approached the harbor of Oran, in French Morocco. Their mission was to capture and secure the port for the off-loading of men and materiel during the imminent Allied invasion, called Operation Torch. Almost a year had passed since Germany and Italy had declared war on the United States. The time at last had arrived for the American army to enter the fight to liberate Europe from fascism. All along the coast of French North Africa that night, tens of thousands of GIs would storm ashore at Algiers, Casablanca, Fedala, Safi, Mehdia, and Oran. Once the Americans seized these cities, it would be on to Tunisia to join the British Eighth Army in its struggle against Erwin Rommel's vaunted *Afrika Korps*.

As the lead ship neared the boom at the mouth of Oran's harbor, a single question animated the mind of all on board: Would the French resist? In the weeks leading up to the invasion, diplomats and intelligence officers had assured the American military that they would not.[2] They were counting on French gratitude earned during the First World War. "Our latest and best information from North Africa," wrote President Franklin Roosevelt to British prime minister Winston Churchill, "is . . . [that] an American expedition led in all three phases by American officers will meet little resistance from the French Army in Africa."[3] But how could the president be so certain? Hadn't the French government signed a shameful Armistice with Germany rather than go into exile and carry on the war from abroad? Hadn't French leaders actively collaborated with their Nazi masters and even shipped valuable supplies to Rommel in Tunisia? In 1941, French colonial troops in Syria had fought savagely for more than a month against a combined British and Free French force. But surely, replied the optimists, the French would rally to the Stars and Stripes once they saw it flying above American forces intent on their liberation.[4]

Then the French guns opened up. Guided by spotlights from shore, machine-gun tracers sprayed out across the jet-black water, followed by a withering artillery barrage. From the docks and jetties, French snipers squeezed off round after round. Neither the large and conspicuous U.S. flags flying from both ships nor the repeated calls over a loudspeaker in American-accented French—"Do not fire! We are your friends! Do not fire!"—had any effect.[5]

As the H.M.S. *Walney* broke through the boom and entered the harbor, a shell smashed through its bridge, killing the French-speaking sailor declaring Franco-American amity through his microphone. With the groans of the wounded filling the air, a French destroyer, *La Surprise*, made straight for the *Walney*. Its powerful guns swept across the crowded decks of the much-smaller ship and tore through its lightly armored sides. Then an artillery shell sliced through the *Walney*'s engine room, causing terrible injuries. Several more shells blew apart both boilers, blasting metal fragments in every direction and drenching sailors with scalding water.

With its engines gone, the ship now drifted with the tide. Sensing the kill, two French submarines and a destroyer began firing mercilessly into the stricken vessel. Although the troops on board managed a courageous final stand with their small arms, the *Walney* was on fire, its bloody deck layered with corpses and its cabins choked with smoke and mangled bodies.

The H.M.S. *Hartland* suffered a similar fate. Already severely crippled and burning from several direct hits, the *Hartland* found itself next to a French destroyer, the *Typhoon*, which raked the cutter with machine-gun fire from bow to stern. The pile of corpses on deck was soon so thick that it impeded access to the fire hoses. At 4 A.M., an hour after the fighting began, the wounded captain ordered the survivors to abandon ship. French sailors rescued some from the oily sea. Sharpshooters and machine-gunners finished off the rest. By dawn, the doomed raid was over. Casualties stood at more than 90 percent, including 307 dead. To add insult to grievous injury, the French would charge the Allies a pilotage fee (per local law) for entering the harbor.[6]

For the next three days, the Americans faced fierce fighting across twelve separate battlefields in Algeria and French Morocco. American GIs comprised the bulk of the landing force on the theory that they would antagonize the French less than the British. But the French premier, Marshal Henri Philippe Pétain, refused to back down. "France and her honor are at stake," he cabled President Roosevelt. "We are attacked. We will defend ourselves. This is the order I am giving."[7] Only superior numbers and American tenacity made Operation Torch a success. "Had the landings been opposed by the Germans," admitted General George S. Patton, "we would never have gotten ashore."[8]

It is widely believed that the Vichy government was a weak puppet regime that cooperated reluctantly with the Nazis and put up only a token resistance to Allied forces. The comical figure of Captain Renault from the movie *Casablanca* epitomizes the image of Vichy officials as opportunists motivated almost entirely by petty corruption rather than fascist ideology. The reality was quite different, as the Americans discovered in North Africa.

One of Vichy's greatest opportunists was Admiral Jean François Darlan, the supreme commander of French naval forces. He finally called for a cease-fire, even though Pétain had expressly forbidden such an order. Yet Darlan and his African comrades could sense further resistance would seal their doom. In August 1941, Darlan had cynically informed an American diplomat: "When you have three thousand tanks, six thousand planes, and five-hundred thousand men to bring to Marseilles, let me know. Then we shall welcome you."[9] Now, facing just such an overwhelming force, Darlan—true to his word—capitulated. As Oran, Algiers, and Casablanca fell into Allied hands, the admiral signed an agreement with Eisenhower promising to provide French forces and equipment for the Tunisian campaign in exchange for continued command over his own troops. His order to the commander of the French fleet at Toulon to steam at once for Africa, however, would be met with defiance. "Merde!" replied Admiral Jean de Laborde, who chose to scuttle his whole fleet rather than entrust them to those attempting to liberate his country. Three battleships, seven cruisers, thirty destroyers, and sixteen submarines were lost.

In the aftermath of their victory, the Americans acted almost remorseful. Although France promptly severed diplomatic relations with the United States, Roosevelt drew a distinction between the collaborationist government and the France of America's imagination. This illegitimate regime, he said in a press release, cannot "sever relations between the American people and the people of France. We have not broken with the French. We never will."[10] Throughout the course of the fighting, it had been difficult for the average soldier to accept that the descendants of Lafayette had become, at least for the moment, the enemy. One naval gunner, hoping to raise the martial spirit of his comrades, suggested they "pretend" that the French were "Japs."[11] Even the hard-driving General George Patton, whose uniform had been stained by the yellow dye of an exploded French shell, found little pleasure in facing his adversary.[12] "I cannot stomach fighting the French if there is a way to avoid it," he said.[13] Indeed, when the conflict was over, he and Admiral Hewitt gave a lavish lunch for their former French adversaries. "They drank $40 worth of champagne," Patton recalled, "but it was worth it."[14]

Even though Francophilia remained a strong current in American culture, the United States had not enjoyed close, uncomplicated relations with France in the two decades following 1919. Indeed, these years were some of the most strained in a difficult history. The unyielding and reckless French program to keep Germany economically and militarily prostrate not only had succeeded in exacerbating lethal tensions in Europe, it had effectively poisoned relations with both the United States and Britain.

In American eyes, the culprit was hypocrisy. The French insisted on wringing Germany dry for reparations but behaved cavalierly about their own war debts to the United States. During the 1930s, France's poorly managed and selfish monetary policies caused further instability in a world still suffering from the aftermath of the Great War and the onset of a global depression. By the middle of the decade, an exasperated secretary of the Treasury, Henry Morgenthau, said that France had become "a bankrupt, fourth class power."[15]

In spite of its many problems, however, 1930s France still reigned over a rich colonial empire in Africa, Asia, and the Middle East and boasted a modernized army and navy. Unfortunately, as Hitler's rise and his vow to undo the Treaty of Versailles made war more likely, France became increasingly reluctant to use its military to confront its threatening neighbor. When Weimar Germany withheld reparations payments in 1923, France had been able to muster the nerve to invade and briefly occupy the Ruhr, but a decade later it balked at flexing the same military muscle to challenge a far more sinister German regime.

As dictators emerged in Germany and Italy, French strategy unaccountably changed from clumsy confrontation to weakhearted appeasement. In 1935, French foreign minister Pierre Laval signed an agreement with Benito Mussolini: In exchange for assurances of consultation if Germany violated the Treaty of Versailles, Laval ceded France's economic interests in Abyssinia (modern-day Ethiopia) to Italy. This paved the way for Italy's invasion of that African country and League of Nations member. By giving Mussolini a free hand, France destroyed what was left of the system of collective security in the absurd hope that fascist Italy would help contain Hitler. It foreshadowed the events of future decades, when the French would choose a narrowly nationalistic foreign policy of weakening both NATO and, during the Iraq crisis, the United Nations.

In 1936, France and Britain vacillated as the Nazis illegally seized the Rhineland. At the infamous Munich Conference two years later, France repudiated its long-standing obligation to protect Czechoslovakia's territorial integrity by agreeing to the German annexation of the Sudetenland. The Czechs were now helpless. Despite further assurances from France and Britain, they would face Hitler alone. When the Nazis marched into Prague on March 16, 1939, the French forgot their promises. The years of bluster and pique over German violations of Versailles were now a distant memory, and limp attempts at pacification substituted for a realistic policy. Still, the French were supremely confident that they could parry anything that Hitler might thrust at them.

When Germany attacked Poland on the morning of September 1, 1939, France declared war—and then did nothing. French leaders passed up an extraordinary opportunity. As the bulk of Germany's forces pummeled France's ally to the east, Hitler had left a mere 25 divisions on his western border to guard against 110 French divisions. Indeed, one reason for the speed and brutality of the Polish invasion—the world's first taste of *Blitzkrieg*—was Hitler's fear of giving France enough time to launch a counterattack. Had France chosen to seize the initiative and invade the industrial heart of western Germany, the most destructive war in the history of mankind might have been stopped in its tracks. But it was not to be.

As the Germans turned picturesque Warsaw into a pile of rubble, France was content to crouch behind its newly built Maginot Line. The Gallic "Sitzkrieg" had begun. To be sure, France had ample reasons for confidence. In May 1940, the combined forces of France, Britain, Belgium, and Holland had more divisions, more tanks, more bombers, more fighters, and considerably more heavy artillery than the Germans.[16] The United States was depending on this bulwark to preserve the peace in Europe and avoid another cataclysmic war. President Roosevelt understood that the United States could not keep itself out of the European conflict indefinitely if things went poorly for France. "Passionately though we may desire detachment," he explained in one of his fireside chats after the Nazi invasion of Poland, "we are forced to realize that every word that comes through the air, every ship that sails the sea, every battle that is fought, does affect the American future."[17] In this sense, the Maginot Line was not only France's last line of defense, but America's first.

Yet few Americans had faith in French assurances. U.S. ambassador William Bullitt had grave doubts about France's ability to stop a head-on German attack. Nor was he convinced, as the French were, that their generals were vastly superior to their German counterparts.[18] The Roosevelt administration could only hope Bullitt was mistaken. In 1940, the United States possessed only the seventeenth-largest army in the world and desperately needed time to convert its awesome industrial capacity toward rearmament.

Bullitt's fears were soon justified. On May 10, 1940, the Germans struck with violence and cunning. After assaulting the Netherlands, they invaded neutral Belgium—luring a large and experienced French force into that country—while they thrust through Luxembourg in the south. Then, moving north and west into France, they outflanked and outmaneuvered the panicked Allied forces.

Much had gone wrong. For starters, French generals had positioned themselves far from the front, while their German counterparts could be found in the thick of the battle (often at the cost of their lives). French communications were dismal because commanders worried about breaking radio silence. The Germans had no such reservations and generally achieved their objectives long before their messages were intercepted, translated, and sent to French field commanders. But the most fatal French mistake—the one that cost them their country—was failing to anticipate the possibility that Germany might attack through Luxembourg, whose heavily wooded Ardennes forest was considered impenetrable. The Germans simply used the roads. Such a strategy remained so far from French thinking that it took them an incredible four days before they realized they had been duped.

By then it was too late. On May 15, French prime minister Paul Reynaud called to inform a stunned Winston Churchill that the Germans had broken through at Sedan and all was lost. Paralysis and indecision reigned among the French high command. "Do anything you like, sir," said a corps commander to General Georges Blanchard, "but for Heaven's sake do something!"[19] In fact, France's hapless commander-in-chief, General Maurice Gamelin, was suffering from syphilis, a malady known to cause disorientation, loss of memory, and "delusions of grandeur."[20] After receiving word that the massive German attack had begun, the normally sedate Gamelin was seen, to the surprise and horror of his subordinates, "striding up and down the corridor of his fort, humming, with a pleased and martial air."[21] Within days, the once-proud French army—syphilitic leader and all—would find itself thoroughly routed. The final tally told the grim tale: 135,000 Allied dead (as many as 90,000 of them French) to only 27,000 on the German side.

By late June, Wehrmacht columns were goose-stepping down the Champs-Elysées. Thanks to a darkly comic touch of German inspiration, French leaders found themselves signing the surrender documents in the same train carriage in which the 1919 Armistice had taken place. The Treaty of Versailles was avenged.

The consequences of France's sudden collapse were profound and far-reaching. In the wake of the German victory, Hitler—one of the main architects of the battle plan—achieved a mythic status in his country. Only a few months before, several of his generals had contemplated toppling the dictator in a coup—such was their lack of faith in his mad plan to invade France. Now, thanks to the speedy fall of France, his murderous plans for the rest of Europe would move forward on an accelerated timetable.

For the United States, the French defeat was terrible and shocking—"a stupefying disappointment" in the words of the president's confidant, Harry Hopkins.[22] In a May 23 speech, as French defenses crumbled, Roosevelt admitted his surprise that the French had not put up more of a fight. "We have to think in terms of [protecting] the Americas . . . infinitely faster," he said.[23]

Although the French would complain that the United States had not rushed to their aid during the German attack, such protests were plainly disingenuous. "If you cannot give to France in the coming hours the certainty that the United States will enter the war in a short time," the emotional French prime minister cabled Roosevelt, "the destiny of the world will change. . . . You will then see France go down like a drowning man and disappear, after having thrown a last look toward the land of liberty where she sought salvation."[24] But French security was first and foremost the responsibility of France. Besides, any American assistance would have arrived too late to stave off the abrupt failure of the French military. Moreover, in light of France's unfulfilled obligations to Czechoslovakia, these recriminations were the height of hypocrisy.

At this moment, France relinquished its great-power status in the minds of Washington's political elite. It would be held in special awe no more. France's defeat also would have profound and lasting consequences for the way France viewed itself. Subsequent French insecurity and resentment, which found frequent expression in anti-Americanism, drew from the national guilt and shame of cataclysmic defeat.[25] Yet illusions of French grandeur would die hard or not at all. France's postwar leaders would continue to nurse the dream of French political and cultural preeminence.

The Third Republic's decision to make peace with the Third Reich was far from inevitable. It most certainly had not been the only option. During the desperate days of early June, Prime Minister Reynaud had argued strenuously that French honor called for the government to retreat to its North African colonies, which held a contingent of troops and about a thousand combat aircraft. There, protected by Britain's navy, the French might continue their fight against the Axis. Hadn't Poland, Belgium, Holland, and Norway sent their governments or their representatives into honorable exile? Besides, the French had signed an explicit agreement with Britain that neither would commit to an armistice without the other.

But the French saw their defeat not only as the conclusion of a great battle, but as the end of the war itself. By routing the glorious French army, the Germans had proven their invincibility. In the view of French leaders, it would be only a matter of weeks before Britain too was swept away and all of Europe would reside securely in the clutches of the Nazis.[26] In the opinion of U.S. ambassador Bullitt, who remained in the capital, French leaders "have accepted completely for France the fate of becoming a province of Nazi Germany . . . Their hope is that France will become Germany's favorite province—a new *Gau* [German for province] which will develop into a new Gaul."[27] The French reasoned that it was better to make peace with the new masters of Europe than engage in a long and pointless struggle.

As support for the armistice grew within the government, Reynaud resigned and was replaced by Marshal Pétain, a dim-witted, eighty-six-year-old childless womanizer and hero of the First World War. He was an overwhelmingly popular choice. His chiseled features, grandfatherly mien, and air of command lifted the spirits of a traumatized nation. "With a heavy heart, I tell you today that it is time to stop the fighting," he announced in a June 17 radio address that was met with outpourings of joy.[28] Even though negotiations had yet to begin, the majority of the French were eager to surrender. They could barely conceal their relief.

As German troops continued to drive forward, French soldiers stood listlessly by the road. "Such will to resist as still remained," reported Bullitt, "is being sapped by the buzzing stories of collapse at the front; by the tales of wholesale disintegration."[29] One French commander was shot by his troops when he ordered them to break out of their encircled positions close to the Maginot Line: "He's going to have us all massacred," they had complained.[30] At Vierzon, French civilians murdered an officer who had tried to thwart the enemy from seizing the city's bridges.[31]

On the surface, the armistice agreement seemed reasonable, even advantageous. The Germans would occupy the northern region of the country while the French government carried on in its new capital, the mountain resort city of Vichy. Although the collaborationist government was expected to aid the German war effort, it retained many civil administrative responsibilities and, most important, was allowed to keep its valuable fleet as well as its numerous colonies. Hitler, after all, had no ideological or racial interest in destroying France. He needed France to provide economic support for his coming war against the Soviet Union. Besides, the Nazi leader admired certain aspects of French culture and history. On June 23, he flew to Paris for a whirlwind tour of the captured city. The highlight of his trip was a visit to the tomb of Napoleon. "That," he said upon emerging from it, "was the greatest and finest moment of my life."[32]

To many in France, it seemed that Pétain had made the best of an impossible situation. Yielding to their national weakness for the authority of generals, the French believed that their beloved war hero would see to it that France would survive, even with the loss of some honor and dignity. Yet in truth, Pétain was little more than a well-groomed thug and bigot with a glamorous pedigree. Although he did manage to retain a small degree of autonomy, he oversaw and implemented an energetic program of collaboration.[33] Throughout his four-year reign, Vichy's aid to the Germans went far beyond the requirements of the armistice agreement.

For all intents and purposes, Vichy France became a part of the Axis. French industries churned out planes and parts for the Luftwaffe as French factories clothed German troops. Valuable raw materials such as magnesium and bauxite were shipped to the Fatherland. Even French wine was distilled into alcohol and added to gasoline for German tanks. "French workers in industry, railroads, internal shipping, and most overseas shipping are working almost exclusively for Germany," said one Nazi bureaucrat.[34] When American diplomats pleaded with France for permission to buy back 106 navy planes that had been sold before the German invasion, they were rebuffed. The planes were simply left to decay on France's single, inactive aircraft carrier.[35]

Pétain even offered to send troops to fight alongside the Nazis during the invasion of the Soviet Union. Although Hitler was wary,

10,000 French volunteers fought on the eastern front, many of them in the uniforms of the Waffen S.S. In 1945, an entire division of French S.S.—the Charlemagne division—was formed. Even after Hitler's suicide in May 1945, fanatical French S.S. could be found slugging it out with the Red Army among the ruins of the Reich chancellery.[36]

Perhaps the most ominous aspect of the Vichy regime, however, was the many ways in which it grew to resemble that of its Nazi conquerors. Even before 1940, most Frenchmen had viewed the Third Republic as a model of weakness, corruption, and inefficiency. The military collapse of 1940 only confirmed that opinion. Against this backdrop of failure, Pétain promised a new authoritarian order that would reinvigorate French society and preserve its civilization. France, in short, willingly became a fascist state.

With genuine and widespread rejoicing, the French majority rallied around the Vichy regime and its dictator. Pétain was arguably more popular than any French leader since Napoleon. In keeping with its anti-democratic platform, the new government repudiated that great document of human freedom—the Declaration of the Rights of Man—and replaced the French revolutionary slogan *Liberté, Egalité, Fraternité* with the more fascistic *Travail, Famille, Patrie* (Work, Family, Fatherland). Pétain's key deputy in these doings was Prime Minister Pierre Laval, a former socialist and leading figure in Third Republic politics. A swarthy man with stooped shoulders and a penchant for cigarettes and white ties, "Dark Peter" was the son of a butcher in the village of Châteldon in the Auvergnat. A lawyer and a sociopath, Laval now favored a virtual betrothal of France to Nazi Germany and took particular relish in crushing dissent and rooting out Jews.[37]

The most shameful legacy of the Vichy regime was its complicity in the German plan to murder the Jews of Europe. During the previous century, French anti-Jewish sentiment had cut across political and cultural divisions and enjoyed an impressive intellectual pedigree that included among its devotees the Utopian socialist Charles

Fourier, the economist Pierre-Joseph Proudhon, psychologist Gustave Le Bon, and the historian Ernest Renan. The issue had crystallized in the 1890s during the infamous Dreyfus Affair, when a Jewish army captain and member of the French general staff, Alfred Dreyfus, was unjustly accused of espionage by the French military. After two trials and several years on Devil's Island, Dreyfus was eventually freed and pardoned by the republic. A half-century later under Vichy, many Frenchmen would line up to take their revenge on what they saw as the traitorous, unassimilable *juifs de France*.

With little or no prodding from Berlin, the Vichy French passed new racial laws such as the *Statut des juifs* (Statute of the Jews), which defined Jewish identity and banned Jews from holding many public offices and professions. In a nation that had been the first in Europe to grant Jews full civil rights (in the 1790s), all foreign Jews—most of them refugees of Nazi persecution—were interned in horrendous conditions. In 1942, yellow armbands were issued. Soon large numbers of Jewish men, women, and children were rounded up by German troops and French police and sent to Auschwitz via Drancy, the notorious French concentration camp in the suburbs of Paris. In all, France deported more than 76,000 Jews to camps in the east. More than a third of them were French-born, 8,000 were under the age of thirteen, and 2,000 were under the age of six. Only 3 percent would ever return to France. Although more than a quarter million Jews residing in France survived the war, Vichy's hands were covered in Jewish blood. By submitting to the long history of anti-Semitism that has never been completely eradicated from France, the country's rulers became accomplices to the Holocaust.[38]

Despite the armistice and Vichy's subsequent collaboration with Hitler, the United States chose to maintain diplomatic relations with the French. Although very unpopular with an American public that correctly sensed the evil at Vichy's core, Roosevelt's decision reflected larger geostrategic considerations. In the end, he made a difficult and defensible choice. By keeping diplomatic relations open, the administration believed it could retain a valuable line of communication to the continent. American spies would have freer access to information and, most important, American diplomats could keep pressure on the French not to hand over their valuable fleet to the Germans.

The fleet was critical. On October 3, 1940, when France refused to transfer the ships to Britain, the Royal Navy sank a portion of it at Mers el-Kébir near Oran in order to keep it away from the Germans. But a number of French ships survived. For the next two years, before their scuttling in the aftermath of Operation Torch, Vichy used them as a bargaining chip in its dealings with both Germany and the United States. Although Pétain at times attempted to play the Americans off against the Germans, he made a habit of giving the Nazis most of what they wanted.[39]

While Vichy represented the constitutional government of France, an alternative soon emerged to compete for American attention and support. It was led by General Charles André Joseph Marie de Gaulle, the self-appointed head of the Free French. He had served under Pétain in the First World War but now repudiated his old superior officer, fleeing to England rather than participating in the armistice. As Pétain and his cronies negotiated with the enemy, the forty-nine-year-old general, who had courageously led a tank battalion during the German invasion, went on the radio on June 18, 1940, and audaciously claimed to speak for the French nation. He vowed to continue the fight against the Axis powers. "Must we abandon all hope? Is our defeat final and irremediable?" de Gaulle asked his countrymen from London. "To those questions I answer—No!"[40]

Nicknamed "The Tall Asparagus" by his schoolmates and once described by a British official as having "the head of a pineapple and the hips of a woman," the gangly de Gaulle made up for his lack of physical grace with a burning ambition and a demeanor that can only be described as a study in Gallic pomposity.[41] Born to monarchist parents in Paris in 1890, two decades after Prussian troops had first marched down the Champs-Elysées, de Gaulle bore the shame of that defeat his entire life. Like many French soldiers, he was an ardent chauvinist who believed in the innate superiority and destiny of

France. Determined to restore his country's glory on the battlefield, he joined the army at an early age, fought bravely in the First World War, and wrote innovative works on tank warfare in the 1930s. Although neither a monarchist nor a fascist like many of his right-wing contemporaries, he was nevertheless heir to a powerful French conservative tradition that still believed its country's true greatness could be found in its imperial past. The political forces that had split France into two starkly divergent camps during the French Revolution were still flourishing in the twentieth century and would provide a backdrop for de Gaulle's political ascendancy. Believing that the French had suffered throughout their history from dissension and disunity, the general offered himself to the nation as the man who could best save France from itself.

Of all the arrogant Frenchmen who had put their thumbs in American eyes, de Gaulle was in some ways the worst. Just two weeks after the German declaration of war on the United States in December 1941, the fateful first episode took place on the small islands of St. Pierre and Miquelon. Just twelve miles off the coast of Newfoundland, they were relics of France's once-mighty North American empire. Now they were home to 5,000 people and controlled by Vichy. Fearing that a radio transmitter on St. Pierre might be used to reveal the positions of Allied shipping to German U-boats, de Gaulle threatened an invasion. The Americans, however, had an agreement with Vichy not to interfere with French colonies. They were also in the process of seeking permission for Canadian observers to monitor the transmitter. After a round of talks, the United States, Britain, and Canada persuaded de Gaulle to call off his plans.

When de Gaulle learned of the existence of a Canadian invasion plan, however, he ordered Free French admiral Emile Muselier to take the islands, which he did without firing a shot. Despite Muselier's success, Roosevelt and his secretary of state, Cordell Hull, were outraged. Vichy, they feared, might react by surrendering its navy to the Germans. When de Gaulle learned that the Roosevelt administration threatened to "force" the Free French off the islands, he stated his willingness to "fire" on the Americans.[42] To preserve Allied unity, the United States backed down—but Hull would continue to seethe over de Gaulle's treachery and arrogance for years.

Most Americans, however, supported de Gaulle. Less interested in large strategic considerations, they were eager for acts of bravado following the recent defeats at Pearl Harbor and in the Western Pacific. When Hull publicly described the invasion as having been carried out by "so-called Free French troops," letters of protest poured in addressed to the "so-called Secretary of State" at the "so-called State Department."[43]

Nevertheless, the episode convinced many in the American leadership that de Gaulle was unreliable. Roosevelt already held a dim view of the French governing elite, whom he associated with instability, corruption, and incompetence. In his opinion, de Gaulle was the worst of the lot. He considered the obnoxious general a great poseur who fancied himself a composite of Joan of Arc, Napoleon, and Clemenceau—and who had done little to earn this exalted opinion of himself and even less to deserve American respect. As a popular leader who had been elected three times, Roosevelt doubted that someone who had been virtually unknown in France before its fall could claim to speak for the French people. Was the general, he wondered, angling to become a dictator after the war?

At times it was difficult to determine which side de Gaulle favored in the conflict, such was his narrow fixation on France's interests. When he was awakened at six in the morning with the news of the Allied invasion of North Africa—just hours after the American disaster in the harbor of Oran—he impulsively replied: "Well, I hope the people of Vichy throw them into the sea. You can't break into France and get away with it."[44] And although he ultimately supported the invasion and its goals (perhaps after a cup of coffee), he was upset that he had not played a part in the invasion planning as well as the subsequent governing of French North Africa. Roosevelt, in fact, had insisted on keeping de Gaulle in the dark: "I . . . consider it essential that de Gaulle . . . be permitted to have no information whatsoever [about Operation Torch] regardless of how irritated or irritating he may become," the president said to Churchill in a cable.[45] When Eisenhower, in the interests of stability, cut a deal giving Admiral Darlan control of French forces in North Africa, de Gaulle was livid. On Christmas Eve 1942, Darlan was assassinated by a twenty-year-old anti-fascist monarchist. Many, including FDR, saw de Gaulle's fingerprints on the act, although definitive proof has never surfaced. All the interrogations and trial records were immediately sealed and may have been destroyed.[46]

Tensions worsened in January 1943, when de Gaulle fumed at Roosevelt for inviting him to a meeting in Casablanca. How dare an American invite a Frenchman to visit French soil? When they finally met in Roosevelt's headquarters, a dozen Secret Service agents were positioned behind a curtain with Tommy guns trained on de Gaulle.[47] The president wanted nothing more than to jettison de Gaulle from the team. "I am fed up with de Gaulle," Roosevelt wrote to Churchill on June 17. "I am absolutely convinced that he has been and is now injuring our war effort and that he is a very dangerous threat to us. I agree with you that he likes neither the British nor the Americans and that he would double-cross both of us at the first opportunity. . . . He has proven to be unreliable, uncooperative, and disloyal to both our governments."[48]

But there were few viable alternatives. The Americans were afraid that too much antagonism might drive de Gaulle into the arms of the Soviets after the war. Besides, as D-Day neared, Eisenhower needed the help of the de Gaulle-dominated French Resistance. Although many in the Resistance were Communists, Moscow had decreed that, for the time being, unity in the war against fascist Germany should override all other priorities.

There is a saying in France that in 1946, everyone was a member of the Resistance. Indeed, de Gaulle and subsequent French leaders did everything they could after the war to spread the comforting belief that France, as a whole, had resisted occupation and remained firmly on the side of the Allies. In this sense, the heroic French Resistance was more myth than reality. In truth, almost as many French citizens were actively working to crush the Resistance as actually participated in it. Many Frenchmen refused to join the Resistance because of their outrage at Allied bombing, which frequently went awry and killed civilians. (In an era before laser-guided bombs, only 20 percent of all ordnance dropped from the air could be counted on to hit its target.) "What sense," asked writer Andre Gide, "do these idiotic destructions make?"[49]

During the occupation of France, the Germans sent relatively few police units to administer order; the French were all too willing to keep their fellow citizens in line. In fact, on the eve of the D-Day landings, the majority of French citizens were either apathetic or downright hostile to the idea of liberation. "The Americans," wrote journalist Hubert Beuve-Méry, who went on to found France's most influential newspaper, Le Monde, "constitute a real danger for France—a danger different in kind from the threat represented by Germany, and the threat that may eventually emerge from Russia." Although Hitler's legions still controlled much of the European continent, Beuve-Méry was more concerned that the United States and its supposed culture of materialism would stand in the way of France's "necessary revolution."[50] During the Cold War, this view would become the bedrock of the French cultural elite's anti-Americanism.

In the months leading up to the Allied landings in Normandy, the Americans tried to keep as much information from de Gaulle as possible. The Free French offices in London were reputedly so infiltrated by spies, it was said that the quickest way to send a message to the Germans would be to mark it "Top Secret" and deliver it to Free French headquarters.[51] Two days before the invasion, when de Gaulle was asked to record a radio message for the French people that would be broadcast after an announcement from Eisenhower, he angrily refused. He was further driven into fits by the Allied plan to use specially minted francs (designed by his nemesis Roosevelt) in post-liberation France. The Frenchman's incredible hauteur at such a critical moment enraged Churchill. "The prime minister," observed

Foreign Secretary Anthony Eden, "made plain his entire lack of confidence in General de Gaulle and his conviction that as long as he was at the head of French affairs there would be no good relations between France, Great Britain, and the United States. He said that the General was an enemy and many other things of like sort."[52]

In the end, de Gaulle agreed to make a radio address on the day of the invasion, but he mentioned neither the Allies nor the requirement that French citizens be prepared to take directions from them. Instead he advised the French to obey their new government—headed by him. "He's a nut," said Roosevelt bluntly, when he heard of de Gaulle's latest act of noncompliance. "This supposed ally . . . has virtually stabbed our troops in the back," railed Secretary of War Henry Stimson.[53]

The D-Day invasion to liberate France and Western Europe succeeded at great cost. In the first month of the assault, the American army alone would sustain 100,000 casualties. De Gaulle did prove useful during these terrible early days. He displayed great vigor in taking over the French civilian administration while the Allies (with some Free French help) concentrated on fighting the Germans. Although the Allies still harbored grave doubts about his ultimate intentions, de Gaulle had become vitally important as a leader who offered the best guarantee of stability in the aftermath of the liberation as well as the ability to keep the resurgent and vengeful Communists from seizing power. (These were very serious concerns. In 1944, as Allied armies moved across France, a veritable civil war raged among French citizens who supported the Vichy regime and those who opposed it.) When Eisenhower learned, however, that de Gaulle was telling crowds that the French were returning to liberate them "with the aid of the British and the Americans," the back of his neck grew red. "He was furious," his son later recalled.[54]

Meanwhile, American generals grew increasingly impatient with Gaullist posturing. As American and British soldiers pushed hard against the Germans in the summer of 1944, de Gaulle insisted that a Free French general, Jacques Leclerc, be allowed to liberate Paris, even though this seemed impractical at the time. Leclerc and his small force were more than 100 miles from the capital, while the Americans had a considerably larger force only ten miles away. Furthermore, Eisenhower felt that liberating the city would be a distraction and result in a costly drain of men and resources when the primary goal should be to defeat the German army.

In the end, Eisenhower relented. In the spirit of unity, he ordered Leclerc and his men to proceed alongside an American division so that both would share in the glory of liberation. Before long, Leclerc was disobeying orders and taking roads that were not assigned to him in a childish attempt to beat the Americans. When the crush of the jubilant crowds and stiffening German resolve slowed his progress, the exasperated Americans decided to seize the city by themselves rather than allow the French to "dance their way in."[55] Panicked, Leclerc (dubbed "Le Jerk" by Ernest Hemingway) managed to rush a small unit of troops to the city center ahead of the Americans on August 24. The Free French had liberated Paris from the collaborationist French (and their German masters)—or, at least, the Americans had allowed them the honor.

Several months later, when the Germans launched a massive surprise offensive against American lines in what became the Battle of the Bulge, Eisenhower ordered the French to pull back from their positions in and around Strasbourg. When de Gaulle refused—arguing that such a retreat would appear cowardly—Eisenhower threatened to cut off his gasoline and supplies, thereby paralyzing his forces. Said one American about a French officer with whom he had been assigned to discuss this disagreement: "If he had been an American, I would have socked him on the jaw."[56] Fortunately for de Gaulle, Eisenhower again would relent in the interests of Allied harmony.

As Allied forces began to enter Germany, French troops continued to be difficult to control. After de Gaulle gave orders to take as much German territory as possible, French columns surged forward with little regard for orders and even less interest in engaging German troops. In the chaos, Eisenhower worried that elements of the German army would retreat into the Alps, where they might wage a long and costly guerrilla campaign.

There was also a fear that French troops would stumble upon German nuclear secrets in the zones of occupation. De Gaulle, after all, had made a disturbing November 1944 visit to Moscow and had threatened the Allies with a possible postwar alliance with Stalin. Special American units were sent ahead of the advancing French army to round up and safeguard German scientists and radioactive material. But thankfully, the ravenous French, as one American put it, "were much more interested in pigs and chickens than in atomic specialists."[57]

When President Roosevelt died in Warm Springs, Georgia, on April 12, 1945, de Gaulle would write in a letter of condolence that "France admired him and loved him."[58] Yet de Gaulle had more tricks up his sleeve. Later that month, he refused to remove French troops who had seized certain strategically important districts in the Italian Alps, ostensibly as payback for Italian incursions into France during the invasion of 1940. A furious Truman called de Gaulle "psychopathic" and shut off all military aid. Allied troops were mobilized. The new president berated de Gaulle for "the almost unbelievable threat that French soldiers, bearing American arms, will combat American and Allied soldiers whose efforts and sacrifices have so recently and successfully contributed to the liberation of France itself."[59] In the face of this pressure, de Gaulle blinked and ordered a withdrawal. (France would later acquire a small portion of the land through negotiation.) Yet he had demolished what little trust the Allies still had in him. The United States refused to lift its ban against military assistance and pointedly informed France that it would not be allowed to participate in the final phases of the war against Japan. In spite of this, General Leclerc, at de Gaulle's insistence, attended the signing of the Japanese surrender document on the U.S.S. *Missouri* in Tokyo harbor on September 2, 1945.

The "alliance" was over, and Franco-American relations would never be the same. No more would Washington view France as a great and consequential power. France would continue as a cultural bea-

con, and in the years after the war Americans would flock to France
in record numbers to savor its cuisine, its museums and monuments,
and its quaint village life. But the image of France as a powerful, self-
assured nation upon which America could rely was a thing of the
past. The shock of the French collapse, combined with the sins of
Vichy and de Gaulle's outrages, had transformed France into more of
a nuisance than a partner. The United States soon would face new
and difficult challenges in its postwar struggle against the Soviet
Union. Would France have the moral fiber to choose the side of freedom or would it instead devote its energies to undermining the
United States and its allies? For France's intellectual elite, still nursing
fantasies of glory, this was no question at all.

TEN

FABLES OF THE DECONSTRUCTION

*Mistaken ideas always end in bloodshed, but in every case it is
someone else's blood. That is why some of our thinkers feel free to say
just about anything.*
—*Albert Camus* [1]

I N SEPTEMBER 1949, the steamship S.S. *Jamaique* made its
way across the Indian Ocean, through the Red Sea and the
Mediterranean to the French port of Marseilles. Among its
passengers were twenty-one Cambodian scholarship students bound
for France and an education in useful trades. One of their number, a
sweet-tempered, polite youth of provincial origins named Saloth Sar,
was destined for Paris and courses in radio-electricity. Although Sar
managed to apply himself in his first year, he took no examinations
and eventually lost his scholarship. In 1952, he returned to Cambodia
having achieved no formal degree. During more than three years in
the French capital, however, Sar would experience a profound political transformation that would have momentous consequences for
his country and the world. For in the smoky bars and cafés of Paris's
Latin Quarter, he became a Communist and almost certainly joined
the ranks of the French Communist Party. It was an ideological commitment from which he never strayed. [2]

By April 1976, Sar had become the leader of the so-called Democratic Kampuchea and had embraced a new revolutionary pseudo-
nym: Pol Pot. The genocide that would ravage his tiny country of

seven million people had been in full swing for many months. In all, one million men, women, and children would be executed and another million would succumb to starvation and disease in the nightmarish work camps of the world's newest "Utopia."

The evil dream of Pol Pot and his Khmer Rouge comrades—most of them former schoolteachers who had also studied in Paris, including three Ph.D.s from the Sorbonne—was to orchestrate a "total" revolution. By razing Cambodian civilization to the ground and returning it to the "Year Zero," the Communists believed they could achieve a level of ideological purity that would surpass their revolutionary predecessors in the Soviet Union, China, and North Korea.

The country's downfall was swift and tragic. Once it was clear that the United States would not intervene, the Khmer Rouge pounced on the weakened Cambodian government of right-wing nationalist Lon Nol—and made prophets of those who saw disaster in America's retreat.

Whole cities were emptied of their inhabitants. In Phnom Penh, the entire population of two million was evacuated in a few harrowing days. Suspected members of the enemy class, the *bourgeoisie*— and this included anyone who could read or owned a watch (or even had a tan line on his wrist)—were singled out and executed. Frequently entire families of the accused were tortured and killed. Children were ordered to murder their parents and teachers. Because bullets were precious commodities, the Khmer Rouge asphyxiated many victims by placing plastic bags over their heads. Others were clubbed to death or doused with gasoline and set ablaze.

Arguably the lowest and saddest moment in American foreign policy, the tragedy in Cambodia resulted not from the effects of American bombing (as some have suggested), but rather from America's failure to live up to its multiple responsibilities in the region, perhaps the most important of which was keeping Communist forces from taking control of their allies' civilian populations. "South Vietnam and Cambodia," President Richard Nixon would write, "were worthy of our help—and the three million people who were killed in the war's aftermath deserved to be saved."[3] But the greatest guilt must surely fall on the killers themselves, who not only carried out the genocide but spent years in their jungle hideouts meticulously planning their murders.

Where did the Khmer Rouge find their inspiration? To be sure, the legacies of their Asian forerunners in totalitarianism, Mao Tse-tung and Kim Il Sung, helped guide them. But the Khmer Rouge were more interested in theory than experience, and it was in Paris—as much the City of Theory as the City of Light—that they had found their true direction. The radically charged climate that dominated the intellectual world of France in the late 1940s and 1950s had a powerful and lasting impact on the minds of these impressionable young Asian revolutionaries. It was in Paris that the first, most important, and most violent ideological influences took root—and it was in Paris that anti-Americanism gained the intellectual pedigree it has enjoyed ever since the end of the Second World War.

It is a tragic fact of history that Pol Pot and his comrades studied in Paris at a time when the French Communist Party was arguably the most Stalinist in Europe. Why the intellectuals of France, a country that had just been liberated from a totalitarian power, fell so precipitously and passionately under the spell of another terrible tyranny is a question for the ages. The self-described heirs of the eighteenth-century Enlightenment found themselves slavish worshipers at the altar of a despotism that had carried out a bloody purge of its own elite, committed genocide in the Ukraine, the North Caucasus, and Kazakhstan (in which up to seven million people died), and erected a vast network of prison camps to house its political prisoners, including many artists and intellectuals. The *crème* of the Parisian intelligentsia—those who came from the best families and had gone to the best schools and universities—looked not to Churchill or Franklin Roosevelt or even their countryman, Charles de Gaulle, for political inspiration. Instead, they turned to the mass murderer Joseph Stalin. All the while, the Cambodians were taking careful notes.

It was certainly understandable that the French cultural elite would turn their back on the Right after the crimes of Vichy. Moreover, many were impressed by the sacrifices and triumphs of the Red Army. Still, the head-first swoon of the French intellectuals for everything Stalinist must be characterized as one of the great moral and intellectual lapses of the twentieth century.

It was during this fateful period that Sar and his comrades found themselves in Paris. Here, in private reading groups (or those sponsored by the Communist-controlled Khmer Student Association), they would have been exposed to French translations of such works as Lenin's *On Imperialism*, Marx's *Das Kapital*, and Stalin's *History of the Communist Party of the Soviet Union*. Indeed, many of the strategies employed by the Khmer Rouge during their four-year rampage of forced collectivization and political purges came right out of the Stalinist playbook. In addition to the seminal texts of Communist thought, the young Cambodian students also read and absorbed the anti-colonial works of Martinique-born Frantz Fanon, author of the bloodthirsty classic *The Wretched of the Earth*.[4]

One of the great preoccupations of French intellectual life in this period was the importance of revolutionary violence as an instrument of positive social change—an astonishing idea in the wake of two world wars. *Humanisme et terreur* was the fitting title of philosopher Maurice Merleau-Ponty's representative work of 1947. Such notions had their original roots in the ideology of the Terror during the French Revolution and later in the highly influential anarcho-syndicalist manifesto of Georges Sorel, *Reflections on Violence*. A former engineer from Normandy, Sorel is a pivotal figure in the history of revolutionary thinking. His combustible mixture of dangerous ideas helps to illuminate much of what went wrong in the twentieth century. Originally a Marxist, he combined the nihilism and anti-rationalism of the German philosopher Friedrich Nietzsche with a fervent call for the violent overthrow of the existing order. A great admirer of both Mussolini's fascism and Lenin's bolshevism, he was the first to formulate the image of a revolutionary elite leading the masses to smash the corrupt world of the *bourgeoisie*. His was a barbaric appeal to the vanity, arrogance, and misanthropy of modern intellectuals (and future totalitarian leaders) on both the Left and Right.

Another of Pol Pot's chief influences was Rousseau. Unlike many of his fellow eighteenth-century *philosophes*, who believed that society could be civilized through the gentle and gradual application of laws and manners, Rousseau considered society to be so irredeemably corrupt that it needed to be completely razed to the ground before it could be built again. The violence of the French Revolution was a direct outgrowth of this belief. The most bloodthirsty Jacobins were almost worshipful of Rousseau. They even removed their prophet's body from its grave and reburied it in the Pantheon, next to the great men of French history. Pol Pot and the Khmer Rouge, however, had almost no interest in the symbolism of political power. In their zeal to perfect the art of annihilation, they left few tangible monuments to their short, unforgettable reign, except, of course, for the endless piles of bleached bones that still dotted the killing fields of Cambodia years after they were driven from power.

Pol Pot was not the only tyrant to find inspiration in the "Ville Lumiere." In 1918, a young man named Nguyen Sinh Cung traveled to Paris and spent six years there. "I am eager to learn and serve France among my compatriots," he wrote on a job application.[5] Like Saloth Sar, he joined the French Communist Party and began writing for several left-wing and nationalist papers, including *L'Humanité*, the French Communist daily. Thereafter, Ho Chi Minh—as he came to be known—turned into a professional revolutionary. Although he would always have a soft spot for the beauty of Paris, his rage against the French for their brutal colonial rule in Vietnam led him to found and direct a regime many times more despotic than that of his former masters.

Southeast Asia is not the only part of the world that can trace a horrific political pedigree to Paris. The founders of the Middle Eastern Ba'athist Party that instituted secular police states in Saddam Hussein's Iraq and Hafez al-Assad's Syria were also educated in the French capital. In the late 1920s and early 1930s, Syrian citizens Michel Aflaq, Salah al-Din Bitar, and Zaki Arsuzi attended the University of Paris at the Sorbonne, where they imbibed the fashionable Marxism that spread through Europe during the global depression. "We came to socialism," Aflaq and al-Din Bitar would write in 1944, "by way of thought and science and found ourselves before a new, masterly, and fascinating explanation for all the political and social problems which harass the world generally and from which we Arabs particularly suffer."[6] Although Aflaq later declared himself anti-Western, his ideological debt to France is clear. The radical socialism he and his peers had learned in Paris would combine with fascist concepts from Vichy—concepts that entered the Arab world during the Second World War through the French-controlled territories of Syria and Lebanon.

France became a vital conduit for the importation of ideas from Nazi Germany to the Middle East, including violent anti-Semitism, virulent anti-Americanism, and strident nationalism. Indeed, the first significant political act of the Syrian Ba'ath Party was its support for the 1941 pro-German coup in Iraq. Although the British and Free French eventually drove the Vichy French and Germans out of Syria, Lebanon, and Iraq, these noxious ideas would remain a central feature of Ba'athist ideology.[7]

Not only did the postwar French intellectuals prepare the tainted broth from which future despots would drink, their poisoned leftism also inspired them to invent modern anti-Americanism—a scourge that continues to cloud the judgment of governments and citizens the world over. While many French in 1945 felt indebted to America for liberating their country, most intellectuals seemed plagued with a deep and seething resentment. The virus of anti-Americanism was not unknown in other parts of Europe after the war, but the French variety was particularly nasty. And, with much of Europe in ruins, France had emerged by default as the continent's cultural leader.

To be sure, French anti-Americanism has a long history, going back to the eighteenth century. The earliest versions labeled the new land as materialistic and culturally backward. Even nature was not exempt. It was a matter of observable fact, said French scientists, that things in the New World were simply inferior to those in the Old. In 1768, one such "scientist," Cornelius de Pauw, wrote that America's dogs actually lacked the ability to bark. Two decades later, while living in Paris, Thomas Jefferson became embroiled in a debate with George Louis Leclerc, the Comte of Buffon, then considered the greatest living naturalist. Buffon insisted that North America contained fewer species than Europe and that they were smaller in size. "In these melancholy regions," he wrote,

> nature remains concealed under her old garments, and never exhibits herself in fresh attire; being neither cherished nor cultivated by man, she never opens her fruitful and beneficent womb. . . . The air and the earth, overloaded with humid and noxious vapors, are unable either to purify themselves, or to profit by the influence of the sun, who darts in vain his most enlivening rays upon this frigid mass, which is not in a condition to make suitable return to his ardor.[8]

Jefferson tried to persuade Buffon that French intellectuals were quite capable of producing their own "humid and noxious vapors." To refute Buffon's theories, he asked his friends back home to weigh and measure North American animals and send him the data. James Madison responded with information on weasels and woodchucks. General John Sullivan, who had quarreled with the French admiral at Newport during the American Revolution, shipped him the skin and boiled bones of a huge moose.

The French myth of American inferiority, however, was not confined to the animal kingdom. "The United States, this republic born yesterday, full of stiffness and Puritan sadness, with its mores so monotonous and so cold, has none of the national memories that lend so much charm and color to our old Europe," wrote the Marquis de Cusine. "That country lacks a past, no monument, no traditions. There, all is serious, cold, and dry."[9] The Abbé Raynal sponsored an essay competition based on the question "Has the discovery of America been useful or harmful to the human race?" Raynal took the negative view—and Jefferson referred to his notions as the "effusions of an imagination in *deliris.*"[10]

There have been, of course, a handful of French intellectuals who did admire the United States. But Tocqueville's *Democracy in America* was virtually ignored in France until the 1960s, and those French readers who knew of it could not resist casting their own anti-American views onto the book. "Our debate," concluded a contemporary after reading Tocqueville's work,

> is not with this hideous gathering of aristocratic bourgeois and bourgeois aristocrats who proclaimed so loudly Christian freedom, and rebelled against the Motherland not to pay a few extra pennies on a pound of tea; this bunch of slave-drivers who speak of fraternity and equality, and engage in the shameful traffic of human flesh; a people of ignorant shopkeepers and narrow-minded industrialists, who do not have on the whole surface of their continent a single work of art . . . who do not have in their libraries a single science book not written by the hand of a foreigner; who do not have a single social institution not patterned after an ancient one, and constituting a flagrant rebuttal of the Christian principle it pretends to emulate.[11]

Whereas many early criticisms of America were tame or even comical, postwar French anti-Americanism would assume a more sinister cast. In the 1920s and 1930s, the rhetoric grew increasingly strident as France felt more and more culturally threatened by the American colossus. Works such as Robert Aron and Arnaud Dandieu's *Le Cancer Américain* (1931) and Georges Duhamel's *America, the Menace* (1931) led the way. For Duhamel, the United States was an "industrial dictatorship," an "ant-heap" that threatened the cultures of the world.[12] For Aron and Dandieu, American "industrial and banking supremacy" was a veritable cancer on the "life of the age."[13]

The tenor of anti-Americanism intensified as French self-loathing reached a fever pitch in the immediate aftermath of the war. As the French reflected on how quickly their army had melted away in 1940 and confronted the cruel reality that so few had actually been part of the Resistance, their normally bloated egos were deflated. "Seen from a distance," said René Etiemble, "we are just forty million losers."[14] In the opinion of journalist and author Jean-François Revel, the postwar French hatred of America was based in part on the demoralizing realization that they had been culturally eclipsed:

> The most humiliating kind of defeat is the cultural defeat. It is the only defeat one can never forget, because it cannot be blamed on bad luck, or on the barbarism of the enemy. It entails not only acknowledgment of one's weakness, but also the humiliation of having to save oneself by taking lessons from the conqueror—one must simultaneously hate and imitate.[15]

Hatred of America was also clearly a reflection of the French intellectuals' ideological commitments—most of all, their enthusiasm for the Soviet Union. Many resented the United States for literally standing in the way of the westward advance of Stalin and the Red Army; the Russians, in their view, had just "liberated" half of Europe. Others believed the Soviet Union had no intention of engaging in any future military action. "I have looked," said Jean-Paul Sartre in the early 1950s, "but I just can't find any evidence of an aggressive impulse on the part of the Russians in the last three decades."[16]

To the intellectuals, the Communist world was simply more legitimate than the West. The wish to believe in a modern-day Utopia was so strong that reality in any of its recognizable forms was casually jettisoned. Whereas Georges Sorel had seen the need for "myths"—the socialist revolution, the General Strike, et cetera—with which revolutionary elites could manipulate and incite the masses, the new Marxist intellectuals actually believed in them. Since the Enlightenment, religious faith had been replaced for many intellectuals with a belief that revolution could usher in a new age of perfection.

Believing in the possibility of Utopia was so psychologically important that they defended and praised beastly regimes in a slavish style that became a hallmark of Cold War leftism. "Our friendship with Russia," wrote Simone de Beauvoir, "was marked by no reticence whatsoever; the sacrifices of the Russian people had proved that the leadership incarnated their will."[17] According to Sartre—perhaps the most famous philosopher of the twentieth century—the Soviet citizen was not muzzled by the state, but actually enjoyed the fullest freedoms in criticizing his country. We may not fully understand the manner of his protests, he argued, but that does not mean that they do not exist. In fact, the Soviet citizen "criticizes more frequently and more effectively than us."[18] Ordinary Russians did not travel, he once said, not because of their own government's totalitarian restrictions, but because they simply had no desire to leave their lovely country. He was even more admiring of Mao—a man responsible for some 65 million deaths, more than anyone in history.

Incredibly, what Sartre said mattered. A short, stocky, ugly little gnome of a man, he ruled over the intellectual life of France like a rock star. As a cultural icon and "moral voice," his beliefs corresponded to many of the trends and nostrums held dear by the Western intellectual elite. Indeed, he strove mightily to lead the way. Anyone interested in understanding the darker chapters of French influence on the twentieth century must first come to grips with Jean-Paul Sartre's tawdry, self-promoting, and ultimately violent legacy.

Like the Khmer Rouge, Sartre was a devotee of Frantz Fanon. He reveled in Fanon's defining belief that it is only through murderous violence that the citizens of the Third World can achieve their ends. After 1952, when he fully embraced Marxism, Sartre could say shamelessly that he found Communist violence "admirable."[19] Sartre would travel the globe with his long-suffering companion in ideological mischief, Simone de Beauvoir, serving up praise to both Communist states and petty dictators of the developing world. Although they certainly were not the first intellectuals to pander to despots, their doggedness in this regard made Moscow, Hanoi, and Havana must-see stops on the left-wing travel circuit.[20] "The country which has emerged out of the Cuban Revolution," he absurdly proclaimed, "is a direct democracy."[21] Ideological legitimacy increased with every new Red Star on one's passport.

Sartre in fact cared little for the unfortunate masses who lived under the thumb of the murderous regimes that received his boundless praise. When Eastern Europe was gripped with a slew of highly publicized show trials (Lászlo Rajk and Cardinal Mindszenty in Hungary, Koci Xoxe in Albania, and others), Sartre famously said nothing. He was livid, however, when Julius and Ethel Rosenberg received the death penalty in the United States for giving nuclear secrets to the Soviet Union: "The execution of the Rosenbergs . . . is a legal lynching which has covered a whole nation with blood and proclaimed once and for all [America's] utter incapacity to assume the leadership of the Western World."[22] When the great Catholic intellectual François Mauriac called on Sartre to condemn the persecution of Jews behind the Iron Curtain, Sartre responded with chilling words: "The problem of the condition of the Jews in the People's Democracies," he said, "must not become a pretext for propaganda or polemic."[23] It was the anti-Communists whom Sartre truly could not bear. "An anti-Communist is a dog," he once said, "I don't change my views on this, I never shall."[24]

From a philosophical perspective, Sartre's support for Marxist doctrine made little logical sense. Sartre was an "Existentialist"—that is, he purported to believe in a philosophy of radical individualism. In Sartre's view, the individual found himself alone in an amoral world and therefore had to make conscious and willful attempts to fashion a valid and courageous existence. At first glance, this would seem the very opposite of Communism, which stressed rigid state control and the suppression of individual liberty. But Sartre knew that Communism was not merely trendy; it was a monolithic presence in French postwar intellectual life, the "unsurpassable philosophy of the times."[25] And Sartre, like so many French intellectuals, would never allow himself to be perceived as out of step with the times. Even if he ran the risk of logical or moral contradiction, Marxism would be made to fit his system.

Late in life Sartre did express some second thoughts about Soviet tyranny, but he never gave up his virulent hostility toward the United States. "America has rabies," he wrote in a 1953 essay. "Let us sever all our links with her, or else we shall get bitten and become rabid."[26] Although he was never known to have returned a royalty check to his American publishers, he did turn down an invitation to speak at Cornell University, explaining that his friends in the Third World would not have appreciated his visiting the "enemy."[27] Not only did he harbor a hatred of the American government and its policies, he displayed a thoroughgoing contempt for American culture and its citizens. In America, he wrote:

> There are the great myths of happiness and freedom, of triumphant motherhood. . . . There is the myth of equality and there is "segregation," the myth of freedom, and the dictatorship of public opinion. . . . There are pretty little clean houses, white-washed apartments with a radio, a rocking chair, a pipe in its case and there are the occupants of those apartments who after dinner leave rocking chair, radio, wife, pipe, and children behind and get drunk all by themselves in the bar next door. Nowhere maybe will one find such a gap between people and myths, between life and the collective representation of life.[28]

By the end of his life, Sartre had become somewhat marginalized by the new wave of French postmodern thinkers. Yet his legacy of anti-Americanism lived on among intellectuals who stressed the moral equivalence of the United States and the Soviet Union. "There exist two distinct forms of totalitarianism, very different in their effects, but equally fearsome," wrote Alain de Benoist. "The Eastern variety imprisons, persecutes and mortifies the body, but at least it does not destroy hope. Its Western counterpart ends up creating happy robots. It is an air-conditioned hell. It kills the soul.[29]

Not all French intellectuals shared in this hostility, however. Political scientist Raymond Aron was born the same year as Sartre (1905), but he took a decidedly different position on Communism and its network of police states. A liberal in the best sense—one of the relatively few France has produced—Aron rejected the nihilism and relativism of his peers. Above all else, he believed in "the power of the man who makes himself by assessing his place in the world and in making choices. Only thus can the individual overcome relativity through the absoluteness of decision, and only thus can he take possession of the history that he carries within him and that becomes his own."[30] In the aftermath of the Second World War, Aron supported the North Atlantic alliance against the Soviet Union and called attention, in his great work, *The Opium of the Intellectuals*, to the delusions of those who had swallowed the Marxist religion whole. Iconoclast Jean-François Revel surprised Western audiences with his spirited defense of American civilization and politics in *Without Marx or Jesus* (1970), his compelling accounts of the Communist threat in the West in *The Totalitarian Temptation* (1976) and *How Democracies Perish* (1983), and his cogent critique of the global hatred for the United States in *Anti-Americanism* (2002). Following the lead of historians like Alain Besancon, Stéphane Courtois and his colleagues would attempt to make amends for the irresponsibility of their countrymen with the publication of their magisterial compendium of Communist crimes, *The Black Book of Communism* (1997). Unfortunately, these bright lights have been all too few.

Irrational anti-Americanism continues to thrive in many parts of the world, and its rhetoric is strikingly familiar. With the fall of the Soviet Union, America has become for many people the world's one true menace—and it is the French intellectuals of the postwar era who bear much of the responsibility for this viewpoint. Indeed, the stain that France's flirtation with totalitarianism and anti-Americanism has left on Western culture undoubtedly will remain for many years. Lionel Trilling was correct in 1952 when he said that "the commanding position of Stalinism in French cultural life . . . makes the artistic and intellectual leadership of France unthinkable."[31] Today, the French have largely and conveniently forgotten their past infatuation with the Soviet dictator. But their attempts to reclaim their long-lost cultural leadership have been nothing short of disastrous.

One of the saddest realities of French intellectual life during the Cold War was that so many of the country's leading thinkers supported the Soviet Union even after its true nature was widely known. Years before the French publication of Alexander Solzhenitsyn's *The Gulag Archipelago* in 1973, events in the East had dramatically revealed the despotic nature of Communism. From the violent suppression of democratic uprisings in Berlin (1953) and Hungary (1956), to the spectacle of the Eastern European show trials and Khrushchev's famous Politburo speech denouncing Stalin's crimes, the evidence of Communist tyranny was there for all to see.[32]

What did the French intellectuals do when the evidence of Communist crimes mounted and the human toll of totalitarianism became clear? Did they repent? Did they lend their pens and their intellects to the cause of freedom around the world?

Sadly, they did none of these things. Desperate to avoid confronting the past, they fled into the obscure realm of language theory and created an ingenious concoction that would become known as Postmodernism. In this sense, the linguistic plague that made its way from France to the English-speaking world began with an act of moral cowardice. The French retreat into abstraction, into the murky thickets of structuralism, deconstruction, and postmodern language games—scourges that have wreaked so much havoc in college classrooms and faculty lounges—was preceded by a wholesale French withdrawal from the great moral questions of the day. Fleeing the immoral into the arms of the impenetrable, the French intellectuals attempted to refashion or even disavow reality through a new-fangled interpretation of language. Unable to rule the world, the French sought to negate it. Unfortunately, the American academic mandarins who were supposedly guarding the ivory walls not only failed to drive the Gallic barbarians away, they invited them in for wine and cheese.

The roots of postmodernism, or *La Nouvelle Critique,* can be found in what has been called structuralism, a mode of thought grounded in the respectable academic contributions of Swiss linguist Ferdinand de Saussure and French anthropologist Claude Levi-Strauss. Following a long tradition of Western language theory, Saussure based his theories on the somewhat self-evident observation that each language divides reality in different ways. One is born not merely into a language, he argued, but into a way of thinking. Beneath the actual words and phrases of a language, there exists an unconscious structure of relations (made up of "signs") of which the speaker is largely unaware. Levi-Strauss would extend these insights into the discipline of anthropology, arguing that beneath the exteriors of human society lay a complex structure of unconscious habits and beliefs, many of which were based on the structural interrelations of a system of binary oppositions (man-woman, raw-cooked, etc.).

In the work of these pioneers, a slew of radical critics saw their opening. Among the first was literary critic Roland Barthes and his generation of Marxist theorists, who would argue that a book was merely a product of its time and place rather than an exposition of an individual author's thoughts or intentions. Most authors, after all, were members of the *bourgeoisie*—and, as every good Marxist knows, the thought of such people is largely (or wholly) determined by the class structures in which they exist. "Language, narrative, structure," wrote intellectual historian J. G. Merquior, "does the willing that we, in our beclouded naiveté, insist on crediting people (real or imaginary) with. . . ."[33] The author was dead, and with him, free will. The French had killed them.

With Jacques Derrida, we have the culmination of the whole illogical chain: *Deconstruction.* As the gods of Communism lay dying, the only path left was one of complete and utter destruction. And Derrida was the perfect arsonist. All texts, discovered the French philosopher-turned-literary-critic, when placed under scrutiny, reveal fatal contradictions that lead inevitably to their unraveling. Because words are assigned arbitrary meanings (*pace* Saussure) and because language was constantly changing, meaning of any kind could never be fixed and therefore determined. "Literature," wrote American Marxist literary critic Frank Lentricchia, "is inherently nothing; or it is a body of rhetorical strategies waiting to be said."[34]

Few did more to spread the new deconstructive gospel in the United States than Paul de Man. "The relationship between truth and error that prevails in literature cannot be represented genetically," wrote the Belgian literary mandarin and former Yale professor, "since truth and error exist simultaneously, thus preventing the favoring of the one over the other."[35] The text, in short, was dead—along with the entire Western tradition of finding reason and meaning in language. Only the critic remained.

Having denounced their old occupation of analyzing and explaining literature as the product of human inspiration, the critics now threw off their long servitude and fashioned a new and infinitely more satisfying role for themselves. With the author and text lying dead in a ditch, the critics found themselves suddenly liberated, free to turn their lectures and monographs into rap sessions on their own narrow interests, obsessions, and neuroses. "No longer," wrote leading American exegete Stanley Fish, "is the critic the humble servant of texts whose glories exist independently of anything he might do."[36] Who cares what Shakespeare thought of love when one can hear an aging dinosaur in tweed opine on what the symbolism of the phallus really means to him? In one fell swoop, the once great field of literary criticism was reduced to a cacophony of professors exposing their own ideological entrails.

Truth be told, Derrida had not really subverted the entire Western metaphysical tradition, as he and his gullible followers had claimed. The flaws of deconstruction are easily exposed. How can one articulate a theory arguing that communication is impossible? In the words of literary scholar George Watson: "It is a contradiction to say that nothing can be said, and a multiple contradiction to say it at length."[37]

The critics' relativist assertion that "truth" was merely a matter of perspective was proclaimed with every bit as much absolutist fervor as the outdated ideologies they purported to overthrow. Intellectual hypocrisy of the most blatant sort lies at the heart of the postmodern project. Paul de Man's legacy would be shaken by the posthumous discovery of fascist and anti-Semitic articles he had written for *Le Soir*, a French-language collaborationist newspaper in Belgium, during the Second World War. Indeed, the radical autonomy and freedom from consequence promised by deconstruction—the ultimate divorce of speech and deed—was powerfully challenged by the rediscovery of de Man's tawdry past.

What is truly shocking is that after all they had done to tarnish their credibility in the preceding decades, French intellectuals still found a wide audience on American college campuses. When the French took the linguistic and cultural plunge, American professors followed closely behind. Apparently afraid of being left with their feet planted on terra firma, they dove into the darkest and most polluted waters in search of the mystique of French ideas. One of their favorite French postwar intellectuals was the historian Michel Foucault, who aimed to subvert what he saw as the Western myths of rationality, progress, and freedom. A seductive writer with a gift for imagery and pseudo-technical jargon, but with decidedly less interest in solid historical evidence, Foucault beguiled his American readers and asked them to contemplate the sinister forces that wielded power in society through the control of language or "discourse." Thanks to his insights, all of history could now be read as a subversive text that cried out to be debunked by the good, the just, and the initiated (i.e., the intellectuals).

In the end, deconstruction claimed the minds of an entire generation of American literary critics and professors. It was the latest manifestation of the French avant-garde impulse, and it appealed to both lazy academics and their students who wished to become cutting-edge literary theorists without having to perform the drudgery of mastering the weighty Western canon. The prestige of deconstruction has declined since its high-water mark in the 1980s and 1990s, perhaps due more than anything else to the fact that it had become part of the new establishment and was, therefore, no longer "cutting edge." Yet the avant-garde impulse, born in France and exported to America, remains a potent and perilous force in modern culture.

ELEVEN

COLD WAR AGAINST AMERICA

War is against our enemies, peace against our friends.
—Charles de Gaulle [1]

DEEP IN THE jungles of Vietnam, a one-armed French officer assured his commander that he and his men would hold the village of Dien Bien Phu. "No Vietminh cannon will be able to fire three rounds before being destroyed by my artillery," boasted Colonel Charles Piroth. On the evening of March 13, 1954, the Vietminh put this promise to the test when several months of preparation culminated in a long-anticipated attack. Within hours, two key French outposts collapsed and Piroth was helpless to stop the Vietminh howitzers hidden in the hills from pouring deadly fire down upon his countrymen. "I am completely dishonored," said the colonel. "We are going to lose the battle." Some hours later, Piroth clutched a grenade in his right hand and yanked out the safety pin with his teeth. The explosion killed him instantly. [2]

Fifteen thousand French soldiers were trapped. Several months earlier, General Henri Navarre had selected Dien Bien Phu as the best place to make a stand against Communist forces in northern Vietnam. It proved to be a fatal blunder, based on the wrongheaded belief that troops under Vietminh general Vo Nguyen Giap would be unable to haul artillery pieces into the highlands surrounding the

French valley garrison. It was in fact the first thing the Vietminh did. Then, after encircling the village, they shelled its airstrip and threw wave after wave of infantry at the defenders. Although the French inflicted far more casualties than they received, their desperation grew by the hour. The grim logic of Communist leader Ho Chi Minh's strategy, announced years earlier, was playing itself out. "You can kill ten of my men for every one I kill of yours," he had said. "But even at those odds, you will lose and I will win."[3]

As the noose tightened around the French, one of their generals flew to the United States to beg for badly needed bombers, fighters, and transports. While these were given, U.S. admiral Arthur Radford suggested the possibility of something even better: U.S. airstrikes on the Vietminh, but only if both countries could agree to a battle plan. President Dwight Eisenhower, however, was reluctant to intervene without France first agreeing to a series of commitments that it had so far resisted, such as hastening Vietnamese independence and granting the Pentagon a greater role in setting military policy in the French colony. To complicate matters, few of Radford's high-ranking colleagues believed American strikes would succeed in lifting the siege. An ineffective attack, they feared, might compel the United States to deploy ground troops—possibly leading to another costly and unpopular stalemate, as in Korea.

Weeks of diplomatic confusion and delay followed, but in the end the United States chose not to come to France's rescue. On May 7, after fifty-four days of savage fighting, Dien Bien Phu fell. For the Vietminh, it provided exhilarating proof that impassioned peasants could rout their colonial masters. For the French, it was another in a long line of mortifying defeats in the last century, from the Cinco de Mayo catastrophe at Puebla in 1862 to the Fall of France in 1940. And yet many in France were only beginning to realize that their country was no longer a world power capable of sustaining a vast colonial empire.

Resentment of this stubborn fact drove countless Frenchmen to blame their misfortune on the United States. Although European graveyards were filled with American soldiers who had died liberating France from the grip of fascism, France seemed driven at almost every turn—in Vietnam and elsewhere—by a chronic distrust of American motives as well as an envy of its power. The Cold War forced the nations of the world to choose between Communist totalitarianism and a coalition of liberal democracies under the aegis of American leadership. Stalin may have promised Roosevelt and Churchill at Yalta that he would permit free elections in Eastern Europe after the war, but in reality he was busy planning its domination and plotting ways to project his influence into Western Europe. As his agents pulled Bulgaria, Czechoslovakia, East Germany, Hungary, Poland, and Romania into Moscow's orbit, Soviet spies in Western Europe worked through the powerful Communist parties and labor unions to subvert free institutions and sow the seeds of revolution. In order to save itself, its friends, and the future of democracy, the United States realized it could ill afford to retreat across the ocean and leave Europe to its fate, as it had a quarter century before. It would take action instead.

France became an especially vital battlefield. It was there that the United States first began to build a bulwark against Soviet totalitarianism by encouraging liberal democracy and market capitalism. Yet many in France were suspicious, believing that America was using this ideological rationale to gain de facto control over their country. Some were fixated on what they called "Coca-Colonization." In 1949, French Communists allied with wine growers pressured the government to ban Coke for alleged health reasons. "Coca-Cola wasn't injurious to the health of the American soldiers who liberated France from the Nazis," responded Coke executive James Farley after the National Assembly approved the measure. "This might be the straw to break the back of the camel hauling billions of American dollars to France."[4] Others, like the Jesuit newspaper *Témoignage chrétien*, saw Coke as only "the advance guard of a tremendous offensive aiming at the economic colonization of France."[5] *Le Monde* declared that "the moral landscape of France is at stake."[6] Only the warnings of the U.S. ambassador David Bruce and intimations in Congress that there might be retaliation against French imports of wine and perfume persuaded the French government to block the bill's final enactment. French expressions of anti-Americanism predated the Second World War, of course. But what infuriated many Americans was the speed and virulence with which it had reasserted itself in the immediate aftermath of France's liberation by American troops. French ingratitude for America's sacrifice became a common theme in postwar relations between the two countries.

Under such circumstances, many felt that France was being given much more aid than it deserved. In 1944, de Gaulle and the French had not been invited to the Yalta conference, where Churchill, Roosevelt, and Stalin had mapped out the postwar world. After all, as the Soviet leader put it, "They had not done very much fighting in the war."[7] Yet Churchill wanted to resuscitate France quickly so that it might counteract the possible rebirth of German ambition. As early as 1944, Britain had convinced the United States, the Soviet Union, and China to assign France one of the five permanent, veto-wielding seats on the Security Council of the newly conceived United Nations.[8] The Allies also provided France with its own administrative zone of occupation in West Germany, again at British insistence. The only thing expected from the French in return was loyalty. In the words of American ambassador Jefferson Caffrey to one French official: "Don't create difficulties for us."[9]

The French, however, had other ideas. Almost from the start, they erected trade barriers against certain products, such as American movies—in this instance, restoring a law from Vichy and foreshadowing a form of cultural protectionism that would intensify over the decades. Worse still, France remained blind to the lessons of Versailles. As the United States and Britain moved to democratize their defeated enemy, the French made endless (and familiar) pleas to sever the Ruhr from Germany and internationalize the Rhineland. General Lucius Clay, the U.S. military governor in Germany, admitted that he found it easier to deal with the Soviets than the French.

In spite of such disagreements, the United States remained steadfast in its commitment to rebuild France and the ruined economies of Western Europe. The most ambitious initiative was the Marshall Plan, announced by Secretary of State George Marshall in 1947. Anxious not to repeat the mistake of disengagement after the First World War, the United States donated more than $13 billion to the cause of European renewal between 1948 and 1952.[10] With the exception of West Germany, which had been completely devastated, no country benefited more than France. Over an eight-year period, it received $5.5 billion from the United States and began to transform itself from a nation of rural farmers into a nation with a fully modernized economy.

But the Marshall Plan was about more than mere economics—it was also about preserving political freedom. After the war, powerful Communist parties surfaced in the democracies of Western Europe, and nowhere were they more threatening than in France, whose Communist Party boasted more than five million members.[11] Stalinist to their core, the French Communists took orders from Moscow, and their rise posed enormous difficulties for democratic France as it tried to reclaim its republic. In the national elections of 1945, they received 25 percent of the vote. In 1946, Charles de Gaulle resigned his premiership rather than participate in a government in which Communists controlled some of the most important ministries. In Washington, the situation was considered so dire that Truman authorized a plan to mobilize U.S. troops in the event that the French Communists carried out a successful coup.

Even nongovernmental organizations in the United States participated in the fight to prevent France from sliding into Moscow's orbit. American labor unions joined the Department of State in their attempts to weaken Soviet control of French unions. "France is the area where we have to fight," declared Irving Brown of the American Federation of Labor.[12] In 1949, when Communist dock workers in France called for strikes in order to thwart the unloading of American weapons bound for NATO forces, the CIA financed "strong-arm squads" to allow their free flow.[13]

America's fight to save France from Communism was also tightly bound to the fate of Indochina, where the French had maintained colonial control for decades. In 1857, Napoleon III had ordered an invasion of Vietnam after missionaries told him that local converts would be willing to assist their fellow Catholics, the French, in toppling the native emperor. The missionaries were wrong. Support for the invasion never materialized and it took until 1883 before France subjugated the entire country. Although economic development was rapid, its beneficiaries were few. Irrigation projects quadrupled the amount of land devoted to rice cultivation in the Mekong Delta, but the typical peasant's food consumption actually declined under French rule as the new land was handed over to a class of exploitative owners. With only half of all Vietnamese families possessing any land at all, most of the natives acquired little beyond an abiding resentment of the French.

Whereas the British left a legacy of self-government, high-quality education, and real economic development in many of their former colonies, the French improved few of the places where they imposed their authority. In Haiti, slaves had revolted against conditions that were much crueler than anything known in the United States. French Guiana, which remains a colony today, was little more than a dumping ground for unwanted criminals. Nicknamed "the dry guillotine" because of the grim fate that awaited those sent there, it is chiefly known nowadays for the fact that the notorious Devil's Island lies off its shore.

Yet the desire for an empire had become such an integral part of the national psyche that the French remained committed to retaining their colonies in order to salve their wounded postwar pride. France can "only be a great power so long as our flag continues to fly in all the overseas territory," said government minister Jean-Jacques Juglas.[14] In the early years of the Cold War, this determination would cost the French dearly in Vietnam. Later on, it would cost the United States as well.

During the Second World War, President Roosevelt had been a

sharp critic of France's brutal and corrupt rule in Southeast Asia. The French had imposed crushing burdens on an impoverished people. "Taxes, forced labor, exploitation," said Ho Chi Minh of the French, "that is the summing up of your civilization."[15] There were hideous tales of individual terror. Vo Nguyen Giap, the general who would crush the French at Dien Bien Phu and later confound the United States, lost most of his family to French viciousness. His young wife had been imprisoned, strung up by her thumbs, and beaten to death.

The French tried to control every aspect of Vietnamese life and governance. There were as many French civil servants in Indochina as there were in British India, even though the native population was only one-fifteenth the size. France's expectations of the people it ruled were frequently absurd. Schoolchildren in Vietnam were required to recite phrases from textbooks that began: "Our ancestors, the Gauls. . . ."[16] The French liked to claim that they were lifting up the masses—they spoke of a high-minded *mission civilisatrice*—but eighty years after Napoleon III ordered the French into Vietnam, 80 percent of the population remained illiterate. "Anything must be better than to live under French colonial rule," Roosevelt had said.[17]

In 1940, Japanese forces had invaded Vietnam and left the internal administration to the French Vichy rulers, just as the Germans had done in France. Soon, an indigenous resistance movement under the leadership of Ho Chi Minh arose. Like many idealistic students from the Third World, Ho had been converted to Communism in the cafés of Paris and believed that Marxism would liberate his people from colonial rule. His hybrid ideology combined nationalism and totalitarianism—an all-too-familiar mix in the twentieth century and fully reminiscent of Stalin, Hitler, and Mao. Initially, Ho received aid from the United States for his fight against the Japanese. He believed that after the war the Americans would help him convince the French to abandon Indochina and grant independence to Vietnam.

Roosevelt was of two minds. Realizing that France "has milked it for one hundred years" in Southeast Asia and left its inhabitants "worse off than they had [been] in the beginning," he recoiled at any plan to "further France's imperialistic ambitions."[18] He proposed an international trusteeship for Indochina, with the region falling under the authority of the United Nations and eventually earning sovereignty. But he also recognized that any push to remove a colony from French dominion had to be weighed against the rising specter of Communism in France itself.

Roosevelt's successor, Harry S. Truman, had fewer qualms about French colonialism. As America's first Cold War president, he chose to support French aims in Vietnam, believing them necessary for France to repair its shattered national pride. The imperatives of geopolitics called for the United States to commit itself to the French program. This meant rejecting its former ally Ho. By the end of 1946, guerrilla warfare had broken out.

In retrospect, the most effective strategy for thwarting a Communist takeover of Vietnam would have been for France to accept some version of Roosevelt's trusteeship plan. But French pride made this impossible and only energized Ho's movement, which merged its Communist ideology with the powerful patriotism of the Vietnamese people. "The biggest Vietminh appeal," said one State Department official "is land, education, and a chance to shoot Frenchmen. It is difficult to match that platform."[19] Even as they stared at defeat, the French remained inflexible. Their military operations in Vietnam stumbled along and required extensive U.S. support. The events of the late 1940s only strengthened American resolve against Communism as Moscow tested atomic weapons and sponsored uprisings in Burma, Indonesia, Malaya, and the Philippines. Although these insurgencies eventually failed, the fear of Communist dominance in Asia was real, especially after the loss of China and the standoff in Korea. (France sent 1,000 volunteers to fight in the Korean War.)

By 1954, the United States was paying for 80 percent of French expenses in Vietnam. To secure this funding, France had repeatedly blackmailed American defense plans for Western Europe. Most notably, it threatened to block the creation of the European Defense

Community, which at the time was viewed as crucial to West Germany's reintegration into Europe. (In the end, the French parliament refused to ratify the EDC, effectively killing it.)

The growing American involvement in Indochina forced the French to make several concessions—or at least to give the appearance of making them. Yet behind it all, France harbored suspicions that the United States wanted to take over Vietnam for itself. Every suggestion that France grant more freedom to the Vietnamese seemed to confirm these fears and fueled French reprisals and pettiness. U.S. military advisors, for example, were not allowed to supervise the use of American equipment. The United States succeeded in prodding France into promising independence for Vietnam, but the French set up a system of crony colonialism through which they retained almost total control. "Revolution will continue and Ho Chi Minh will remain a popular hero so long as 'independence' leaders with French support are simply native mandarins who are succeeding foreign mandarins," predicted a U.S. diplomat in 1951.[20] One notorious appointment was Prime Minister Nguyen Van Xuan, a French citizen who, despite his name, spoke almost no Vietnamese. His successor, Nguyen Van Tam, formed a cabinet that the U.S. consul in Saigon described as packed with "opportunists, nonentities, extreme reactionaries, assassins, hirelings, and, finally, men of faded mental powers."[21]

It was an awful paradox: France insisted on retaining its colony as an emblem of national strength but quickly showed itself incapable of hanging on, even with massive assistance from a superpower. American officials constantly wondered whether they were naively footing the bill for what Eisenhower called France's "frantic desire" to demonstrate its influence in the postwar world.[22] "Whether the French like it or not, independence is coming to Indochina," said one State Department memo in 1950. "Why, therefore, do we tie ourselves to the tail of their battered kite?"[23] Eisenhower always came back to the same conclusion: Years of colonial mismanagement had led to France's dire predicament. The French have used "weasel words in promising independence," wrote Eisenhower shortly before the fall of

Dien Bien Phu, and for this they "have suffered reverses that have been inexcusable."[24] The final reversal came when the Vietminh raised a red flag over what had once been French headquarters in their valley redoubt. In an effort to appear strong in the eyes of the world, France instead had demonstrated its profound weakness.

Much might have been different if the French had listened to Roosevelt's counsel a decade earlier. "Roosevelt's proposal had a certain eccentricity of detail," wrote the historian Arthur M. Schlesinger, Jr., "but it was founded in realism and wisdom, and, if its essence had been carried out, the world might have been spared much bloodshed and agony."[25] But because of the French failure in Indochina, the United States was forced to take responsibility for the region and guarantee the borders of the non-Communist South.[26]

As France lost one colony, others were beginning to throw off the Gallic yoke. In November of 1954, Algerian insurrectionists began an eight-year struggle for independence. France soon devoted half a million soldiers to suppressing them, the largest force the country had ever committed overseas. Yet no amount of manpower seemed able to contain the Algerian desire for self-determination. France found the experience maddening. Whereas Vietnam was on the other side of the planet, Algiers was just across the Mediterranean from Marseilles. Almost a million European settlers lived in the colony and many of them considered *Algérie française* an integral part of *la France*. Losing it would be an especially painful blow to national pride.

As Algeria was slipping out of French control, Morocco and Tunisia gained sovereignty for themselves—in large measure because France did not have the military capacity to fight for more than one colony at a time. Then, in 1956, another crisis erupted in North Africa that inflicted further damage on Franco-American relations. Looking for ways to finance the Aswan Dam, Egyptian strongman Gamal Abdel Nasser seized on the idea of nationalizing the Suez Canal. France and Britain had financial stakes in the canal and planned with Israel to take it back through military force. Eisenhower was furious. He had not been consulted—possibly because he felt that in the long term the best way to deal with a prima donna like Nasser was with indifference. In his view, negotiations held a better chance of securing international use of the canal than violence.

When Israel launched the initial attack on October 29, Eisenhower could barely contain his rage: "Damn it, the French, they're only egging the Israelis on—hoping somehow to get out of their own North African troubles [in Algeria]. Damn it . . . we tried to tell them they would repeat Indochina all over again in North Africa."[27] This would be no Indochina, however. The adventure collapsed after barely a week, as draconian economic threats from the United States proved decisive. When the Arab nations cut off British and French oil, Eisenhower responded with characteristic firmness and a rare expression of humor. They can "boil in their own oil," he said.[28] There would be no American intervention. Later, the American chief of naval operations admitted that when preparing the Sixth Fleet for possible action in the region, he really "didn't know who the damn enemy was."[29] In the aftermath of the crisis, Eisenhower actually felt it necessary to remind Secretary of State John Foster Dulles that "the 'Bear' is still the central enemy."[30]

Instead of trying to ease tensions with the United States following Suez, the French chose the path of rivalry. In November 1956, Guy Mollet, the previously antinuclear prime minister, sped up plans for a French atomic bomb and tried to improve relations with the Soviet Union. Up to this point, the United States had opposed France's nuclear program on the grounds that French Communists in government positions might share information with Moscow. Where the Suez Crisis had forcibly conveyed to both Britain and France that their imperial pasts were coming to a close, only Britain would have the good sense to put aside parochial interests for the sake of unity during the long bitter struggle with Communist tyranny. France, however, would strive to become a spiteful nuclear power. This initiative was to prove politically shortsighted, strategically dangerous, and fiscally unwise.

By the late 1950s, France had compiled a record of postwar disgrace. One veteran soldier neatly summarized the French public's frustration: "Seven years in Indo[china], two years in Algeria, three weeks in Egypt. Result: nothing!"[31] This pattern of failure led to an insurmountable political crisis for the Fourth Republic. Much as France had turned in desperation to the reassuring figures of Napoleon III in 1848 and Marshal Pétain in 1940, it now looked to another monarchical personality. In 1958, Charles de Gaulle came out of retirement to save his country once more. Serving briefly as prime minister, he was elected president of France's Fifth Republic before the year was over. Realizing that Algeria was lost, de Gaulle overcame intense opposition from hard-liners—including several assassination attempts—and arranged for a cease-fire, followed by full Algerian independence in 1962. He was perhaps the only Frenchman with enough prestige to convince his country to accept this necessary decision.

In many respects, de Gaulle was good for France. Whereas the years of the Fourth Republic had been marked by instability and indecision, de Gaulle gave his country a badly needed sense of direction. He began with nationwide referenda to legitimize his position and consecrate a new constitution in which the office of the president was substantially strengthened. Cutting government expenditures and encouraging investment, he built on the legacy of the Marshall Plan and oversaw a period of stunning economic renewal and modernization. In the realm of politics, his reforms created the foundation for the most stable political era in modern French history. Although he supported the United States during confrontations with the Soviet Union over Berlin and Cuba, his actions in these instances stand out only because they contrast so vividly with his usual antagonism.

Indeed, de Gaulle's return to power proved catastrophic for Franco-American relations. Even after twelve years, many U.S. officials still regarded the imperious Frenchman as a divisive and duplicitous figure due to his behavior during the Second World War, when his incessant grandstanding and obstructionism had created dangerous rifts in the Allied ranks. And while the American public knew tensions existed between de Gaulle and the Roosevelt administration, the true depths of that antagonism had been kept under wraps in the interest of maintaining unity. In private, however, American leaders could be remarkably blunt. A month into his presidency, an exasperated Harry Truman had called his French counterpart an "S.O.B."[32]

De Gaulle did great harm to the West and thus, ultimately, to France. To be sure, his arrogant disregard for the interests of the United States in its global battle against Communist totalitarianism secured him an honored place in the hearts of many of his countrymen. In his drive to increase his political power and execute his program of narrow nationalism, he exploited France's unique position in the Western alliance to tweak and, at times, wound the country that should have been its natural ally. Both presidents Eisenhower and Kennedy had held out the prospect of closer relations with France, but de Gaulle, still fuming over Yalta and any number of old indignities, rejected their overtures. Few men held deeper or longer grudges. On the twentieth anniversary of D-Day, he refused to attend a commemoration in Normandy because the Allies had not consulted him on the original operation. In time, he became the model for all of France's subsequent nose-thumbing anti-American statesmen. There was simply no way an American leader could capture both his esteem and friendship. "My personal tragedy is that I have respect only for those who stand up to me," he liked to say. "But those persons I find intolerable."[33]

The fundamental problem with de Gaulle was not his bad manners but his conception of the world—or, perhaps more accurately, his notion of France's place in it. "All my life I have thought of France in a certain way," he wrote in his wartime memoirs. "France cannot be France without greatness."[34] There is certainly nothing exceptional about expressions of national pride, which may be found in all times and places. Yet de Gaulle, like many French leaders before him, managed to magnify Frenchness into a chauvinistic posture distinct from garden-variety patriotism. Unlike Christianity or Marxism,

"Gaullism" possesses no sacred scripture, but its basic beliefs are clear. At home, France should be politically united, socially stable, and led by a strong executive authority. Abroad, it must be a cultural and political beacon that influences the destiny of all mankind. Apologists maintain that Gaullism has helped France perform a useful role in world affairs by mediating between the superpowers during the Cold War and highlighting the dangers of America's hegemonic power afterward. Its one constant has been anti-Americanism.

Upon returning to power, one of de Gaulle's top priorities was to increase his country's self-esteem. "At this critical moment," he said, "there is nothing more important for the French people than to be made to believe again that France is a great power."[35] Unfortunately for him, French power was a fantasy, and strutting around as if it were otherwise drew valuable resources away from the primary mission of the Western alliance: to contain and defeat Soviet Communism.

In 1960, to the great consternation of the United States, France exploded its first atomic bomb.[36] By creating its own independent nuclear arsenal, the so-called *force de frappe,* or "striking force," de Gaulle hoped to arrest his country's decline and reenter the upper tier of nation-states. He also intended to show that France stood apart from both the United States and the Soviet Union.

But this was an illusion. Just as France had leaned on American strength during two world wars, de Gaulle continued to depend heavily on U.S. security assurances in the Cold War. De Gaulle knew that however disloyal or aloof France might behave, it would always be protected from the Red Army by the thousands of American troops manning the front lines in West Germany. This provided him with a measure of freedom to pursue goals that were often at odds with the interests of the United States, Western Europe, and even France.

His loftiest aspiration—"the vast plan I have formed for my country"—was to lead a bloc of nations in continental Europe as "one of three world powers and, if need be one day, the arbiter between the two camps, the Soviet and the Anglo-Saxon."[37] In more outlandish moments, de Gaulle even spoke of France leading a "Europe from the Atlantic to the Urals."[38] Exactly what made him think the rest of Europe would willingly follow his lead is unclear, especially as he refused to acknowledge the true nature of the conflict. De Gaulle dismissed altogether the ideological struggle that lay at the heart of the Cold War. In his view, the Communist masters of the Soviet Union were motivated less by the radical tenets of Marxism than the national interests of old Russia. "I know as many trustees of the Communist ideology as there are fathers of Europe," he once explained. "The standard of ideology in reality does no more than cover ambitions." Yet he never sought to inquire what those ambitions might be. He professed, "Between France and Russia, there is no conflict of interest."[39] De Gaulle's view of international politics was an expression of the enlightened cynicism that so thoroughly pervades French culture and politics. In the climate of the Cold War, such cynicism was ultimately a form of naïveté. On the mistaken assumption that everyone else in the world was as cynical as themselves, the French badly underestimated the degree to which the Communists were serious about their stated ideological goals.

In addition to leading Europe, de Gaulle wanted his country to become a champion of the Third World, even if it required supporting despots. His *bête noire* was not tyranny, but the United States. "France," he proclaimed, "is violently opposed to blatant American imperialism now rampant in the world. France will continue to attack and to oppose the United States in Latin America, in Asia, and in Africa."[40] Although the French had demanded American aid during their own colonial ordeal in Vietnam, they offered no support to the United States in its Cold War struggle to stop Communist aggression against South Vietnam in the 1960s. Instead, de Gaulle carried on a genial correspondence with Ho Chi Minh, delivered pious lectures condemning American intervention, and, in 1966, gave a rousing speech in Phnom Penh demanding a complete U.S. withdrawal. De Gaulle's hypocrisy was at times shocking. In 1965, when the United States sent Marines into the Dominican Republic to protect

American nationals during a violent civil war, de Gaulle publicly jeered. In secret, however, he sent an urgent message to the Johnson administration: "Won't you please move your Marines four blocks and protect the French Embassy?"[41] Always accommodating, the United States complied with the request, although de Gaulle never expressed his gratitude, even privately. His anti-American rages only worsened.

The most provocative act of de Gaulle's presidency involved the North Atlantic Treaty Organization. Although France had blocked the establishment of a European Defense Community right after the Second World War due to its fear of American military dominance, it had agreed to join NATO. But de Gaulle almost immediately began to limit the French commitment. In 1959, he announced that France's Mediterranean fleet would not operate under NATO authority. He wanted to be free to project French power into the Red Sea and sub-Saharan Africa, which NATO restrictions might have made difficult. Although he assured NATO members that France's fleet would coordinate its operations in the event of a war with the Soviets, he publicly abandoned this pledge four years later.

The biggest blow of all came in 1966. In February, de Gaulle announced that although France considered the Atlantic alliance "useful to her security," it could no longer tolerate an "American protectorate" that masqueraded "under cover of NATO." The next month, de Gaulle informed Western leaders that France was withdrawing from NATO's military integration. Although nominally still a member of the organization, for all practical purposes, France had quit. French troops were promptly removed from NATO commands, and foreign soldiers on French territory were told to leave. In all, the United States shut down thirty military bases in France and removed more than 60,000 soldiers. NATO headquarters shifted from Paris to Brussels. In congressional hearings on the future of NATO, the eminent statesman Dean Acheson, who had been Truman's secretary of state, declared publicly that France was not "a dependable or effective ally." He advised an "empty chair" policy—which is to say, the

United States would have to wait for a more reasonable French leader.[42] President Lyndon Johnson cooperated with de Gaulle's demands, but they incensed him. He instructed his secretary of state, Dean Rusk, to ask the French president: "Do you want us to move American cemeteries out of France as well?"[43] To this, de Gaulle lapsed into an embarrassed silence. He knew that if the Soviet Union launched a future attack on Western Europe, thousands of American boys would die defending France.

In 1967, France took an even more ominous step when General Charles Ailleret declared that its small nuclear arsenal "should not be directed . . . at one theoretical enemy, but be able to strike . . . in any direction."[44] Such provocative action was necessary, France argued, because it needed to defend itself against any foe that might covet its territory during a war—including the United States. This doctrine was called *tous azimuts*, meaning the missiles would target all points of the compass. Because the only real threat came from the East, it was less a strategic position than a political one that appealed to French vanity and chauvinism. The announcement astonished Washington. "Should we Americans take that statement into account with the targeting of our weapons?" asked Rusk of a French diplomat. As Rusk recalled, the French official "smiled rather tightly and let the matter drop."[45] But the policy of *tous azimuts* would continue.

Later that year, during the Six Day War, France stabbed its democratic ally Israel in the back by supporting the Arab dictatorships. De Gaulle calculated that French national interests no longer lay with its former partner from the Suez crisis, which he now called "a martial state determined to expand," but with Israel's more numerous (and oil-rich) enemies. The French president even stooped to utter anti-Semitic canards: The Jews, he said, are "an elite people, sure of itself and domineering."[46] The strength of Israel and the United States, de Gaulle argued, was upsetting the delicate balance of power in the region. When the Soviets voted in the United Nations to condemn Israel's preemptive actions against its hostile neighbors, France supported them.

De Gaulle's threat to destabilize the dollar by exchanging French dollar reserves for gold—an action he eventually took—was the last straw for many Americans. The French president's anti-American policies had reached an unbearable level. In the opinion of Democratic congressman and chairman of the House Armed Services Committee L. Mendel Rivers: "He [de Gaulle] is the most ungrateful man since Judas Iscariot betrayed his Christ." Rivers suggested disinterring America's war dead in France and burying them back home. Democratic congressman Armistead Sheldon, Jr., inveighed against de Gaulle for his "implacable hostility toward the United States— obstructionism in Atlantic and American affairs—cynically promoting distrust among neighbors and instability abroad when the interests of France seem to be served thereby." Daniel Button, a Republican, said that the French president's "anti-Semitic approach," his embrace of Soviet policy in the Middle East, and his snub of NATO "all smack of opportunism and an extremely narrow-minded view of political and sociological matters." Democrat Roman Pucinski called de Gaulle "sick," adding: "He may think he can walk on water, but I don't think he can."[47] Some American officials were beginning to believe his virulent anti-Americanism reflected some deep-seated psychological problem. "Really, the old boy is off his rocker," said Charles Bohlen, the U.S. ambassador to France.[48]

Spontaneous boycotts of French products broke out across the United States as restaurants refused to serve French wine, women returned their French handbags to department stores, and people stopped traveling to France. "I cancelled two trips to Paris because of de Gaulle," said the president of a retail clothing company, "and I won't buy a nickel's worth from France until they get rid of that guy."[49] Said Dallas radio host Gordon McLendon: "It is clear to everyone that, in de Gaulle, the United States is dealing with an ungrateful fourflusher whose hand should have been called years ago." When the French started criticizing comedian Johnny Carson for his disparaging quips about their president, the late-night television host retorted that blaming him for de Gaulle's lack of popularity was "like

Sophia Loren claiming that Twiggy stretched out one of her sweaters."[50] Some Americans, however, were careful to distinguish between de Gaulle and his policies and the views of the French public. Wrote one vice president of a travel agency: "We know that the French people are probably not behind their Führer in this instance and that he may be a senile old man, but the fact is he is doing a lot of damage."[51]

De Gaulle's vision for Europe began to unravel in 1968, when the Soviet Union invaded Czechoslovakia. Although de Gaulle publicly condemned the aggression, he continued to underestimate the unique and real threat of Communism. In doing so, he reverted back to one of his clichéd grievances. The true cause of the Soviet invasion, he explained, was not naked aggression but "the policy of blocs that was imposed in Europe by the effect of the Yalta agreements." It was a jaw-dropping statement (and a swipe at Roosevelt) that combined the dangerous doctrine of moral equivalence with the usual dose of French self-importance. Running through a list of international problems during his New Year's Eve address in 1968, de Gaulle mentioned the U.S.-Soviet standoff, the war in Vietnam, the Arab-Israeli conflict, China, the plight of "French people in Canada," and even self-determination for Biafra. He conspicuously failed to say a single word about the brutal and bloody Soviet attack on Czechoslovakia. By the late 1960s, French Cold War hypocrisy had been elevated to an art form.

When de Gaulle had returned to power in 1958 at the age of sixty-seven, he told a friend that he was "twenty years too old to face up to destiny."[52] A decade later, however, he really was an old man. Physically and mentally tired, he began to lose control of his political universe. The student riots of 1968 nearly cost him his presidency, and he found himself less and less able to carry on his bitter struggle with the United States. The crippling economic cost of maintaining a separate nuclear force combined with the new American push toward détente with the Soviet Union rendered France less influential and more vulnerable. When Richard Nixon became president in 1969, he vowed to extricate the United States from Vietnam and make peace with America's enemies. It was perhaps natural that he immediately reached out to France, traveling to Paris to consult with the man whom Henry Kissinger fawningly called "the Colossus" and thereby making the first state visit to the country in five years.[53] Nixon admired de Gaulle, but he would have little time to develop strong personal ties. When a plebiscite turned out a bad result, de Gaulle resigned his presidency. A year and a half later he was dead.

De Gaulle's successor, Georges Pompidou, was a well-fed banker who, like many Frenchmen, fancied himself an intellectual. Although he had been de Gaulle's protégé, he carried none of his mentor's debilitating psychological baggage. Relations between the United States and France improved under his watch, even though he irritated the Americans with his Gaullist view that greater Soviet influence in the Middle East would provide a healthy counterbalance to American and Israeli power. On other issues, most notably the American pullout from Vietnam and the warming relations between the United States and the Soviet Union, he and Nixon saw eye to eye. It was a time for trying to get along.

Nixon, however, was preoccupied with Vietnam and domestic concerns and put France and Western Europe on the back burner. Tensions erupted briefly during the short Yom Kippur War of 1973: During the surprise Egyptian and Syrian attack on Israel, France refused to let U.S. supply aircraft into French airspace. But American annoyance quickly subsided and that same year, in an attempt to cement relations, the Nixon administration offered France technical information on how to launch missiles from submarines. In return, the French agreed to coordinate their nuclear arsenal with NATO's. It was a diplomatic breakthrough for the United States that, in many ways, resembled the new era of cooperation that had begun with the Soviet Union.

The elevation of the elegant Valéry Giscard d'Estaing, the "French Kennedy," to France's presidency in 1974 also improved relations. Rising through the ranks of the Gaullist government, he often clashed with his party's true believers. When the United States wanted to place intermediate-range nuclear missiles in Europe to counter the threat of Soviet SS-20s, the French announced their support (though they insisted that the missiles not be deployed on French soil). "Yes. I can see it now," said one of Giscard d'Estaing's aggravated foes. "France will become the 51st state before Puerto Rico."[54]

Important differences remained, however. When the Soviet Union invaded Afghanistan in 1979, France refused to join President Jimmy Carter in imposing sanctions on the Communist superpower. As with Czechoslovakia, the French instead chose to look the other way. Later in the year, France refused to join an American-sponsored embargo on Iran after Islamic revolutionaries seized the U.S. embassy and held sixty-six American hostages at gunpoint for more than a year. In Central America, the French recognized the Communist Sandinista regime in Nicaragua and refused to take a hard line on the Communist insurgency in El Salvador.

The early 1980s saw both countries making important political transitions at home. In the United States, Ronald Reagan, a strong anti-Communist conservative, replaced the liberal Democrat Carter. In France, the socialist François Mitterrand came to power at the head of a coalition whose ranks included members of the Communist Party. (He was also a former official in the Vichy regime, an embarrassing fact he kept hidden until late in life.) At first, Reagan was skeptical of the left-leaning Mitterrand, who had nationalized several industries and viewed America's "jungle capitalism" with profound skepticism.[55]

Yet Mitterrand developed into a more reliable ally of the United States than any of his predecessors since the first part of the century, though he did not exactly face stiff competition for the honor. In one of the most significant Cold War decisions of the 1980s, Mitterrand supported American efforts to base medium-range nuclear missiles in Europe as a response to the Soviet deployment of similar weapons in the east—a decision he made in the face of fierce opposition from Europe's large and energetic nuclear-freeze movement. On the domestic front, he worked to marginalize his country's Communists and oversaw a decline in their influence.

Yet there were points of significant disagreement. In 1983, Reagan proposed pouring massive resources into research on missile defense, in a program known as the Strategic Defense Initiative but which critics dubbed "Star Wars." By demoralizing the Kremlin, SDI would become a significant factor in ending the Cold War on the terms of the United States and its allies. Both Britain and West Germany endorsed the project. The French, however, feared it would inspire the Soviets to enlarge their arsenal and make France more vulnerable. Perhaps they were also wary of the tactical advantage that the United States might enjoy if SDI proved successful. Though American diplomacy softened French resistance, Paris never embraced the concept. In 1985, French defense minister Paul Quiles warned that U.S. and Soviet antimissile technology would force France to counter with its own weapons capable of beating the defensive systems. "The more the two superpowers emphasize programs of strategic defense," he said, "the more will the penetration capacity of our missiles become the fundamental criterion of the credibility of our deterrent."[56] By the 1980s, such statements asserting an American threat equal to that of the Soviets were so typical they hardly drew special notice.

Nevertheless, as the Cold War ended, Franco-American relations were arguably more amicable than at any time during the course of the conflict. The honeymoon was a short one, however, for the Age of Terror was about to arrive—and Franco-American affairs would return to old antagonisms.

TWELVE

THE AGE OF TERROR

Is France an ally or an adversary of the United States?
—*Vice President Dick Cheney to French ambassador Jean-David Levitte*[1]

IN MARCH 1986, the government of Libyan dictator Muammar al-Qaddafi sent an urgent order to its agents in Europe: Launch terrorist attacks inflicting "maximum and indiscriminate casualties" on American civilian and military targets. Although the United States decoded the ghastly message and went on alert, a bomb exploded early in the morning of April 5 in the bathroom of La Belle, a West Berlin discotheque patronized by American GIs. The blast killed two U.S. Army sergeants and a Turkish woman. Another 229 people, including seventy-eight Americans, were injured. There could be no doubt about Qaddafi's involvement. A few days before the detonation, British intelligence had intercepted a cable from Libya's bureau in East Berlin boasting of "a joyous event" that was about to occur. After the attack, the British intercepted another indiscreet communiqué in which Qaddafi's henchmen gleefully reported on their success and even mentioned the time it had taken place.[2]

Here at last was a clear set of fingerprints. The Americans had suspected for a long time that Libya was sponsoring terrorism, but until the West Berlin bombing they had lacked irrefutable evidence. Within days of the deadly explosion, President Ronald Reagan called for a hard-hitting response and asked the Pentagon to draw up a list of potential targets in Libya, including military facilities and terrorist training camps. "We're going to defend ourselves," Reagan promised at an April 9 press conference.[3]

Defending the United States, however, would require international cooperation. Aware of her role as America's staunchest ally, British prime minister Margaret Thatcher immediately granted Reagan's request to unleash U.S. Air Force planes based in Great Britain. "The U.K. came through like gang-busters," said Navy Secretary John Lehman.[4]

The French were not so cooperative. President François Mitterrand flatly denied permission for U.S. warplanes to fly over his country on their way to Libya. "The refusal upset me," wrote Reagan in his memoirs, "because I believed all civilized nations were in the same boat when it came to resisting terrorism."[5] Others remembered the incident with more anger: "Everyone connected with the attack was furious with [Mitterrand's] casual refusal," wrote Secretary of Defense Caspar Weinberger.[6]

Reagan believed that economics lay behind the rebuff: "France conducted a lot of business with Libya and was typically trying to play both sides."[7] Whatever the motive, French obstruction proved more of an inconvenience than an impediment. American planes on their way to Libya were forced to take a much longer route around the Iberian Peninsula and through the Straits of Gibraltar, adding about 1,200 extra miles to the journey and six or seven hours of additional flight time. (Spain also refused to let American planes into its airspace because it did not then support military responses to terrorism.) For American pilots based in Britain, the operation lasted more than fourteen hours from takeoff to touchdown, making it the longest fighter mission in U.S. history.

Although two American airmen were killed over Tripoli, the attack was a success, weakening Qaddafi at home and reducing the number of terrorist incidents linked to him in later years. (There were two awful exceptions: The bombings of Pan Am flight 103 over

Lockerbie, Scotland, in 1988 and UTA Flight 772 over Niger in 1989.)[8] Reagan showed that a swift and muscular response to terrorism could produce results. Yet France remained defiant. In a fit of moral equivalence following the raid, the foreign ministry announced that it "deplores the intolerable escalation of terrorism which has led to an action of reprisal which in itself renews the chain of violence."[9]

The French certainly knew something about terrorism. Indeed, the words *terrorism* and *terrorist* both entered the English language in references to the French revolutionaries who perpetrated the Reign of Terror.[10] Acts that might be described as examples of terrorism have occurred throughout history. By the early twentieth century, most terrorists were anarchists or nationalists who believed they could achieve political goals through violence. The 1914 assassination of Archduke Franz Ferdinand sparking the First World War is perhaps the best-known example of this. The influence of the anarchists eventually faded (many of them were absorbed by the Communist movement). The nationalist impulse to inflict terror remained powerful throughout the twentieth century, though in recent years Islamic radicalism has eclipsed it as a force for death and destruction.

France was one of many countries increasingly seared by terrorism in the years following the Second World War, despite France's own strenuous efforts to pacify Muslim nations. After Algerian independence, the French reversed their strategic calculus in the Middle East. They abandoned their former allies in Israel and opposed U.S. policies in the region, aiming to become the best friends of oil-rich Arab dictators. They wanted to leverage this friendship into influence on the world stage, transforming France into the global powerbroker it craved to be.

This cynical policy was not without its moral costs for France. It meant tolerating a certain amount of terrorism and even assisting the terrorists themselves when it promoted good relations. In 1977, French police captured Abu Daoud, the Palestinian militant who had planned one of the most notorious terrorist incidents of the twentieth century: the murder of Israeli athletes at the 1972 Olympics in Munich. Although Israel and West Germany immediately began extradition proceedings, French authorities put the evil mastermind on a plane to Algeria, where he promptly disappeared. According to the *New York Times*, "The French reportedly released Mr. Daoud because their secret services feared losing valuable contacts among radical Arab groups."[11]

France was not always so forgiving of other international criminals, yet over the years it followed a more lenient policy toward terrorism than any other Western country. In the 1970s and 1980s, French leaders feted PLO radicals and negotiated with the sinister Abu Nidal (whose terrorist organization had been credited with some 900 deaths). In one startling incident, Mitterrand paid a state visit to Syria, stood beside Syrian president Hafez al-Assad, and declared in the face of overwhelming evidence that there was no link between Damascus and terrorism. Mitterrand's own intelligence agency believed that Syrian-sponsored groups were behind a bombing in Beirut that had killed fifty-eight French soldiers a year earlier as well as the assassination of the French ambassador to Lebanon. But the French president decided to ignore such inconvenient information.

Despite such willful denials of reality, France discovered to its horror that it was not immune to terrorist violence. By 1986, bombs were going off in Paris, and Islamic extremists held several French citizens hostage in the Middle East. Indeed, the country was experiencing its worst round of attacks since the Algerian conflict a generation earlier. And yet the imperative of maintaining positive ties with Arab despots remained so strong that France dared not even lend its airspace for the purpose of helping the Americans punish Qaddafi, one of the world's leading terror-masters. The commitment to accommodation and appeasement was simply too much to overcome.

The war on terrorism is often said to have begun on September 11, 2001, but in truth it began decades earlier. In a fundamental way, 9/11 was a new Pearl Harbor, awakening Americans to a serious and ongoing problem that Europe had failed to contain. The twin challenges of Islamic radicals committing terrorist atrocities and rogue states plotting to acquire weapons of mass destruction could no longer be overlooked. What would happen if a man like Qaddafi got his hands on a nuclear device? Surely the result would be much worse than a Berlin disco bombing. During the post–Cold War era, however, the Americans and the French would spend much of their time arguing not about how to confront these menaces but whether to confront them at all. In the end, they would find themselves bitterly confronting each other.

The man at the center of the dispute was Mitterrand's successor, Jacques Chirac. The story begins in the 1970s, during Chirac's first term as French prime minister. Born in Paris in 1932, Chirac went to good schools and was once described by a history teacher as having "a lively and curious mind but more spontaneous than reflective."[12] After a youthful flirtation with Communism, he thought about becoming a writer but instead volunteered for military service in Algeria and fell under the spell of Gaullist chauvinism. In the 1960s, he threw himself into politics and won a seat in the National Assembly as a member of de Gaulle's faction (defeating, coincidentally, Mitterrand's brother). He rose in the party ranks, became the minister of agriculture, and then, in 1974, prime minister. Fiercely ambitious, Chirac wanted nothing less than to inherit the Gaullist mantle as French president, though he would have to wait two decades to achieve this goal.

One of the most significant developments in Chirac's political career was the close personal bond he formed in the 1970s with an ambitious official from Iraq. Vice President Saddam Hussein had come to France during those years to shake hands and sign oil contracts, and few were as keen to accommodate him as Chirac. The two men met frequently in Baghdad and Paris while brokering a massive set of trade agreements in which Iraq agreed to supply France with 700 million barrels of oil over ten years and spend billions on French military equipment, including tanks, missiles, and Mirage F-1 fighters. In addition, Iraq bought 100,000 French-made cars and invited French companies to develop a billion-dollar resort complex near Baghdad. Hussein, of course, wanted something in return: French assistance in building a nuclear reactor plus a source of weapons-grade uranium to use as starter fuel. Chirac was so eager to oblige that Hussein's infamous Osirak nuclear reactor earned the nickname "O'Chirac" among French critics of the deal.

There was ample cause for concern. "The agreement with France is the first concrete step toward production of the Arab atomic bomb," said Hussein, ominously.[13] In 1981, Israel came to believe the plant posed a threat to its national survival and destroyed it in a daring airstrike. Although many now view the raid as an act of providential foresight, at the time most governments criticized the attack (including that of the United States). Few issued more vituperative condemnations than Paris: "Unacceptable, dangerous, and a serious violation of international law," said Foreign Minister Claude Cheysson.[14]

There is evidence to suggest that Chirac offered to rebuild the reactor for his "personal friend," as he called Hussein, though Chirac has denied this, and the plant was never reconstructed.[15] Yet the French continued to support Hussein and—along with the United States—endorsed Iraq's war against its neighboring terror state, Iran. In the first six years of that bloody conflict, French companies sold more than $20 billion in military and civilian materials to Iraq, accounting for as much as 40 percent of all French military exports.[16] By the time Hussein turned his rapacious gaze to Kuwait in the summer of 1990, France had supplied the dictator with about one-quarter of his military arsenal. Only the Soviet Union had done more to arm him.

Iraq's invasion of Kuwait on August 2, 1990, turned French thinking about the Middle East on its head. Smaller than Vermont, the little country on the western shore of the Persian Gulf had done nothing to provoke the attack other than sit atop oil reserves that Hussein coveted for himself. Within twelve hours, Kuwait fell to the overpowering force of Iraqi arms. Thousands of foreign nationals from the United States and Europe became Hussein's hostages.[17]

In truth, France had stopped arms sales to Iraq some months earlier—not because of any moral or foreign-policy qualms but rather because Hussein had fallen nearly $5 billion behind on his payments.

The size of this debt, however, did nothing to prevent French leaders from praising the Ba'athist tyrant and long-time friend of France. "President Saddam Hussein has a clear and interesting outlook, which he qualifies by leading his people towards peace," said French defense minister Jean-Pierre Chevenement a few months before the invasion of Kuwait. Hussein, he added, "has the respect and esteem of French leaders."[18]

Who was this man of peace? Born in 1937, Saddam Hussein threw himself into radical politics at an early age, joining with the violent Ba'ath Party of pan-Arab socialists. In 1959, he tried to assassinate Iraq's president but failed. He fled to Egypt, where he stayed until a 1963 Ba'athist coup in Iraq made his return possible. His steady rise in the Ba'ath Party was aided by his ability to woo foreign investment, especially from France. In 1979, he seized control of the country for himself and butchered dozens of political rivals. A year later, he ordered the invasion of Iran. Despite Hussein's willingness to deploy chemical weapons, the war dragged on inconclusively for eight years, leaving more than a million people dead or wounded. When it ended, Hussein initiated a campaign of terror against ethnic Kurds within his own borders. More than 100,000 Kurdish men, women, and children were killed, many of them slaughtered in what is believed to be the first case of a country using poison gas on its own citizens since the Holocaust.

French defense minister Chevenement was just the sort of man to overlook this record of brutality. He was one of many French secularists who praised Hussein as a latter-day Jacobin. Others, perhaps including Chirac, saw the strongman as an Iraqi version of de Gaulle. (Hussein himself admired de Gaulle, ranking him alongside Nebuchadnezzar, the ancient king of Babylon, as one of history's greatest leaders.) Chevenement was also a founding member of the Franco-Iraqi Friendship Alliance, a shadowy group that promoted business contacts between the two countries and which was believed to have spent millions of francs buying influence in Paris. Chevenement certainly had become a man to reckon with: He led a bloc of nationalist-minded socialists who shared power in Mitterrand's government. So when Iraq invaded Kuwait, France found itself in the awkward position of having an admirer of Hussein in charge of the nation's war-making capabilities.

A day after the invasion, France joined the United States and the rest of the United Nations Security Council in demanding an immediate and unconditional withdrawal. Three days later, the Security Council unanimously approved a trade and financial embargo on Iraq and occupied Kuwait. Although the West appeared to be acting in concert against Hussein's aggression, close observers spotted some strains. The French followed the United States and Britain in sending military forces to the region, but they also insisted that they were acting on their own initiative. It was a classic case of France trying to have it both ways, a practice it perfected in its previous dealings with Arab states and which it would continue throughout the showdown with Hussein. When the United States and Britain threatened to turn the trade embargo into an armed blockade, Mitterrand declared that his country could not possibly endorse such drastic action. The French president dispatched a dozen envoys to Arab capitals to emphasize that his country's actions were purely defensive. France's military contribution was negligible. Much was made of the aircraft carrier *Clemenceau* being ordered to the Persian Gulf, and less of the fact that it came with only forty-two helicopters of limited value and no fighter jets.

Defense Minister Chevenement spoke out publicly against doing even this much. As the crisis unfolded in August, he actually went on vacation. "They don't need me to carry out Bush's policies: I'm going back to Tuscany," he groused.[19] But he did not take any time off from his campaign against united action: "No legal basis exists today for armed intervention against Iraq or even to liberate Kuwait," he claimed. Chevenement also warned of "getting carried away by irresponsible ideas" and predicted that a war "would cost 100,000 lives and would engulf the entire Middle East."[20]

Mitterrand not only refused to rebuke his minister, he embarked on a subtle campaign of accommodation. In a speech to the United Nations on September 24, the French president reiterated that Iraq must withdraw from Kuwait. Instead of keeping this demand unconditional, however, Mitterrand responded to a suggestion that Hussein had made in August. Iraq would withdraw from Kuwait, the dictator had promised, if Israel first removed its forces from the Palestinian territories. Mitterrand now proposed that if Hussein were to call his troops home, he would be rewarded with an international conference to discuss, among other things, "the Palestinians who are prey to despair." In essence, the French president was offering to enhance Hussein's prestige in the Arab world as the man whose devotion to Palestine and ability to bully the West had compelled America and Europe to drag Israel to the bargaining table.

Next, Mitterrand suggested that the UN guarantee "the restoration of Kuwait's sovereignty and exercise of the democratic will of the Kuwaiti people." It was a bizarre statement. Kuwait was a sheikdom ruled by the al-Sabah family. Was Mitterrand actually proposing regime change *in Kuwait*? If the French had their way, their friend Hussein might actually exit the scene as a liberator, which in fact was what he had claimed to be when his tanks bore down on the tiny country. "Everything might become possible," promised Mitterrand.[21] Secretary of State James Baker branded Mitterrand's address "an appeasement speech, like those heard in Europe in the 1930s."[22]

President Bush nevertheless wanted the French to serve as full partners in an international coalition against Iraq. This was easier said than done. As Bush wrote in his diary: "The Brits are strong, and the French are French."[23] Meanwhile, Hussein devised a diplomatic strategy for driving a wedge between Anglo-American resolve and French vacillation. In October, Iraq released all of its 330 French hostages, while still holding thousands of American and British citizens. A few weeks later, Iraqi troops captured three Saudi-based French soldiers who seemed to have wandered across the border. Hussein let them go as well. "It is very clear that the Iraqis released the French soldiers because they consider France a weak link and are trying to divide the alliance," said one U.S. diplomat. "If it had been an American, they would have paraded him through the streets of Baghdad."[24] Suspicions abounded that France had engaged in secret talks with Hussein and cut a special deal for French hostages. Paris denied the charges, but it could not refute the basis for them. It was well known that in August one of France's special envoys—Claude Cheyson, the man who had reproached Israel for destroying Iraq's nuclear facility a decade earlier—had traveled to Tunis, met with Yassir Arafat, and asked the PLO leader to intervene personally with Hussein on behalf of the French captives.

As the months wore on, France assembled its military in the Gulf and cooperated on a Security Council resolution authorizing war if Iraq did not leave Kuwait by January 15, 1991. At the same time, however, it continued to distance itself from the United States. "I have respect for Mr. Bush, but I do not feel I am in the position of a second-class soldier who must obey his commanding general," said Mitterrand as Iraq's deadline drew near.[25] When the coalition needed to show a united front, France continued to press for a deal with Hussein. Mitterrand remained fixated on the idea of an international peace conference (a venue in which the French had never distinguished themselves). He also pushed for another Security Council meeting, whose only possible purpose could be to delay the ultimatum. One prominent member of the French Senate—Philippe de Gaulle, son of the late president—lent his prestigious name to the antiwar faction and voted against French military involvement. On the eve of the deadline, Defense Minister Chevenement suggested that the Americans should offer "the very small gesture" of an international conference, as if they, and not Hussein, were responsible for preventing a war.

Meanwhile, the defense minister was making several gestures of his own, all in the service of obstructing the United States. Although France had positioned 10,000 soldiers in the desert, it refused to follow Britain's lead and place them under U.S. command. The French wanted to emphasize their independence from the coalition, and so their top officer reported instead to Saudi commander Prince Khaled.

Chevenment also made sure French forces were stationed far from U.S. bases, apparently to disassociate them even further from the coalition. On January 9, Mitterrand continued his long-standing sensitivity to airspace issues when he announced that French forces would neither fly over Iraqi territory nor march into it. "The mission is to fulfill the mandate of the United Nations," he said. "It does not mean launching some kind of war of destruction against Iraq. It means the liberation of Kuwait."[26] When the bombs started dropping on the seventeenth, however, France rushed to place its personnel under American command, though it continued to insist that they not violate Iraq's borders.

The French restriction made no military sense. If the United States and Britain had not been allowed to enter Iraqi territory, much of Iraq's war capability would have remained untouched and Hussein could have led his forces from the luxury of a palace sanctuary rather than the confines of a cramped bunker or a tent in the desert. Mitterrand's decision baffled former French president Valéry Giscard d'Estaing. "Why strike the country under occupation yet spare the aggressor?" asked Giscard d'Estaing. "What would have happened in World War II if the United States decided only to attack France and not strike inside Germany?"[27]

Even French officers began to complain about Mitterrand's strategy—though not out of a wish to degrade the enemy or defend Gallic honor. As the *Washington Post* reported: "Senior French officers in the Gulf reportedly have been unhappy with the restraints, which they contended would lead to more casualties among their troops than necessary. Air strikes at installations in Kuwait, they contend, represent some of the most hazardous duty of the campaign, as French pilots swooping low over munitions depots outside Kuwait City encounter heavy machine-gun fire."[28] Mitterrand was persuaded. On January 20, he announced on national television that the airspace ban was lifted. Four days later and a week after the start of the air war, French pilots flew over Iraq for the first time. They also appeared to meet their safety goals. The Americans, British, and Italians all lost planes in the early days of Operation Desert Storm, but the French emerged unscathed.

There was, however, one French casualty: Defense Minister Chevenement resigned his post on January 29. He had tried to quit twice before out of frustration with his country's decision to go to war against Iraq, but both times Mitterrand had refused to let him go. Chevenement used the occasion of his departure to criticize the coalition effort, even as it stood on the threshold of unprecedented success against what was once advertised as the world's fourth-largest army. "The logic of war risks driving us ever further from the objectives established by the United Nations," the defense minister complained in a letter that was made public.[29] He was hardly the only one to announce his objections. "Our foreign policy in Europe, Africa, and the Middle East is null," said Philippe de Gaulle. "Our credibility with Arab countries is very compromised."[30]

As the start of ground operations approached, French soldiers in Saudi Arabia were assigned the task of capturing the Iraqi town of As Salman, about 200 miles west of Kuwait City and estimated to have a population of 7,000. They were given two days to meet this objective. Major General Jim Johnson of the 82nd Airborne Division said that his men could accomplish the same task in less than twenty-four hours. His superiors decided that coalition politics outweighed the need to achieve every military goal as rapidly as possible. The French would have their two days to get to As Salman.

When the ground war began on February 24, the 2nd Brigade of the 82nd Airborne Division sent a message to their French comrades: *Côté à côté soldats français et américain nous écrirons une page d'historie.* "Side by side, French and American soldiers will write a page of history."[31]

"It would be written slowly," deadpanned Rick Atkinson in his account of the Persian Gulf War. Because French commanders were under considerable pressure to limit their casualties, their portion of the offensive crept forward at a snail's pace. Within hours of the first friendly message, Colonel Frank Akers radioed the French: "Francois, get your ass moving! Why are you guys taking so long?"[32]

The French achieved some of their objectives on the first day, but irritated American commanders by quitting early: They had bivouacked when there was still an hour of sunlight in the sky. "To avoid mistakes," explained French brigadier general Bernard Janvier, "it's better to delay."[33] When they finally reached the outskirts of As Salman on February 25, they set up their tents for the night instead of taking the city. As they moved into As Salman at dawn on the next day, the French discovered a ghost town: Only a dozen civilians and fifteen soldiers were still there. There had been no reason for hesitation.

The overall war effort succeeded brilliantly: Iraqi troops abandoned Kuwait and Hussein submitted to UN sanctions. Moreover, the war resulted in less than 1 percent of the 100,000 fatalities Chevenement had predicted half a year earlier. When the fighting went much more smoothly than even optimists in the Bush administration had hoped, American war planners considered a more ambitious goal than merely removing Iraq from Kuwait. Should the coalition also march on Baghdad and eliminate the root problem? When Bush and his advisors decided against it, they gave a variety of rationales: The coalition's UN charter called for liberating Kuwait rather than deposing Hussein, Arab states might oppose broadening the coalition's aims, and many people believed that Hussein had put himself in imminent danger of being overthrown by his own military. Yet one of the most persuasive reasons for not expanding the war had to do with France: It could not be counted on to remain a part of the coalition, no matter how much sense going after Hussein might have made at the time or how many problems it would have averted later.

Leaving Hussein in power may have served the interests of diplomatic expediency, but it was a short-term compromise with long-term consequences. Over the course of the next decade, that fateful decision set in motion a series of events that would exacerbate the tensions already existing between the United States and France. It finally tore open a wide rift that forced many Americans to wonder whether France was an ally or an adversary.

After the Persian Gulf War, the U.S.-led coalition imposed no-fly zones over parts of Iraq as a way of containing Hussein. Almost all of the enforcement resources came from the United States and Britain, though France made a symbolic commitment of about a dozen planes. At the same time, the French returned to their traditional practice of cultivating relations with the despotic regimes of the Arab world, including the one in Baghdad. Their government took the first steps toward reconciliation with Hussein when it reopened its Baghdad embassy at the chargé d'affaires level and signaled its support for lifting the oil embargo that had cut off Iraq's main source of hard cash. By 1996, the Ba'ath Party was once more favorably disposed to its old friend in Europe. Iraqi oil minister Amir Rasheed visited Paris to discuss development deals. "Friendly countries who have supported us, like France and Russia, will certainly be given priority," he said. Rasheed indicated that lifting the embargo would result in France winning billions of dollars in oil contracts.[34]

These years also witnessed the return of Chirac. Although he had never actually left politics, the rapid progress that had characterized his ascent in the 1960s and 1970s had come to a halt in the 1980s when he lost two presidential elections, both to Mitterrand. Between the defeats, Chirac served another short term as prime minister, but many believed his career had stalled, perhaps permanently. There were rumors of crooked financial dealings, and it was later revealed that during his eighteen-year reign as mayor of Paris, his family had billed the city $3 million for food and wine purchases—nearly $1,000 per day. There were also allegations of intricate schemes to enrich himself and his political allies through lavish kickbacks and clever expense-account frauds.

Despite this—or perhaps because of it—Chirac continued to lead the Gaullists, and in 1995 he was finally elected to succeed the retiring Mitterrand. In America, there was some hope that he would become a French version of Ronald Reagan or Margaret Thatcher and revive a moribund economy that had suffered through fourteen years of socialist experimentation. Instead, Chirac would prove not to be the hero of a free-market revolution but the champion of a revived nationalism. As ever, his true role model was de Gaulle. "Let us be tolerant and fraternal, but let us also be inventive, audacious, and conquering," he said on the night of his election victory.[35] One of his first acts as president was to resume French nuclear tests in the South Pacific, which Mitterrand had suspended. The *force de frappe* was alive and well. Chirac even redecorated his office with de Gaulle's desk and furniture.

In these early days, Chirac expressed a fondness for the United States that his idol never shared. During interviews with American reporters, he would share warm remembrances of that magical summer of 1953, when he had attended summer school at Harvard and worked as a soda jerk at Howard Johnson's. He also seemed genuinely interested in healing some of France's historical differences with the United States by inching back into NATO, though not as a full member, because France continued to keep its troops outside the alliance's command structure.

On the subject of Iraq, however, Chirac made sure that France kept its distance from U.S. policy. In September 1996, Iraqi forces infiltrated Kurdish territory and went door-to-door executing political leaders. It was Hussein's most provocative military action since the end of the war. In response, President Bill Clinton ordered cruise-missile strikes targeting Iraqi military installations, and Hussein pulled back. Britain and Germany praised the American effort, but France refused to endorse the action even though Clinton personally had lobbied for Chirac's support. French officials did not even content themselves with keeping mum. Instead, they charged that Clinton was trying to boost his reelection prospects with a cynical show of force aimed more at American voters than Iraq's thugocracy. When Clinton extended the no-fly zone over southern Iraq from the 32nd parallel to the 33rd—about sixty miles, to a position just below Baghdad—the French responded with petulance, announcing that their planes would not observe the new boundary. In the fall of 1997, when the Security Council considered a resolution on Iraq's transparent failure to cooperate with UN weapons inspectors, France abstained.

In the future, Hussein might be in the position to hand out big oil contracts. Why alienate him?

Then, in 1998, Iraq announced that it was ending all participation with UN monitors hunting for evidence of biological, chemical, or nuclear weapons programs. In a devastating report to the Security Council, chief inspector Richard Butler described the regime's systematic efforts to deny access to various sites. What was the dictator hiding? Had he stockpiled biological and chemical weapons? Had his nuclear scientists made swift advances in their research? On December 17, the United States and Britain began what was by far the most concerted and powerful attack on Iraq in more than seven years.

Once again, France questioned the need for military force. Within days of the bombing, it proposed ending economic sanctions in exchange for the return of arms inspectors. Perhaps believing that Western resolve was about to fall apart, Iraq rejected the idea. Unperturbed, France made another offer to lift the oil embargo and implement a weakened inspections system. It also hinted that part of the bargain might include banning American personnel from the inspection teams. Iraq spurned this suggestion as well. The reason was simple: Hussein knew he had finally split the Security Council and undermined the international will to contain him.

The United States understood that it had to salvage the Security Council's crumbling determination to maintain at least some pressure on Hussein. In the fall of 1999, the Americans worked with France and other countries to craft a new UN resolution that loosened economic constraints and installed a watered-down system of inspections. These were substantial concessions, but the Americans believed they served the larger purpose of restoring a lost consensus among Security Council members. France promised to vote in favor of Resolution 1284. When the measure actually came up for a vote, however, the French government broke its pledge and abstained. It believed that this hedge would benefit French companies pursuing contracts in Baghdad. "The signal sent to Saddam was an unfortunate one," wrote Butler. "If even this compromise resolution couldn't be passed unanimously, what hope was there that the Security Council might be resolute in the next challenge from Iraq?"[36] The UN's resolve had been permanently smashed.

France was juggling several agendas at once, from its long-standing habit of pandering to Arab dictators to its hope that it might get a large chunk of Iraqi trade, then valued at $17 billion. The most important factor in opposing Anglo-American resolve, however, was a geopolitical calculus. Since the end of the Cold War, France had tried to claim a grand role for itself in global affairs. "The bipolar world we have known is finished, and the world of tomorrow will be multipolar," said Chirac in 1995. "One of the essential poles will be Europe."[37] Needless to say, France intended to provide political and intellectual leadership for the whole continent. The dream of Charles de Gaulle was reborn.

One of the chief obstacles to France's goal, however, was the United States. In the post–Cold War world, America stood squarely in the way of French aims. At least that is what many French officials believed. "The United States of America today predominates on the economic level, on the military level, on the technological level, and in the cultural area in the broad sense of the word," said French foreign minister Hubert Vedrine in 1999. "It is not comparable, in terms of power and influence, to anything known in modern history."[38] Vedrine declared that the United States was not a mere superpower, but a dangerous "hyperpower"—a word he coined and deployed freely. His envy was palpable. So was his fear.

The American hyperpower threatened the Gaullist vision of an international order maintained by multiple poles of influence, including one headquartered along the banks of the Seine. The French clearly saw the Americans as adversaries. "Their weight carries them towards hegemonism, and the idea they have of their mission is unilateralism," said Vedrine. "And that is not acceptable."[39]

The problem was not merely that the United States was a political or military giant but a cultural and economic one as well. Since the conclusion of the Second World War, France had felt profoundly threatened by America's growing influence in virtually every area of human activity. These fears only grew in the wake of the Cold War, and the French were determined to react against it. In the early 1990s, France hindered world trade talks by demanding a right to subsidize French movies and discriminate against American ones. Hostility toward all things American manifested itself most flamboyantly and absurdly in the figure of Jose Bove, a mustachioed sheep farmer who attacked a McDonald's franchise with a group of men wielding pick axes and power saws. Bove himself drove a tractor. Together, they inflicted $120,000 worth of damage on the restaurant, which they saw as an emblem of American capitalism (even though it happened to be owned by a fellow Frenchman who bought his food almost exclusively from French sources). Bove was arrested, and promptly became a national folk hero. Some 30,000 people turned out to support him at one of his court appearances. He was invited to dinner with the prime minister. Even Chirac proclaimed his support for the vandal: "I am in complete solidarity with France's farm workers and I detest McDonald's."[40]

Chirac and the French wanted to do more than fight a rearguard action against what they saw as the "McDomination" of their country. They longed for France to make its Gaullist mark on the world by challenging the great American hyperpower. This would not be done through military strength but through mediating bodies such as the United Nations, where France still held one of five precious vetoes on the Security Council. Rather than a David-and-Goliath duel between France and America, the French envisioned a Lilliputian assault upon Gulliver, with France serving as the pint-sized ringleader. Paris imagined that it could tie America down by forcing it to bow to the authority of the UN as well as international agreements on climate change, war crimes, and arms control.

On the day Osama bin Laden's henchmen brought unimaginable terror to the United States, Chirac seemed genuinely moved. In a display of goodwill and solidarity, he rushed to the side of President George W. Bush. His government supported American military action in Afghanistan and sent peacekeepers to assist the post-Taliban government. Yet September 11 did nothing to alter France's fundamental approach to global affairs. Chirac made it clear that he was skeptical of extending the war on terrorism beyond the borders of Afghanistan. When Bush spoke of an "axis of evil" that included Saddam Hussein's Iraq in early 2002, Paris snickered with contempt: "The rhetoric of good and evil is not suitable for the reality of today's world," said a Chirac confidant.[41] One top French official, Charles Josselin, told a Saudi newspaper that the Bush administration suffered from "Texas-style diplomacy"—a phrase meant as an insult in European circles.[42] Vedrine was even more outspoken: "Today we are threatened by a simplicity that reduces all the problems of the world to the struggle against terrorism that is not properly thought through," he said.[43]

Franco-American relations deteriorated at the popular level as well. In France, ugly conspiracy theories about September 11 became disturbingly prevalent. One of the most sinister and irresponsible was concocted by Thierry Meyssan, a self-styled investigative journalist who claimed in his book *L'Effroyable Imposture—The Big Lie*—that the common understanding of what happened was based on "nothing more than a cover-up" and "lies put forward by officials."[44] According to Meyssan, "The attacks of September 11 were masterminded from inside the American state apparatus"—that is, George W. Bush—as a justification for reckless warfare.[45] By the summer of 2002, *L'Effroyable Imposture* had sold more than 200,000 copies in France.

As the first anniversary of September 11 approached, Chirac tried to minimize his profound differences with the United States by invoking the enduring myth of Franco-American friendship. "When the chips are down," he declared, "the French and Americans have always stood together and have never failed to be there for one another." At the same time, he proved incapable of hiding his disdain for what he took to be America's hamfisted approach to international problems. "I am totally against unilateralism [i.e., American foreign policy] in the modern world," he said. The emerging American doctrine of pre-emptive action to thwart national-security threats, he added, was "extraordinarily dangerous."[46] But after the carnage of

9/11, the United States was not interested in waiting for its enemies to strike. It would move against them before they could mount an effective attack.

Far from acting unilaterally, Bush won the support of Britain's Tony Blair and many other world leaders. On September 12, 2002, a year and a day after the worst terrorist attacks in history, Bush spoke at the United Nations and promised to seek UN approval for a new resolution on Iraq, which he did at the behest of France and other countries. Although Bush had been an advocate of regime change in Iraq before 9/11, he narrowed his argument in front of the international body to focus on weapons of mass destruction rather than more comprehensive strategic goals about the importance of installing regimes that would cooperate in the war on terrorism or spreading democracy in the Middle East. This was done in part because if Bush had made a broad case about how despotism threatened freedom, he would have alienated UN members that did not grant political rights to their citizens, such as China. So he committed the United States to seeking a resolution that would grant international sanction to disarming Iraq by force if necessary. But he added that the United States would not hesitate to act alone. "Iraq has answered a decade of UN demands with a decade of defiance," said Bush. "Are the Security Council resolutions to be honored and enforced, or cast aside without consequence?"[47]

It was a bold challenge to the UN, as well as to France, which sought to influence world affairs from its permanent seat on the Security Council. Two months of frustrating negotiations ensued. Chirac's point man in this endeavor was his new foreign minister, Dominique de Villepin. Born in Morocco when it was still a French colony, Villepin was a generation younger than his boss, who was said to adore his handsome silver-haired deputy like the son he never had. Whereas Chirac had pushed aside his dream of becoming a writer to pursue a career in politics, Villepin managed to do both. He became an amateur poet who published several volumes at personal expense. "From the bottom of my pockets, stuck to the back of my smock, hidden in the corner of abacuses, poetry gushed out," he once wrote. (For his odd prose style, London's *Daily Telegraph* labeled him an "obviously dangerous lunatic.")[48] The foreign minister achieved wider notice for a nostalgia-choked book on Napoleon, whom he lionized over the course of 600 pages as a kind of French superman. Villepin even described the emperor's final battle at Waterloo with a phrase that only a Frenchman could write: "a defeat which gleams with the aura of victory."[49]

During negotiations over Iraq, Villepin took to lecturing the United States on the finer points of national sovereignty—arguments that the belligerent Napoleon would have found absurd. The Americans continued to believe that weapons inspections would fail if they were not backed by the credible threat of war. Villepin thought that this was too imposing and said that the Security Council should begin with a resolution that did not mention military force. A couple of weeks later, Chirac announced that he was "totally hostile" to anything giving "an automatic character to military intervention."[50] France insisted on two resolutions, one that would create a new inspection formula and another requiring further debate in the Security Council before any hostilities.

Bush stood his ground. "Those who choose to live in denial may eventually be forced to live in fear," he warned. "The time has arrived once again for the United Nations to live up to the purpose of its founding to protect our common security."[51] The United States did not budge on the need for a single Security Council resolution, but it did agree to compromise on some of its wording. An early proposal called for using "all means necessary" against Iraq in the event of continued noncompliance. The phrase was changed to say that Iraq would suffer "serious consequences" instead. This semantic wrangling went on for several weeks. The negotiations were often tense and progress seemed slow. "That's the French way," remarked Richard Holbrooke, the U.S. ambassador to the UN under Clinton. "It is the classic play out of the Charles de Gaulle playbook: hold out to the end, get more leverage."[52] He might have said the *French* playbook: France has been jockeying for advantage against its supposed allies since the days of Vergennes and the American Revolution. Clemenceau had used much the same tactic against Wilson at Versailles.

On November 5, the United States proposed a resolution giving Iraq a "final opportunity" to disarm or face "serious consequences"—in other words, military action. Secretary of State Colin Powell and other American officials made sure that everybody understood this U.S. interpretation. When the Security Council approved Resolution 1441 by a vote of 15–0 on November 8, there could be no mistaking what it meant: The United States had won multilateral authorization to go to war if Iraq continued to behave as it had for a decade. It was a tremendous diplomatic triumph, or so it seemed.

Iraq needed only a month to show that it had no intention of meeting its new obligations. One of these, the submission of a detailed weapons report to the United Nations, was disgorged on December 8—all 12,000 pages of it. Inspections chief Hans Blix reviewed the massive document and said that it "failed to answer a great many questions." Although this alone would have been enough to trigger Resolution 1441's "serious consequences," there were other breaches as well. Investigators turned up evidence that Iraq had bought missile engines and fuel. They also found a dozen warheads designed for chemical weapons. All were flagrant violations of the UN decree.

While the United States gathered its military strength in the region, France saw the interlude as an opportunity to undermine Resolution 1441. As it happened, France was scheduled to chair the Security Council in January 2003. On the twentieth, it called a meeting, supposedly to discuss terrorism. The night before, Powell listened to his French counterpart Villepin discuss the French public's opposition to war. Most Americans continued to support the Bush administration's stance, but Villepin pressed his point. "Listen to the world's people," he lectured Powell, as if American foreign policy should be dictated by polls in other countries.[53]

At the meeting the next day, France sprang what the *Washington Post* labeled, "a diplomatic version of an ambush."[54] The French had no intention of discussing anything but Iraq, and they used the occasion to announce their opposition to military force, no matter what Resolution 1441 said. "If war is the only way to resolve this problem, we are going down a dead end," said Villepin.[55] "As long as you can make progress with the inspectors and get cooperation, there's no point in choosing the worst possible solution—military intervention."[56] French resistance was so strong, said Villepin, that he could not even imagine a circumstance in which it might be necessary: "We believe that today nothing justifies envisaging military action."[57]

Although blindsided by the French, Powell responded with vigor: "We cannot be shocked into impotence because we are afraid of the difficult choices that are ahead of us."[58] In truth, French intransigence actually made war more likely because it demonstrated to Hussein once again that the Security Council was divided. Even as Villepin was springing his trap in New York—an action that earned him the nickname "Slick Villy"—Iraq was imposing conditions on surveillance planes that the inspectors deemed a further violation of 1441.

On January 21, President Bush made a blunt assessment of the situation. "It is clear to me now that [Hussein] is not disarming," he said. "This looks like a rerun of a bad movie and I'm not interested in watching it."[59] He expanded on this thought the next day: "If Saddam Hussein will not disarm, the United States and friends of freedom will disarm Saddam Hussein."[60] Spoken for the benefit of the Iraqi dictator, these lines were a stark statement of American resolve, in case Hussein suffered under any illusions that opposition to his regime was about to fade away. Powell had his own words for the French: "There are some nations in the world who would like simply to turn away from this problem, pretend it isn't there."[61]

At this point, France returned to its tired practice of accusing the United States of unilateralism, even though the Americans and British had assembled a large coalition of countries favoring Hussein's forced removal, including Australia, Italy, Spain, and much of Eastern Europe. When Secretary of Defense Donald Rumsfeld characterized those opposing the war as "old Europe," many, including the French, were stunned.[62] Chirac, after all, still clung to the Gaullist fantasy that all of Europe might fall in line behind his leadership and unite against the American behemoth. In February, Chirac became so upset with the Czech Republic, Hungary, Poland, and a dozen other European countries that he flew into a rage: "It is not really responsible behavior," he said of their public support for the United States. "It is not well-brought-up behavior. They missed a good opportunity to keep quiet."[63] He also threatened countries seeking to join the European Union that they might not be welcome if they failed to obey Paris. Although most officials held their tongues, several spoke out against Chirac's intemperance. "We are not joining the EU so we can sit and shut up," said Czech foreign minister Cyril Svoboda.[64] Several months later, when France criticized Silvio Berlusconi for refusing to meet with Yassir Arafat on a tour of the Middle East, the Italian prime minister threw Chirac's words right back at him. The French, he said, had missed a good opportunity to keep quiet.

Relations between the United States and France had almost reached the point of no return. On February 9, a Monday, Powell gave Iraq until the weekend to disarm. It was a last-ditch effort to let France save face by saying it had bought Hussein a little more time before joining the international coalition against Iraq. France, however, insisted on allowing more time for inspections. The difficulty was not that Chirac doubted the contents of Hussein's arsenal: "There is a problem—the probable possession of weapons of mass destruction by an uncontrollable country," he said. "The international community is right to be disturbed by this situation, and it's right in having decided Iraq should be disarmed."[65] The question for Chirac was how to achieve disarmament, and he believed a new round of inspections at last might succeed, despite their long track record of failure. In the coming weeks, Chirac hardened his position, and France moved from merely opposing the United States to actively obstructing its goals.

As the United States built its "coalition of the willing," France toiled to organize a coalition of the unwilling. Chirac's most important partners in opposition were Germany and Russia. The French president suddenly was living the Gaullist dream of dominating an alliance that stretched from the Atlantic to the Urals, but it was sheer fantasy. Although the Germans had bought into Chirac's vision of a Europe that would limit American influence in the world, the Russians certainly did not view themselves as taking orders from Paris. They merely believed that their own interests temporarily converged with those of the French. And Europe as a whole was far from unified, as the spat over "Old Europe" and "New Europe" demonstrated.

Yet France was able to complicate the efforts of the United States and its allies. In February, when Turkey asked its NATO allies to supply it with defensive equipment in case war broke out, France (along with Belgium and Germany) voted to deny the appeal. The French argued that honoring Turkey's request would acknowledge the inevitability of military conflict, and this was unacceptable. In reality, Paris was trying to thwart a country that might serve as a staging ground for invasion. Apparently it was not enough for the French to keep one foot outside of NATO: They also had to subvert it from within. The alliance ultimately approved sending Patriot missiles and other supplies, but only by routing the decision through a subcommittee where France had no say because it remained only a partial member of NATO. Two months later, a senior member of the Bush administration would call the episode "a significant crisis, probably the greatest in NATO history," because France had nearly blocked the alliance from assisting a member state in a time of need.[66]

France did not confine its troublemaking to Europe or NATO, either. At a summit meeting with African leaders in February, Chirac produced a document allegedly showing that more than fifty African countries supported the French position on Iraq. Three of them— Angola, Cameroon, and Guinea—then held rotating seats on the Security Council, so their opinions were especially important. Yet the document was a ruse. It merely stated that war should be considered only after all the alternatives had been exhausted, something the United States and its allies already believed had happened. Moreover, some leaders publicly denied that they had given France their support. "Nobody asked me my opinion," said President Paul Kagame of Rwanda. "We didn't even discuss it."[67] His government actually supported the United States. So did Eritrea, Ethiopia, and Uganda. Most of the rest, including the three on the Security Council, never declared themselves one way or the other.

On February 24, the United States, Britain, and Spain tendered a resolution holding Iraq in defiance of UN accords. The time at last had come for Hussein's regime to face "serious consequences." France countered with a proposal to allow four more months of inspections, followed by a new round of chatter at the UN. This was totally unacceptable to the Americans and their allies, but they still hoped that France might be enticed to join their cause. On March 7, they offered Iraq ten more days to comply. Then Chirac finally announced that France would veto any new resolution threatening war against Iraq.

On March 16, Vice President Dick Cheney found it "difficult to take the French seriously and believe that this is anything other than just further delaying tactics."[68] That same day, Bush met with Blair and Spanish prime minister José María Aznar in the Azores, where they agreed to spend one more day trying to persuade Security Council members to support military intervention. "Tomorrow is a moment of truth for the world," said Bush. The three leaders were especially frustrated with France and its veto threat. "We have an expression in Texas that says 'Show your cards,'" said Bush at a press conference. "France has shown its card. Now we have to see tomorrow what that card meant."[69] All Villepin could do was quibble about the use of an American idiom. "This expression is unfortunate," he sniffed. "I don't think we can compare war to any kind of game. It's not a game."[70]

Chirac did make a final plea to avoid war and offered a one-month deadline for inspections. But by now the French position had slipped into caricature, and the Americans had stopped paying attention. On March 18, the day before the war began, Chirac went on national television to condemn the United States for acting "outside the authority of the United Nations."[71] The criticism from Paris continued even after the first bombs started falling. On March 27, when the war was barely a week old, Villepin gave a speech blasting American foreign policy. Afterward, a British reporter asked him if he wanted the U.S.-led forces to prevail. "I'm not going to answer," Villepin snapped, "because you have not listened carefully to what I have said before." A simple "yes" would have cleared up the considerable confusion that followed. As the *New York Times* pointed out, the text of Villepin's speech "gave no particular clue as to what he meant," except for a picayune comment hoping for "a swift conclusion with the minimum possible number of casualties."[72] The French minister's apparent indifference (if not antagonism) to American victory over Iraq was widely reported around the United States. The next day, under obvious pressure, Villepin insisted that France wished for an American victory. Yet many French hoped for a U.S. defeat—25 percent of them, according to one survey.[73]

That victory came after three weeks of fighting. In Baghdad, jubilant Iraqis pulled down a statue of the tyrant who had oppressed them for more than twenty years. Hussein went into hiding. As the United States and its allies struggled to restore order in a nation whose civil society had been systematically destroyed, the French government said that it found the war's outcome pleasing, or at least an undeniable fact. "We can clearly see that the page on Iraq has been turned and now we must look towards the future," said Villepin.[74]

Within a few weeks, however, the French were back to their old games. In May, their ambassador to the United States, Jean-David Levitte, distributed a letter accusing the Bush administration and the American media of waging a "disinformation campaign aimed at sullying France's image and misleading the public."[75] In June, Chirac reiterated his view that the war was "illegitimate and illegal."[76] Then, over the summer, France demanded that the United States transfer governing authority to the Iraqis by the fall. This obviously impractical proposal was aimed at making France appear to be the champion and friend of Arab peoples. Having done everything in their power to prop up the previous regime, the French now saw fit to lecture Iraq's liberators on creating a new one. They also took a perverse delight in the American failure to discover weapons of mass destruction, as if evidence of a somewhat less imminent threat meant that Iraq was no threat at all or that the world had not become a safer place following the end of Hussein's rule.

But the French were living in a spider hole of denial. By the end of the year, Saddam Hussein had been captured. Despite continued violence inside Iraq, Americans were making significant progress in the war on terror around the world. Pakistan was helping track down al Qaeda renegades who had previously operated inside its borders with impunity. The government also admitted that its scientists had contributed to nuclear proliferation. Iran opened its secret nuclear program to international weapons inspectors and agreed to stop enriching uranium. Relations with Syria began to thaw, however slightly. Most important was a development in Libya, where America's old scourge Muammar al-Qaddafi announced his intention to abolish his program of nuclear-weapons development. Soon after, UN inspectors were surprised to learn that Qaddafi was just a few years away from building a bomb. He had accumulated huge quantities of uranium-processing equipment, and his country had even produced a small amount of plutonium. The man who had sponsored so much terrorism in the past had stood on the threshold of unprecedented power, and yet he stepped back from the brink. He knew that the United States and its allies, after their striking display of resolve in Iraq, would not allow a rogue regime like his own to develop such deadly capabilities. Qaddafi decided the time had come to disarm. It was one retreat the French simply did not know how to explain.

CONCLUSION

THE FRENCH DECISION

O N NOVEMBER 24, 2003, six Democratic presidential candidates gathered in Des Moines, Iowa, to debate prescription drugs, free trade, and foreign policy. Two more joined them by way of video hookup, including Massachusetts senator John Kerry. About midway through the forum, moderator Tom Brokaw asked a question of Kerry: "What about the French? Are they friends? Are they enemies? Or something in-between at this point?"

"The French are the French," Kerry responded, in a line that drew knowing laughter from the audience. "Very profound, Senator," said Brokaw to more chuckles. "Well, trust me," explained Kerry, "it has a meaning and I think most people know exactly what I mean."[1]

Seven months after the successful completion of Operation Iraqi Freedom, most Americans perhaps would have shown more candor: The French had been insufferable obstructionists during the recent crisis and had behaved nothing like the age-old allies they so often claimed to be. When Kerry went on to promise that his presidential goals included patching up relations with Paris, many of his listeners must have wondered whether that was really possible.

More than thirty years earlier, another man who had served as a senator from Massachusetts, John F. Kennedy, made a celebrated state visit to France with his glamorous French-speaking wife, Jacqueline. Although most of the press coverage focused on how the former Miss Bouvier had captivated Charles de Gaulle and the French public with her beauty, style, and charm—the president would jokingly introduce himself as "the man who accompanied Jacqueline Kennedy to Paris"—few remember that relations between France and the United States deteriorated in those same years. When Kennedy was assassinated, de Gaulle was in the first row of world leaders who followed the caisson on foot to Arlington National Cemetery. Yet in reality he had little respect for the inexperienced young leader and had spurned Kennedy's attempts to draw the French into a closer alliance with the United States, a rejection that culminated several years later in the dramatic French decision to abandon NATO.

Can France ever become America's steadfast ally? The lessons of history call for cautious pessimism. For three centuries, the French have pursued their perceived self-interest with little regard for any supposed ties to their North American "allies." More often than not, they have treated Americans as their inferiors, criticized their culture, maneuvered against them across the globe, threatened hostilities, and, in several instances, engaged them in bloody combat. Many of these disputes were kept partially hidden from the public, such as when Georges Clemenceau tangled with Woodrow Wilson at the Versailles peace talks or when Charles de Gaulle clashed with Franklin Roosevelt during the Second World War. At other times, disagreements between the two countries burst into full view, such as during the XYZ Affair of 1798 or, most recently, when Jacques Chirac sought to derail American efforts to remove Saddam Hussein.

There have been periods of relative amity as well. In the late nineteenth and early twentieth centuries, America's most important ambassadors to France were not government officials but writers, artists, and tourists, and relations between the two countries were defined largely by cultural exchange. In the 1970s, following the death of de Gaulle, Richard Nixon succeeded in strengthening bonds between France and the United States when he simultaneously pursued détente with the Soviet Union.

After the successful invasion of Iraq in 2003, initial signs hinted at superficial improvements in relations. This was perhaps inevitable as the immediacy of the war loosened its grip on the American conscience and bracing examples of French intransigence no longer led the evening news. Consumers lost interest in boycotting French products, late-night jokes about France began to peter out, and freedom fries became french fries once more.

Yet there were numerous reminders that the successful ouster of Saddam Hussein had resolved nothing between the two countries. "A war that lacks legitimacy does not acquire legitimacy just because it has been won," said Chirac a few days before his first postwar meeting with George W. Bush.[2] Perhaps even more maddening was the French insistence that their opposition to the war had actually been an act of true loyalty. "I think we are the best ally of the U.S. in this war," said France's ambassador to the United States, Jean-David Levitte, in a speech at Harvard.[3] Those who disagreed were tutted like children: "I don't understand why there was so much French-bashing. It seems to me that in a family, there may be disagreements. . . . But that is no reason to insult us."[4] On another occasion, Levitte ascribed dark motives to American critics of French policy: "When you insult the French people, simply because they are French, then it's kind of a racist campaign."[5]

But French actions after the war continued to display the antagonism and hypocrisy that had come before it. Although they never had demonstrated a sincere interest in Iraqi democracy during Saddam Hussein's brutal dictatorship, the French suddenly cast themselves as the champions of the Iraqi people in a cynical bid to thwart U.S. plans. Foreign Minister Dominique de Villepin demanded an immediate transfer of sovereignty to a nonexistent provisional government, to be followed by elections that would occur much sooner than the American-led coalition thought possible. For *New York Times* columnist Thomas L. Friedman, the true breaking point with Paris came not during the escalation to war, but in its aftermath: "It's time we Americans came to terms with something: France is not just our annoying ally. It is not just our jealous rival. France is becoming our enemy."[6]

Perhaps most frustrating of all, the French grew increasingly sure of themselves and their anti-American policy as the United States and its allies began to experience problems in the wake of major combat operations. As terrorist attacks and guerrilla ambushes increased, Hussein remained at large for months and investigators learned that Iraq's weapons programs did not appear to be as advanced as prewar intelligence estimates had indicated. There was a growing sense in Paris and elsewhere that the French had been right all along.

But had they been right? After all, a full accounting of Iraqi weapons became available only through American resolve and battlefield success. "We don't need more inspectors with flashlights," said Dutch minister of foreign affairs Jaap de Hoop Scheffer a month before the invasion. "We need Saddam to turn the lights on."[7] But the dictator had chosen to keep the world in the dark. It took a force of arms, rather than a UN mandate, to shine the klieg lights on a totalitarian society and discover its true nature, which included mass graves, a safe haven for terrorists like Abu Nidal, and a chilling fascination with the most lethal weapons ever invented. Hussein's removal also provided the West with an unprecedented opportunity to coax the Arab states of the Middle East away from despotism and toward democracy, an interest the French have done precious little to advance despite their avowed concern for the people of the region.

Regime change in Iraq has made the world a decidedly safer place, though the French are loath to admit it. Just as American commitments to the defense of Western Europe gave de Gaulle the freedom to pursue his shameless diplomatic freelancing during the Cold War, present-day French grandstanding is performed within a womb of security built, maintained, and paid for by the citizens of the United States.

This latest episode of French intransigence may be explained at least in part by domestic politics, which are increasingly shaped by a growing population of French Muslims—currently 5 million in number, or about 8 percent of the country's population. Unlike the United States, France does not have a proven tradition of assimilating immigrants into the national culture and recently has resorted to desperate measures of coercion such as banning headscarves in public schools. These policies may ultimately backfire if they encourage Muslims to resist integration with renewed fervor. Perhaps Islam's true believers represent a unique challenge to models of assimilation that have worked with such success in the United States. Whatever the case, the political interests of French Muslims are sure to add an unhelpful dimension to Franco-American tensions in the years ahead as France's Muslim voters push their government toward more extreme manifestations of anti-Americanism.

Meanwhile, the French government has failed to grapple with a rising tide of anti-Semitism that is a direct product of the country's new demography. In 2002, arsonists destroyed the main synagogue in Marseilles. Jewish schools have suffered similar fates. The leading rabbi in Paris advised Jewish boys to wear hats over their yarmulkes so as not to draw attention to their Jewish identities. Although the curse of anti-Semitism is by no means confined to France, the French appear to suffer from it more than the rest of Europe. In the twenty-first century, the challenge for the French will be to overcome this burden before it becomes more deeply rooted in their national culture. Given their historic levels of anti-Semitic sentiment, however, it is not clear whether they have the will to do so.

In the end, it may not even matter whether France is an ally of the United States. For three centuries, the Franco-American rivalry has seen the French nation decline to a faint imprint of what it was in the age of the Bourbon kings. As the United States rose to the position of the world's most powerful country, France often has been relegated to the role of a mere irritant.

At other times, however, France has seriously threatened the security of the United States. If Napoleon III had persuaded the European powers to support the Confederacy in the Civil War or had succeeded in creating a French foothold in Mexico, the entire history of the United States would have been different. American democracy itself might have been imperiled. If the French had treated Franklin Roosevelt's advice regarding their Southeast Asian colonies with something other than contempt, one of the hottest and deadliest struggles of the Cold War might have been avoided and perhaps millions of lives saved—tens of thousands of them belonging to Americans. And if unforeseen circumstances had led the Soviet Union to invade Western Europe in the 1960s, no one can say for sure whether de Gaulle would have rushed to the aid of NATO forces or instead proven a tragic hindrance.

The future undoubtedly will bring new challenges, including many that cannot be anticipated. In a volatile world filled with dangerous regimes, it is reasonable to hope that the leading democratic nations of the West can work together in securing peace and prosperity against the challenges of terrorism, nuclear proliferation, and Islamic radicalism. In keeping with this, the United States has a clear incentive not to let Paris emerge as the capital city of a new axis of anti-Americanism. Democratic France must finally be persuaded that its long-term interests correspond with those of the United States and Britain. Yet given the distorted prism through which the French view their role in the world, this may be difficult. The basic problem with the French is not their blatant hypocrisy so much as the fact that they have adopted a shortsighted view of their own national interest, feeding on fantasies of greatness and living in denial about strategic realities that affect them profoundly.

Will the French continue to follow a path of narrowly defined self-interest or will they aspire to a foreign policy based on the shared values of the West? Will they remain chained to the cynicism of Talleyrand and Clemenceau or will they embrace the idealism of Lafayette? Will they awake from the anti-American delusions of Gaullism and Euro-leftism and see that the twenty-first century requires a wholly different vision? Will the French, in short, continue to be the French? In the end, the choice is theirs.

ACKNOWLEDGMENTS

N O BOOK IS the product of a single person—or in this case, two people. We owe many thanks to a long list of friends and colleagues who read drafts, chased down obscure references, and provided generous amounts of moral support: Andrew Alexander, Rachel Alexander, Alex Berenberg, David Bernstein, Bracy Bersnak, Nicholas Brown, Ed Capano, Linda Chavez, Jenny Choi, Roger Clegg, Gabriela de la Rosa, Brian Domitrovic, Donald Fleming, Chris Fortunato, Bruce Gibson, Arthur Herman, Brian Hooper, Russell Jenkins, Dominic Johnson, Meghan Keane, Richard Lowry, Suzanne Lye, Jennifer Marshall, Cliff May, Peter Miskech, Luke Moland, Kate O'Beirne, Andrew Pacelli, Ramesh Ponnuru, Kalev Sepp, Matthew Spalding, Bill Thomas, Søren Toft, Stephen J. Tonsor, Ken Weisbrode, James Justin Wilson, Ken Wilson, and Jay Winik.

Our resourceful agent, Michael Carlisle, was enthusiastic for this project from the start. We thank him for his unflagging encouragement as well as his diligence in guiding us through the puzzling world of book publishing.

Our outstanding editor, Adam Bellow, gave of his deep reservoir of historical knowledge and helped us write the best book we possibly could and a much better one than we would have written without him. We are also grateful to Doubleday for its unstinting support and creative input.

We owe a special thanks to the *Michigan Review*, a student publication at the University of Michigan and a member of the Collegiate Network. If it did not exist, we might never have met as undergraduates—and we surely would not have run into each other at a reunion dinner in Ann Arbor, where the idea of this book was hatched.

The uncredited authors of any book are family. Amy Miller put up with a husband scribbling away for long stretches at odd hours. Brendan, Josie, and Patrick Miller tolerated a father writing a book of his own when they probably thought he should have been reading other people's books to them.

Mary Jane Molesky, Thomas Molesky, and Jonathan Molesky are owed more than a son and brother can adequately express. Their generous helpings of enthusiasm and encouragement sustained the author during long hours of writing and research.

NOTES

INTRODUCTION: "A WAR WITHOUT DEATH"

1. William Drozdiak, "World Leaders Condemn Carnage, Take Precautions," *Washington Post*, September 11, 2001, p. A20.

2. White House press release, "President Chirac Pledges Support," September 18, 2001. http://www.whitehouse.gov/news/releases/2001/09/20010918-8.html

3. Elaine Sciolino, "In France, Glory Meets Fear," *New York Times*, October 13, 2002, section 4, p. 5.

4. An English-language translation of the column may be read here: http://www.worldpress.org/1101we_are_all_americans.htm

5. Fouad Ajami, "The Falseness of Anti-Americanism," *Foreign Policy*, September/October 2003, pp. 52–61.

6. Kevin Phillips on *Morning Edition*, National Public Radio, March 4, 2003.

7. Josephine Humphreys, "No Reason to Spoil a Friendship," *New York Times*, April 6, 2003, section 5, p. 15.

8. Remarks at U.S.-CREST Franco-American Seminar Series, April 29, 1998, http://www.ttc.org/cgi-binloc/getfile.cgi?0+richard.htm

9. Carla Power, "Chirac's Great Game," *Newsweek*, April 28, 2003, p. 34.

10. Laura Secor, "Lionel Jospin Questions Bush, Chirac," *Boston Globe*, December 7, 2003.

11. Quoted in speech by French ambassador to the United States François Bujon de l'Estang, November 15, 2001. See "Might can be right," *Sunday Telegraph*, September 8, 2002, p. 20.

CHAPTER 1: OLD FRANCE IN THE NEW WORLD

1. John Demos, *The Unredeemed Captive: A Family Story from Early America*, New York: Alfred A. Knopf, 1994, p. 19. See also: Evan Haefeli and Kevin Sweeney, *Captors and Captures: The 1704 French and Indian Raid on Deerfield*, Amherst: University of Massachusetts Press, 2003.

2. Richard I. Melvoin, *New England Outpost: War and Society in Colonial Deerfield*, New York: W. W. Norton and Co., pp. 212–13. See also Edward P. Hamilton, *The French and Indian Wars: The Story of Battles and Forts in the Wilderness*, Garden City, N.Y.: Doubleday and Co., p. 48: "The total English losses this summer, both in slain and captured, were possibly in the nature of one hundred and fifty, mostly women, children, and old men. The attacks were usually made on lonely houses while the menfolk were absent."

3. Melvoin, pp. 220–21. These figures can vary. Demos puts them at 48 people killed and 112 captured. There are no accurate casualty figures for the French and Indians, though they may have suffered as many as several dozen deaths.

4. Demos, p. 23

5. Melvoin, p. 235.

6. Demos, p. 29.

7. Crane Brinton, *The Americans and the French*, Cambridge, Mass.: Harvard University Press, 1968, p. 50.

8. H. W. Brands, *The First American: The Life and Times of Benjamin Franklin*, New York: Doubleday, 2000, p. 234.

9. James Thomas Flexner, *George Washington: The Forge of Experience (1732–1775)*, Boston: Little, Brown, and Co., 1965, p. 86.

10. When Washington's remark was printed in a London magazine, King George II replied: "He would not think so if he had been used to hear many."

11. Flexner, p. 86.

12. Fred Anderson, *Crucible of War: The Seven Years' War and the Fate of Empire in British North America, 1754–1766*, New York: Alfred A. Knopf, 2000, p. 65.

13. Gilbert F. Leduc, *Washington and the "Murder of Jumonville,"* Boston: Le Société Historique, Franco-Americaine, 1943, p. 195.

14. Flexner, p. 105.

15. Douglas Southal Freeman, *Washington*, New York: Simon & Schuster, 1968, p. 63.

16. Flexner, p. 92.

17. Ian K. Steele, *Betrayals: Fort William Henry and the "Massacre,"* New York: Oxford University Press, 1990, p. 76.

18. Anderson, p. 151.

19. Anderson, p. 190.

20. Hamilton, p. 198. See also Louis-Antoine de Bougainville, *Adventures in the Wilderness: The American Journals of Louis Antoine de Bougainville, 1756–1760*, translated and edited by Edward P. Hamilton, Norman: University of Oklahoma Press, 1964.

21. Hamilton, p. 203.

22. Anderson, p. 156.

23. Hamilton, p. 203.

24. Hamilton, p. 209.

25. Hamilton, p. 206.

26. Hamilton, p. 207.

27. Technically, France ceded Louisiana to Spain in 1762 at the secret Treaty of Fontainebleau; the transfer was made public at the Treaty of Paris. By giving away Louisiana, France hoped both to prevent it from going to Britain and to curry favor with the Spaniards.

CHAPTER 2: REVOLTING ALLY

1. Thomas A. Bailey, *A Diplomatic History of the American People*, 2nd ed., New York: F. S. Crofts & Co., p. 28, note 10. Alternate translation in Arthur Burr Darling, *Our Rising Empire, 1763–1803*, New Haven, Conn.: Yale University Press, 1940, p. 26: "We do not desire by a great deal that the rising new republic remain exclusive mistress of this whole immense continent."

2. H. W. Brands, *The First American: The Life and Times of Benjamin Franklin*, New York: Doubleday, 2000, p. 542.

3. C. H. Van Tyne, "Influences Which Determined the French Government to Make the Treaty with America, 1778," *American Historical Review*, volume 21, issue 3 (April 1916), p. 529.

4. Russell Kirk, *Edmund Burke: A Genius Reconsidered*, Wilmington, Del.: Intercollegiate Studies Institute, 1997, p. 64.

5. Edward S. Corwin, *French Policy and the American Alliance of 1778*, Hamden, Conn.: Archon Books, 1962, pp. 57–58.

6. Corwin, p. 56.

7. Samuel Flagg Bemis, *The Diplomacy of the American Revolution: The Foundations of American Diplomacy, 1775–1823*, New York: D. Appleton-Century Company, pp. 17–18, note 6.

8. Bemis, p. 24.

9. Bailey, pp. 18–19.

10. Van Tyne, p. 539.

11. Darling, p. 25.

12. Bailey, p. 20.

13. Gilbert Chinard, ed., *George Washington as the French Knew Him: A Collection of Texts*, New York: Greenwood Press, 1969, p. 30.

14. William C. Stinchcombe, *The American Revolution and the French Alliance*, Syracuse, N.Y.: Syracuse University Press, 1969, p. 18.

15. Stinchcombe, p. 19.

16. James Breck Perkins, *France in the American Revolution*, Boston: Houghton Mifflin, 1911, p. 189.

17. Stinchcombe, p. 28.

18. James Thomas Flexner, *George Washington: In the American Revolution (1775–1783)*, Boston: Little, Brown, and Company, 1967, p. 325.

19. Harlow Giles Unger, *Lafayette*, Hoboken, N.J.: John Wiley and Sons, 2002, p. 81.

20. Flexner, p. 326.

21. Unger, p. 82.

22. Piers Mackesy, *The War for America, 1775–1783*, Cambridge, Mass.: Harvard University Press, 1964, p. 218.

23. Stinchcombe, p. 53.

24. Stinchcombe, p. 51.

25. Stinchcombe, p. 52.

26. Mackesy, p. 232.

27. Evan Thomas, *John Paul Jones: Sailor, Hero, Father of the American Navy*, New York: Simon and Schuster, 2003, pp. 191–92.

28. Thomas, p. 265.

29. Perkins, p. 456.

30. Samuel Eliot Morison, *The Oxford History of the American People*, New York: Oxford University Press, New York: Oxford University Press, 1982, p. 262.

31. Stinchcombe, p. 27.

32. Stinchcombe, p. 196.

33. Bailey, p. 31.

34. Stinchcombe, p. 202.

35. Robert Middlekauff, *The Glorious Cause: The American Revolution, 1763–1789*, New York: Oxford University Press, 1982, p. 401.

36. Stinchcombe, p. 201.

37. Bailey, p. 18, note 20.

CHAPTER 3: THE FIRST FOREIGN SUBVERSIVE

1. Thomas A. Bailey, *A Diplomatic History of the American People*, 2nd ed., New York: F. S. Crofts and Co., 1942, p. 76.

2. James Thomas Flexner, *George Washington: Anguish and Farewell*, Boston: Little, Brown, and Company, 1972, p. 42.

3. Genet's last name is often spelled with an accent: Genêt. This usage is a twentieth-century invention and not correct. See Harry Ammon, *The Genet Mission*, New York: W. W. Norton and Co., 1973, p. vii, note 1.

4. Merrill D. Peterson, *Thomas Jefferson and the New Nation: A Biography*, London: Oxford University Press, 1970, pp. 385, 480. On another occasion, Jefferson famously said: "The tree of liberty must be refreshed from time to time with the blood of patriots and tyrants." These words are commonly believed to refer to the French Revolution. In fact, they were related to Shays' Rebellion in the United States.

5. Matthew Spalding and Patrick J. Garrity, *A Sacred Union of Citizens: George Washington's Farewell Address and the American Character*, Lanham, Md.: Rowman and Littlefield, 1996, p. 134.

6. Flexner, p. 37.

7. David McCullough, *John Adams*, New York: Simon and Schuster, 2001, pp. 417–18.

8. Alexander Hamilton, "The Spectacle of Revolutionary France," in Russell Kirk, ed., *The Portable Conservative Reader*, New York: Penguin Books, 1982, p. 79.

9. Harry Ammon, *The Genet Mission*, New York: W. W. Norton and Co., 1973, p. 2.

10. Meade Minnigerode, *Jefferson, Friend of France, 1793: The Career of Edmond Charles Genet*, New York: G. P. Putnam's Sons, 1928, p. 117.

11. Charles Marion Thomas, *American Neutrality in 1793: A Study in Cabinet Government*, New York: Columbia University Press, 1931, p. 82.

12. Marge Howlett Woodfin, "Citizen Genet and His Mission," Ph.D. dissertation, University of Chicago, August 1928, p. 121. This dissertation is an important source on Genet; among other original observations, it shows that Genet did not meet with acclaim everywhere he traveled.

13. Ammon, pp. 55–56.

14. Flexner, pp. 44–45.

15. Flexner, p. 45.

16. Charles Marion Thomas, *American Neutrality in 1793: A Study in Cabinet Government*, New York: Columbia University Press, 1931, p. 92.

17. Thomas, pp. 120–21.

18. Ammon, p. 73.

19. Ammon, p. 74.

20. Harold Cecil Vaughan, *The Citizen Genet Affair, 1793: A Chapter in the Formation of American Foreign Policy*, New York: Franklin Watts, 1970, p. 29.

21. Thomas, pp. 138–39.

22. Flexner, p. 57.

23. Flexner, p. 58.

24. Flexner, p. 59.

25. Ammon, p. 108.

26. Donald Barr Chidsey, *Louisiana Purchase*, New York: Crown Publishers, 1972, p. 93.

27. Woodfin, p. 551.

28. Daniel J. Boorstin, ed., *An American Primer*, New York: New American Library, 1966, p. 224.

CHAPTER 4: FIRST IN WAR

1. Thomas A. Bailey, *A Diplomatic History of the American People*, 2nd ed., New York: F. S. Crofts and Co., 1942, p. 73.

2. George Washington, letter to Congress, January 4, 1796.

3. Alexander DeConde, *Entangling Alliance: Politics and Diplomacy Under George Washington*, Durham, N.C.: Duke University Press, 1958, p. 436. The rodents and insects, in fact, may have made a meal of it, as the whereabouts of Adet's gift are currently unknown.

4. James Thomas Flexner, *George Washington: Anguish and Farewell*, Boston: Little, Brown, and Company, 1972, p. 324.

5. Gilbert Chinard, *George Washington as the French Knew Him: A Collection of Texts*, New York: Greenwood Press, 1969.

6. DeConde, *Entangling Alliance*, p. 428.

7. Chinard, p. 109.

8. Alexander DeConde, *The Quasi-War: The Politics and Diplomacy of the Undeclared War with France, 1797–1801*, New York: Charles Scribner's Sons, 1966, p. 9.

9. DeConde, *Entangling Alliance*, p. 496.

10. DeConde, *Entangling Alliance*, p. 457.

11. Evan Cornog and Richard Whelan, *Hats in the Ring: An Illustrated History of American Presidential Campaigns*, New York: Random House, 2000, p. 12.

12. David McCullough, *John Adams*, New York: Simon and Schuster, 2001, pp. 443–44.

13. DeConde, *Entangling Alliance*, p. 440.

14. DeConde, *Entangling Alliance*, p. 475.

15. John Patrick Diggins, *John Adams*, New York: Times Books, 2003, p. 74.

16. DeConde, *Entangling Alliance*, p. 488.

17. DeConde, *The Quasi-War*, p. 23.

18. DeConde, *The Quasi-War*, p. 25.

19. Jean Edward Smith, *John Marshall: Definer of a Nation*, New York: Henry Holt and Company, 1996, p. 194.

20. J. F. Bernard, *Talleyrand: A Biography*, New York: G. P. Putnam's Sons, 1973, p. 207n.

21. DeConde, *The Quasi-War*, p. 48.

22. DeConde, *The Quasi-War*, p. 49.

23. William Stinchcombe, *The XYZ Affair*, Westport, Conn.: Greenwood Press, 1980, p. 58. See also DeConde, pp. 50–51.

24. Smith, pp. 217–18. Smith describes the evidence of a romance as "circumstantial." "It would be surprising if Marshall had not been attracted to Madame de Villette. . . . If [they] were intimate, it would not have been an unusual occurrence in the Paris of the 1790s. But whatever the extent of their relationship, it remained private, and the attachment, if there was one, ended when Marshall returned to America."

25. DeConde, *The Quasi-War*, p. 53.

26. DeConde, *The Quasi-War*, p. 62.

27. On June 18, 1798, Congressman Robert Goodloe Harper said: "Millions for defense, but not one cent for tribute." Matthew Spalding, ed., *The Founders' Almanac: A Practical Guide to the Notable Events, Greatest Leaders, and Most Eloquent Words of the American Founding*, Washington, D.C.: Heritage Foundation, 2001, p. 180.

28. McCullough, p. 500.

29. Thomas A. Bailey, *A Diplomatic History of the American People*, 2nd ed., New York: F. S. Crofts and Co., 1942, p. 85.

30. Michael A. Palmer, *Stoddert's War: Naval Operations During the Quasi-War with France, 1798–1801*, Columbia, S.C.: University of South Carolina Press, pp. 30–31.

31. McCullough, p. 504.

32. The nickname derives from its performance during the War of 1812; sailors on board the *Constitution* claimed that British shot could not penetrate "Old Ironsides." Today, the boat is a tourist attraction in Boston and about 20 percent of the timber is original—an astonishing fact given that a ship of its vintage was considered antiquated after three or four decades of service.

33. Palmer, p. 110.

34. "Any minister sent by the United States to France would be received with the respect due to the representative of a free, independent, and powerful nation," wrote Talleyrand, in language that echoed Adams's own demand. See James Alton James, "French Opinion as a Factor in Preventing War Between France and the United States, 1795–1800," *American Historical Review*, volume 30, issue 1 (October 1924), p. 54.

35. Bailey, p. 89.

CHAPTER 5: THE LONG SHADOW OF NAPOLEON

1. Charles A. Cerami, *Jefferson's Great Gamble: The Remarkable Story of Jefferson, Napoleon, and the Men Behind the Louisiana Purchase*, Naperville, Ill.: Sourcebooks, Inc., 2003.

2. Thomas Jefferson, letter to Madame de Staël, May 1813.

3. "In 1792 only a scant dozen flatboats came down to New Orleans from

the American West, and maritime commerce with the United States was prohibited. The one ship that sailed from New Orleans for a port of the United States in that year did so by special dispensation of the governor-intendant. In 1802, more than 550 river craft arrived at New Orleans from the American West, and more than half of the sea-going vessels in that port flew the American flag." Arthur Preston Whitaker, *The Mississippi Question, 1795–1803: A Study in Trade, Politics, and Diplomacy*, New York: Appleton-Century, 1934, p. 150.

4. George W. Kyte, "A Spy on the Western Waters: The Military Intelligence Mission of General Collot in 1796," *Mississippi Valley Historical Review*, volume 34, issue 3 (Dec. 1947), pp. 427–42.

5. E. Wilson Lyon, *Louisiana in French Diplomacy, 1759–1804*, Norman, Okla.: University of Oklahoma Press, 1934, p. 112.

6. Joseph J. Ellis, *American Sphinx: The Character of Thomas Jefferson*, New York: Vintage Books, 1998, p. 100.

7. Ellis, pp. 127–28.

8. Thomas Jefferson, *The Portable Thomas Jefferson*, ed. Merrill D. Peterson, New York: Penguin Books, 1975, p. 293.

9. Alexander DeConde, *The Quasi-War: The Politics and Diplomacy of the Undeclared War with France, 1797–1801*, New York: Charles Scribner's Sons, 1966, p. 315.

10. Cerami, p. 51.

11. Jefferson, pp. 485–88.

12. Ralph Ketchum, *James Madison: A Biography*, Charlottesville, Va.: University Press of Virginia, 1990, p. 417.

13. Lyon, p. 131.

14. Lyon, p. 196.

15. Ketchum, p. 418.

16. Dumas Malone, *Jefferson the President: First Term, 1801–1805*, Boston: Little, Brown, and Company, 1970, p. 286.

17. Jon Kukla, *A Wilderness So Immense: The Louisiana Purchase and the Destiny of America*, New York: Knopf, 2003, pp. 224–25.

18. Lyon, p. 194.

19. Felix Markham, *Napoleon*, New York: New American Library, 1963, p. 87.

20. Malone, p. 284.

21. Cerami, p. 237.

22. Lyon, p. 207.

23. Lyon, p. 206.

24. Cerami, p. 240.

25. Malone, p. 295.

26. Thomas Jefferson, letter to Robert Livingston, October 1808.

27. Samuel Flagg Bemis, *A Diplomatic History of the United States*, rev. ed., New York: Henry Holt and Company, 1942, p. 155.

28. Thomas A. Bailey, *A Diplomatic History of the American People*, 2nd ed., New York: F. S. Crofts and Co., 1942, p. 136.

29. Lawrence S. Kaplan, "France and Madison's Decision for War, 1812," *Mississippi Valley Historical Review*, volume 50, issue 4 (March 1964), p. 658.

30. Ketchum, p. 505.

31. Bailey, p. 136.

32. Napoleon's oldest brother, Joseph Bonaparte, lived mainly in New Jersey between 1815 and 1841. He died in Italy in 1844. Napoleon's youngest brother, Jérôme Bonaparte, served in the French navy and visited the United States in 1803, where he met and married Elizabeth Patterson at the age of nineteen. When the couple arrived on the shores of France in 1805, the emperor said his brother had been too young to marry and refused to let Elizabeth disembark. She left for England and gave birth to their son. The emperor annulled the marriage in 1806 and arranged for Jérôme to wed Catherine of Württemberg. Charles Joseph Bonaparte, the grandson of Jérôme and Elizabeth, was born in Baltimore and served in the administration of Theodore Roosevelt, first as navy secretary and later as a trust-busting attorney general.

33. Noble E. Cunningham Jr., *The Presidency of James Monroe*, Lawrence, Kan.: University Press of Kansas, 1996, pp. 159–60.

34. Bailey, pp. 189–90.

35. John M. Belohlavek, *"Let the Eagle Soar!" The Foreign Policy of Andrew Jackson*, Lincoln: University of Nebraska Press, 1985, p. 95. "*Collision* is one of diplomacy's less obscure synonyms for war." (Emphasis added.) See Marquis James, *Andrew Jackson: Portrait of a President*, New York: Grosset & Dunlap, 1971 [orig. 1937], p. 387.

36. Belohlavek, p. 115.

37. Robert V. Remini, *The Life of Andrew Jackson*, New York: Harper and Row, 1988, p. 290.

38. David B. Cole, *The Presidency of Andrew Jackson*, Lawrence: University Press of Kansas, 1993, p. 126.

39. He may not have said these exact words. Bailey, p. 202.

40. Remini, p. 292.

41. Bailey, p. 203.

42. Belohlavek, p. 122.

CHAPTER 6: THE NEXT NAPOLEON

1. Ulysses S. Grant, *Memoirs and Selected Letters*, New York: The Library of America, 1990, p. 776.

2. William S. McFeely, *Grant: A Biography*, New York: Norton, 1981, p. 221.

3. Grant, p. 775.

4. His full name was Charles-Louis-Napoleon Bonaparte; he was the son of the French emperor's brother, King Louis Bonaparte of Holland.

5. Daniel Dawson, *The Mexican Adventure*, London: G. Bell & Sons, 1935, pp. 48–49.

6. Dawson, p. 49.

7. Alfred Jackson Hanna and Kathryn Abbey Hanna, *Napoleon III and Mexico: American Triumph over Monarchy*, Chapel Hill: University of North Carolina Press, 1971, p. 8.

8. Robert E. May, *The Southern Dream of a Caribbean Empire, 1854–1861*, Athens, Ga.: University of Georgia Press, 1989, p. 8.

9. Elizabeth Brett White, *American Opinion of France from Lafayette to Poincaré*, New York: Alfred A. Knopf, 1927, p. 131.

10. There was a Napoleon II. He was born in 1811, the son of Napoleon I and Marie-Louise. Although he never ruled anything, he was variously known as the king of Rome, the prince of Parma, and the duke of Reichstadt. In 1832, at the age of twenty-one, he died of tuberculosis in Vienna. In 1940, Adolf Hitler had his remains moved to Paris as a gift to the French people.

11. Radepont received inspiration and support for his plan from the French minister to Mexico, the Vicomte de Gabriac. Nancy Nichols Barker, *The French Experience in Mexico, 1821–1861: A History of Constant Misunderstanding*, Chapel Hill: University of North Carolina Press, 1979, pp. 148–56.

12. Hanna and Hanna, p. 17.

13. Lynn Case and Warren Spencer, *The United States and France: Civil War Diplomacy*, Philadelphia: University of Pennsylvania Press, 1970, p. 50.

14. Belle Becker Sideman and Lillian Friedman, eds., *Europe Looks at the Civil War: An Anthology*, New York: Orion Press, 1960, pp. 76–77.

15. Case and Spencer, p. 333.

16. Case and Spencer, p. 333.

17. Case and Spencer, p. 341.

18. Case and Spencer, p. 514.

19. Hanna and Hanna, p. 73.

20. Hanna and Hanna, pp. 74–75.

21. Hanna and Hanna, p. 82.

22. E. C. Corti, *Maximilian and Charlotte of Mexico*, Volume 1, New York: Knopf, 1928, p. 332.

23. Hanna and Hanna, p. 183.

24. Hanna and Hanna, pp. 197–98.

25. White, p. 155.

26. One of them slipped through—but the C.S.S. *Stonewall* arrived in American waters only after the war was over. In its twenty-seven years of service, the ironclad flew six different flags and finished its career as a Japanese training vessel.

27. White, p. 157.

28. Glydnon G. Van Deusen, *William Henry Seward*, New York: Oxford University Press, 1967, p. 368.

29. Philip Henry Sheridan, *Personal Memoirs of P. H. Sheridan*, New York: Da Capo Press, 1992, p. 402.

30. Ephraim D. Adams, *Great Britain and the American Civil War*, volume 2, New York: Longmans, Green, 1925, p. 155.

31. Sheridan, p. 404.

32. Sheridan, p. 408.

33. Sheridan, p. 410.

34. Hanna and Hanna, p. 256.

35. Percy F. Martin, *Maximilian in Mexico: The Story of the French Intervention (1861–1867)*, London: Constable and Company, 1914, p. 390.

36. Hanna and Hanna, p. 301.

CHAPTER 7: DECADENCE AND DEMOCRACY

1. Mark Twain, *Notebooks and Journals, II (1877–1883)*, eds. Frederick Anderson, Lin Salamo, Bernard Stein, Berkeley: University of California Press, 1975, p. 320.

2. Glydnon G. Van Deusen, *William Henry Seward*, New York: Oxford University Press, 1967, p. 558.

3. Neil G. Kotler, "The Statue of Liberty as Idea, Symbol, and Historical Presence," in Wilton S. Dillon and Neil G. Kotler, eds., *The Statue of Liberty Revisited*, Washington, D.C.: Smithsonian Institution Press, 1994, p. 6.

4. Elizabeth Brett White, *American Opinion of France from Lafayette to Poincaré*, New York: Knopf, 1927, p. 124.

5. White, p. 179.

6. White, p. 184.

7. White, p. 184.

8. White, p. 209.

9. White, p. 210.

10. Marvin Trachtenberg, *The Statue of Liberty*, New York: Elizabeth Sifton Books, 1986, p. 31.

11. Alexis de Tocqueville, "On American Literature," in Sidney D. Braun and Seymour Lainoff, eds., *Transatlantic Mirrors: Essays in Franco-American Relations*, Boston: Twayne Publishers, 1978, p. 39.

12. Charles Baudelaire, "New Notes on Edgar Allan Poe," in Braun and Lainoff, p. 198.

13. Henry James believed that after the Civil War, Americans were free to "pick and choose" from the best of European culture. James Buzard, *The Beaten Track: European Tourism, Literature, and the Ways of Culture, 1800–1918*, Oxford: Oxford University Press, 1993, p. 224.

14. Henry James, *Portraits of Places*, London: Duckworth, 2001, p. 72.

15. Henry Adams, *The Education of Henry Adams*, Boston: Houghton Mifflin, 1961, p. 96.

16. Dixon Wecter, ed., *The Love Letters of Mark Twain*, New York: Harper, 1949, p. 313.

17. Mark Twain, "What Paul Bourget Thinks of Us," in Braun and Lainoff, p. 178.

18. Twain, *Notebooks & Journals*, II, p. 326.

19. Modris Eksteins, *Rites of Spring: The Great War and the Birth of the Modern*, New York: Houghton Mifflin, 1989, p. 47.

20. Eric C. Hansen, *Disaffection and Decadence: A Crisis in French Intellectual Thought, 1848–1898*, Washington, D.C.: University Press of America, 1982, p. 20.

21. Matei Calinescu, *Five Faces of Modernity: Modernism, Avant-Garde, Decadence, Kitsch, Postmodernism*, Durham, N.C.: Duke University Press, 1987, p. 112.

22. Henry Blumenthal, *American and French Culture, 1800–1900, Interchanges in Art, Science, Literature, and Society*, Baton Rouge: Louisiana State University Press, 1975, p. 286; Jean Renoir, *My Father*, Boston, pp. 252–53.

23. Blumenthal, p. 286; Robert H. Sherard, "American Artists in Paris," *Magazine of Art*, XVIII (1895), p. 225.

24. From January 1919 to July 1926, the exchange rate increased from 5.45 francs to the dollar to more than 50. In 1927, it would plateau at 25 francs, where it would stay into the 1930s. Tony Allan, *Americans in Paris*, Chicago: Contemporary Books, 1977, p. 13.

25. White, p. 231.

CHAPTER 8: GREAT WAR, POOR PEACE

1. Ray Stannard Baker, *Woodrow Wilson and World Settlement*, volume 2, New York: Doubleday, Page, and Company, 1923, p. 8.

2. Thomas Fleming, *The Illusion of Victory: America in World War I*,

New York: Basic Books, 2003, pp. 112–15; Frank E. Vandiver, *Black Jack: The Life and Times of John J. Pershing*, volume 2, College Station: Texas A&M University Press, 1977, pp. 715–22.

3. Fleming, p. 215.

4. It was Friday the 13th. Wilson considered the date a good omen. To him, thirteen was a lucky number—there were thirteen letters in his name. On his voyage to Brest, he had actually ordered his ship's captain to slow down because he did not want to arrive in France on the 12th.

5. Thomas A. Bailey, *A Diplomatic History of the American People*, 2nd ed., New York: F. S. Crofts & Co., p. 610.

6. Paul Johnson, *Modern Times: The World from the Twenties to the Eighties*, New York: Harper and Row, 1983, p. 23.

7. Fleming, p. 179.

8. Johnson, p. 24.

9. Johnson, p. 29.

10. Johnson, p. 23.

11. George Bernard Noble, *Policies and Opinions at Paris, 1919: Wilsonian Diplomacy, the Versailles Peace, and French Public Opinion*, New York: Macmillan Company, 1935, pp. 1–2.

12. Margaret MacMillan, *Paris 1919: Six Months That Changed the World*, New York: Random House, 2003, p. 27.

13. MacMillan, p. 27.

14. MacMillan, p. 30.

15. MacMillan, p. 30.

16. Fleming, p. 324.

17. Perhaps apocryphal. MacMillan, p. 27.

18. MacMillan, p. 31.

19. Bailey, p. 662.

20. Johnson, p. 24–25.

21. MacMillan, p. 174.

22. MacMillan, p. 174.

23. MacMillan, p. 197.

24. Baker, vol. 2, p. 34.

25. Baker, vol. 2, p. 35.

26. MacMillan, p. 199.

27. Fleming, p. 358.

28. Charles W. Brooks, *America in France's Hopes and Fears, 1890–1920*, vol. 2, New York: Garland Publishing, 1987, p. 645; Dorothy Shipley White, "Franco-American Relations in 1917–1918: War Aims and Peace Prospects," Ph.D. dissertation, University of Pennsylvania, 1954, pp. 475–86.

29. Baker, vol. 2, p. 40.

30. MacMillan, p. 200.

31. Baker, vol. 2, p. 45.

32. MacMillan, p. 200.

33. Fleming, pp. 375–76.

34. MacMillan, p. 461.

35. Fleming, p. 377.

36. MacMillan, p. 477.

37. In 1920, Clemenceau was defeated in the French presidential election and retired from politics. In November 1922, he toured the United States, including battlefields where French soldiers had fought during the American Revolution.

38. John Maynard Keynes, *The Economic Consequences of the Peace,* New York: Harcourt, Brace and Howe, 1920, p. 55.

39. Johnson, p. 27.

40. MacMillan, p. 479.

41. Charles Bracelen Flood, *Hitler: The Path to Power,* Boston: Houghton Mifflin, 1989, p. 60.

42. Flood, p. 97.

43. MacMillan, p. 483.

CHAPTER 9: FRENCH RESISTANCE

1. Frank Costigliola, *France and the United States: The Cold War Alliance Since World War II,* New York: Twayne Publishers, 1992, p. 39.

2. One secret army estimate warned of 1,700 killed and 4,000 wounded on the first day of combat in Morocco. Rick Atkinson, *An Army at Dawn: The War in North Africa, 1942–1943,* New York: Henry Holt and Company, 2002, p. 106.

3. Milton Viorst, *Hostile Allies: FDR and Charles de Gaulle,* New York: Macmillan Company, 1965, p. 101.

4. An opinion poll of North African residents ordered by President Roosevelt and administered by a Princeton, New Jersey, company had given added reason for optimism. See Atkinson, p. 27.

5. Atkinson, p. 73.

6. Atkinson, pp. 69–78. See also George F. Howe, *The Mediterranean Theatre of Operations, Northwest Africa: Seizing the Initiative in the West,* Washington, D.C.: Center of Military History, 1957, pp. 202–4.

7. Viorst, p. 114.

8. Atkinson, p. 136.

9. Henry Blumenthal, *Illusion and Reality in Franco-American Diplomacy, 1914–1945,* Baton Rouge, La.: Louisiana State University, 1986, p. 277.

10. Blumenthal, p. 296.

11. Atkinson, p. 106.

12. Artillery shells contained dye of various colors so that gunners could more easily make out the splash of near misses.

13. Atkinson, p. 136.

14. Atkinson, p. 150.

15. Blumenthal, p. 200.

16. Although the Germans had almost twice as many light tanks as their opponents, the French and British had nearly twice as many medium ones. And there was no comparison among heavy tanks. The French and British had 584; the Germans had none. Ernest R. May, *Strange Victory: Hitler's Conquest of France,* New York: Hill and Wang, 2000, p. 478.

17. James MacGregor Burns, *Roosevelt: The Lion and the Fox*, New York: Harcourt, Brace, and World, 1956, p. 395.

18. William L. Langer, *Our Vichy Gamble*, New York: Knopf, 1947, p. 5.

19. Julian Jackson, *The Fall of France: The Nazi Invasion of 1940*, Oxford: Oxford University Press, 2003, p. 224.

20. Paul Johnson, *Modern Times: The World from the Twenties to the Nineties*, New York: Harper Perennial Classics, 1992, p. 364.

21. Jackson, p. 11.

22. Blumenthal, p. 304.

23. Frank Friedel, *Franklin Roosevelt: A Rendezvous with Destiny*, Boston: Little, Brown, and Company, 1990, p. 333.

24. Viorst, p. 22.

25. For a classic contemporary account and analysis of France's defeat, see Marc Bloch, *Strange Defeat: A Statement of Evidence Written in 1940*, New York, W. W. Norton & Company, 1968.

26. "When I'm beaten here," de Gaulle quotes General Maxime Weygand as saying, "England won't wait a week to negotiate with the Reich." Viorst, p. 15.

27. Langer, p. 69.

28. Robert D. Paxton, *Vichy France: Old Guard and New Order*, New York: Columbia University Press, 1972, p. 8.

29. Langer, p. 52.

30. Paxton, p. 9.

31. Paxton, p. 9.

32. Martin Gilbert, *The Second World War: A Complete History*, New York: Henry Holt and Company, 1989, p. 102. On the visit to Paris, Hitler also ordered the body of Napoleon's son—the so-called Napoleon II—to be moved from Austria to France. Three years later, as Allied armies approached Paris, Hitler demanded that the city be razed to the ground. "Paris must not fall into the hands of the enemy, or, if it does, he must find there nothing but a field of ruins," said his directive. Thankfully, his order was disobeyed. See Larry Collins

and Dominique Lapierre, *Is Paris Burning?*, New York: Pocket Books, 1965.

33. The word "collaboration" appears in the armistice agreement.

34. Paxton, p. 144.

35. Blumenthal, p. 279.

36. Bertram M. Gordon, *Collaborationism in France During the Second World War*, Ithaca, N.Y.: Cornell University Press, 1980, pp. 244–78.

37. After the Liberation, Laval was tried for high treason. He was found guilty and sentenced to death. He was executed on October 15, 1945.

38. Michael R. Marrus and Robert O. Paxton, *Vichy France and the Jews*, New York: Basic Books, 1981. See also Lucy S. Dawidowicz, *The War Against the Jews, 1933–1945*, New York: Bantam Books, 1976, pp. 359–63.

39. Pétain was put on trial in France in 1945 for collaborating with the Nazis. He was condemned to death but immediately had his sentence commuted to a life sentence of solitary confinement. He was imprisoned on an island fortress and died in 1951, at the age of 95.

40. Charles de Gaulle, *The Complete War Memoirs of Charles de Gaulle*, vol. 1, New York: Simon and Schuster, 1964, p. 83.

41. Viorst, p. 2. See also Julius Jackson, *France: The Dark Years, 1940–1944*, New York: Oxford University Press, 2001, p. 389.

42. Costigliola, pp. 17–18. See also Douglas G. Anglin, *The St. Pierre and Miquelon Affair of 1941*, Toronto University Press, 1966.

43. Costigliola, p. 18.

44. Costigliola, p. 20.

45. Kenneth S. Davis, *FDR: The War President, 1940–1943*, New York: Random House, 2000, p. 661.

46. Davis, p. 709.

47. Costigliola, p. 23.

48. François Kersaudy, *Churchill and De Gaulle*, New York: Atheneum, 1983, p. 288.

49. Costigliola, p. 29.

50. Jean-Francois Revel, *Anti-Americanism*, San Francisco: Encounter Books, 2003, p. 52.

51. Marvin R. Zahniser, *Uncertain Friendship: American-French Diplomatic Relations Through the Cold War*, New York: John Wiley and Sons, 1975, p. 249.

52. Kersaudy, p. 347.

53. Costigliola, p. 30.

54. John S. D. Eisenhower, *General Ike: A Personal Remembrance*, New York: Free Press, 2003, p. 163.

55. Costigliola, p. 34.

56. Costigliola, p. 36.

57. Costigliola, p. 38.

58. Viorst, p. 234.

59. Costigliola, p. 39; Viorst, p. 238.

CHAPTER 10: FABLES OF THE DECONSTRUCTION

1. Tony Judt, *Past Imperfect: French Intellectuals, 1944–1956*, Berkeley: University of California Press, 1992, opening inscription. See also: François Furet, *The Passing of an Illusion: The Idea of Communism in the Twentieth Century*, Chicago: University of Chicago Press, 1999. David Caute, *The Fellow Travellers*, London: Weidenfeld and Nicolson, 1973. Jeannine Verdès-Leroux, *Au service du Parti: Le Parti communiste, les intellectuels et la culture (1945–1956)*, Paris: Fayerd-Minuit, 1983.

2. David P. Chandler, *Brother Number One: A Political Biography of Pol Pot*, Boulder, Colo.: Westview Press, 1992, pp. 27–31.

3. Richard Nixon, *No More Vietnams*, New York, 1985, p. 210.

4. See Karl D. Jackson, *Cambodia 1975–1978: Rendezvous with Death*, Princeton: Princeton University Press, 1989. See also Stephane Courtois, et al., *The Black Book of Communism: Crimes, Terror, Repression*, Cambridge: Harvard University Press, 1999, p. 577–635.

5. Stanley Karnow, *Vietnam: A History*, New York: Penguin Books, 1984, p. 131.

6. Hanna Batatu, *The Old Social Classes and the Revolutionary Movements of Iraq: A Study of Iraq's Old Landed and Commercial Classes and Its Communists, Ba'thists, and Free Officers*, Princeton, N.J.: Princeton University Press, 1978, p. 725.

7. Bernard Lewis, *The Crisis of Islam: Holy War and Unholy Terror*, New York: Modern Library, 2003, p. 70.

8. Merrill D. Peterson, *Thomas Jefferson and the New Nation: A Biography*, New York: Oxford University Press, 1970, p. 253.

9. Jean-Philippe Mathy, *Extrême Occident: French Intellectuals and America*, Chicago: University of Chicago Press, 1993, p. 27.

10. William Howard Adams, *The Paris Years of Thomas Jefferson*, New Haven, Conn.: Yale University Press, 1997, p. 131.

11. Mathy, p. 33.

12. Georges Duhamel, *America the Menace: Scenes from the Life of the Future*, Boston: Houghton Mifflin Company, 1931, pp. 200, 214.

13. Robert Aron and Arnaud Dandieu, *Le cancer américaine*, Paris: Les Editions Rieder, 1931, pp. 16–17.

14. Judt, p. 257.

15. Mathy, p. 38.

16. Judt, p. 154.

17. Judt, p. 161.

18. Judt, p. 156.

19. Judt, p. 126.

20. Paul Johnson, *Intellectuals*, New York: Harper & Row Publishers, 1988, p. 245.

21. For an excellent account of such left-wing pilgrimages, see Paul Hollander, *Political Pilgrims: Travels of Western Intellectuals to the Soviet Union, China, and Cuba 1928–1978*, Oxford: Oxford University Press, 1981.

22. Mathy, p. 154.

23. Judt, p. 185.

24. Judt, p. 180.

25. Mathy, p. 137.

26. Henry Astier, "La maladie française," *Times Literary Supplement*, January 10, 2003, pp. 3–4.

27. Marie-Christine Granjon, "Sartre, Beauvoir, Aron: An Ambiguous Affair," in Denis Lancorne, Jacques Rupnik, and Marie-France Toinet, eds., *The Rise and Fall of Anti-Americanism: A Century of French Perception*, New York: St. Martin's Press, 1990, p. 123.

28. Mathy, pp. 119–20.

29. Mathy, p. 34.

30. Tony Judt, *The Burden of Responsibility: Blum, Camus, Aron, and the French Twentieth Century*, Chicago: University of Chicago Press, 1998, pp. 142–43.

31. Lionel Trilling, *The Partisan Review*, "Our Country and Our Culture: A Symposium," May–June, 1952, p. 319.

32. Even the French Right, which is still influential in contemporary France, would say remarkably little. "The fate of those close to us," said one right-winger in 1952, "interests us more than the misfortunes of Czech and Jewish vermin. Those people poisoned Europe; they are now the source of our ills and their own enslavement." Judt, *Past Imperfect*, p. 184.

33. J. G. Merquior, *From Prague to Paris: A Critique of Structuralist and Post-structuralist Thought*, London: Verso, 1986, p. 135.

34. R. V. Young, *At War with the Word: Literary Theory and Liberal Education*, Wilmington, Del.: ISI Books, 1999, p. 21.

35. Roger Kimball, *Tenured Radicals: How Politics Has Corrupted Our Higher Education*, New York: Harper and Row, 1990, p. 102.

36. Young, p. 21.

37. George Watson, *The Literary Critics: A Study of English Descriptive Criticism*, London: Hogarth Press, 1986, p. 209.

CHAPTER 11: COLD WAR AGAINST AMERICA

1. Brian Crozier, *De Gaulle*, New York: Charles Scribner's Sons, 1973, p. 547.

2. Bernard B. Fall, *Hell in a Very Small Place: The Siege of Dien Bien Phu*,

New York: Da Capo Press, 1985, pp. 102, 155–56. See also Stanley Karnow, *Vietnam: A History*, New York: Penguin Books, 1984, p. 212.

3. Karnow, pp. 197–98.

4. Frank Costigliola, *France and the United States: The Cold War Alliance Since World War II*, New York: Twayne Publishers, 1992, p. 78.

5. Costigliola, p. 77.

6. Costigliola, p. 77.

7. Costigliola, p. 36.

8. John W. Young, *France, the Cold War and the Western Alliance 1944–49: French Foreign Policy and Post-War Europe*, New York: St. Martin's Press, 1990, pp. 23–24.

9. Costigliola, p. 47.

10. In 2004 dollars, that would be worth more than $75 billion.

11. They were also very strong in Italy, but the loss of France to Communism would have dealt a bigger blow.

12. Costigliola, pp. 66–67.

13. Costigliola, p. 67.

14. George C. Herring, *America's Longest War: The United States and Vietnam, 1950–1975*, 2nd edition, New York: Knopf, 1986, p. 6, note 4.

15. Paul Johnson, *Modern Times: The World from the Twenties to the Nineties*, Revised Edition, New York: Perennial, 2001, p. 149.

16. Geoffrey Perret, *Eisenhower*, New York: Random House, 1999, p. 466.

17. Young, p. 4.

18. Karnow, p. 147. See also Gary D. Hess, "Franklin D. Roosevelt and Indochina," *Journal of American History*, LIX, 1972, pp. 353–68.

19. Costigliola, p. 106.

20. Karnow, p. 203.

21. Karnow, p. 195.

22. Costigliola, p. 107.

23. Karnow, p. 193.

24. Herring, p. 36.

25. Hess, p. 366.

26. The U.S. Senate approved the Southeast Asia Collective Defense Treaty in February 1955. The treaty obligated the United States to aid member nations against Communist aggression.

27. Costigliola, p. 113.

28. Costigliola, p. 114.

29. Costigliola, p. 114.

30. Costigliola, p. 115.

31. David Reynolds, *One World Divisible: A Global History Since 1945*, New York: W.W. Norton, 2000, p. 95.

32. Costigliola, p. 47. Here is how Dean Rusk characterized de Gaulle in

his memoirs: "De Gaulle himself was a most extraordinary man, but what can a mere mortal say about Charles de Gaulle? I had many talks with him in the sixties, but I would hardly call them diplomatic exchanges. Talking with de Gaulle was like crawling up a mountainside on your knees, opening a little portal at the top, and waiting for the oracle to speak." See Dean Rusk, *As I Saw It*, New York: W.W. Norton, 1990, p. 268.

33. Rusk, p. 269.

34. Charles de Gaulle, *The Complete War Memoirs*, New York: Simon and Schuster, 1968, p. 1.

35. Costigliola, p. 121.

36. French nuclear forces reached their apogee in the early 1990s with approximately 500 warheads.

37. Crozier, p. 547.

38. Crozier, p. 548.

39. John Newhouse, *De Gaulle and the Anglo-Saxons*, New York: Viking, 1970, p. 146.

40. Costigliola, pp. 139–40.

41. Rusk, p. 270.

42. James Chace, *Acheson: The Secretary of State Who Created the American World*, New York: Simon & Schuster, 1998, pp. 416–17. Acheson also said of France leaving NATO: "It's a curious situation of a recovered patient, a convalescent who has been weak, who has been ill and has finally been built up and had good food and good care, been in a warm house and warm bed and suddenly says, 'I'm a big man, I don't need any more food, no more doctors, no more house, I want to get out in the wind and the rain, the ice, and the snow. I don't need any of this protection.'"

43. Rusk, p. 271.

44. Costigliola, p. 146.

45. Rusk, p. 249.

46. Henry Tanner, "Paris Due to Lift Arms Ban on Iraq in a Deal for Oil," *New York Times*, December 8, 1967, p. 2. The quote is from a speech by de Gaulle on November 27, 1967. This infamous comment prompted Raymond Aron to publish *De Gaulle, Israël et les juifs* (1968), expressing his outrage at the suggestion that Jews could not be fully French.

47. Roy Reed, "De Gaulle Scored by Congressman: Retaliation Against France Is Demanded Anew," *New York Times*, December 8, 1967, p. 26.

48. Costigliola, p. 146.

49. Gloria Emerson, "French Are Fearful of a U.S. Boycott," *New York Times*, December 29, 1967, p. 8.

50. Douglas Robinson, "Americans Voice Anger at De Gaulle, but Active Francophobia Seems Limited," *New York Times*, February 7, 1968, p. 4.

51. Emerson, p. 8.

52. Crozier, p. 520.

53. Costigliola, p. 163.

54. Costigliola, p. 180.

55. Jim Hoagland, "Remembering the 'Sphinx,'" *Washington Post,* January 9, 1996, p. A15. During the Los Angeles race riots of 1992, Mitterrand offered a left-wing critique of the mayhem: "It's very nice to promote the capital, profits, and investment in business, but these riots show that the social needs of any country must not be neglected. . . . American society is conservative and economically capitalist. Here are some of the results of that." "Bush proposes to offer no new initiatives," *Manchester Guardian Weekly,* May 10, 1992, p. 1.

56. "Paris to Try to Counter a Russian Space Shield," *New York Times,* November 13, 1985, p. A9.

CHAPTER 12: THE AGE OF TERROR

1. Peter Slevin, "U.S. and France Find Making Up Is Hard to Do," *Washington Post,* September 23, 2003, p. A1.

2. Joseph T. Stanik, *El Dorado Canyon: Reagan's Undeclared War with Qaddafi,* Annapolis, Md.: Naval Institute Press, 2003, pp. 142–44.

3. Stanik, p. 157.

4. Fred Hiatt, "Use of Air Force Planes Raises Questions," *Washington Post,* April 20, 1986, p. A24.

5. Ronald Reagan, *An American Life,* New York: Simon & Schuster, 1990, p. 519.

6. Caspar W. Weinberger, *Fighting for Peace: Seven Critical Years in the Pentagon,* New York: Warner Books, 1990, p. 195.

7. Reagan, p. 519.

8. "The number of terrorist incidents linked to Libya dropped from nineteen in 1986 to six each in 1987 and 1988." See Stanik, p. 227. There were 270 people killed on Pam Am Flight 103 and 170 people killed on UTA Flight 772.

9. Stanik, p. 173.

10. Edmund Burke, *Letters on a Regicide Peace,* 1795: "Thousands of those Hell-hounds called Terrorists . . . are let loose on the people."

11. Richard Bernstein, "The Terror: Why France? Why Now?" *New York Times Magazine,* October 19, 1986, p. 31.

12. Craig R. Whitney, "The Conservative 'Bulldozer': Jacques Rene Chirac," *New York Times,* May 8, 1995, p. A8.

13. Con Coughlin, *Saddam: King of Terror,* New York: HarperCollins, 2002, p. 134.

14. Rodger W. Claire, *Raid on the Sun: Inside Israel's Secret Campaign That Denied Saddam the Bomb,* New York: Broadway Books, 2004, p. 227. Reagan was not very upset by the raid. When reporters asked him about it, he respond-

ed with indifference: "Well, I haven't given very much thought to that particular question here." Then he added that he could not "envision Israel as being
a threat to its neighbors." Claire, p. 232.

15. William Drozdiak, "Gulf Crisis Ends 15 Years of French-Iraqi Closeness;
Paris Was Baghdad's Prime Patron in West," *Washington Post*, October 12, 1990,
p. A13.

16. Lawrence Freedman and Efraim Karsh, *The Gulf Conflict 1990–1991:
Diplomacy and War in the New World Order*, Princeton, N.J.: Princeton
University Press, 1993, pp. 23–24; Dilip Hiro, *Iraq: In the Eye of the Storm*, New
York: Thunder's Mouth Press, 2002, p. 160.

17. A few days later, the French newspaper *Le Monde* printed a cartoon on
France's long-standing ties to Hussein's regime. It was a picture of Western hostages
being taken away by an Iraqi tank labeled "Made in France." Alan Riding,
"Europe and Japan Support Embargo," *New York Times*, August 8, 1990, p. A10.

18. Stuart Wavell, "Breaking up is hard to do as Paris ends 20-year love affair
with Baghdad," *The Sunday Times*, August 26, 1990.

19. Wavell, August 26, 1990.

20. Freedman and Karsh, pp. 158–59.

21. E. Lauterpacht, C. J. Greenwood, Marc Weller, and Daniel Bethlehem
(eds.), *The Kuwait Crisis: Basic Documents*, Cambridge International Document
Series, vol. 1, Cambridge: Grotius Publications, 1991, pp. 287–88.

22. Freedman and Karsh, p. 167.

23. George Bush and Brent Scowcroft, *A World Transformed*, New York:
Knopf, 1998, p. 383.

24. Michael R. Gordon, "Iraqis Capture 3 French Soldiers and Return
Them to Diplomats," *New York Times*, November 3, 1990, p. A6.

25. Alan Riding, "French Maneuvering: Taking the Lead for Europe," *New
York Times*, January 6, 1991, p. A4.

26. Rone Tempest, "Ready to Fight to Free Kuwait, Mitterrand Says," *Los
Angeles Times*, January 10, 1991, p. A8.

27. William Drozdiak, "France Suggests It Will Alter Gulf Doctrine, Attack
Iraq Directly," *Washington Post*, January 21, 1991, p. A26.

28. Drozdiak, Jan. 21.

29. Alan Riding, "French Defense Chief Quits, Opposing Allied War
Goals," *New York Times*, January 30, 1991, p. A11.

30. Rone Tempest, "French Revive a Pastime: Fretting About U.S.
'Imperialism,'" *Los Angeles Times*, February 15, 1991, p. A9.

31. Rick Atkinson, *Crusade: The Untold Story of the Persian Gulf War*,
Boston: Houghton Mifflin Co., 1993, p. 381.

32. Atkinson, p. 382.

33. Atkinson, p. 384.

34. David Makovsky, "Behind Chirac's foreign policy activism," *Jerusalem Post*, October 25, 1996, p. 9.

35. William Drozdiak, "Chirac Wins Presidency of France," *Washington Post*, May 8, 1995, p. A1.

36. Richard Butler, *The Greatest Threat: Iraq, Weapons of Mass Destruction, and the Crisis of Global Security*, New York: Public Affairs, 2000, pp. 226–27.

37. Jacques Chirac (interview), "Pragmatism and Power," *Time*, intl. ed., December 4, 1995, p. 56.

38. Craig R. Whitney, "NATO at 50: With Nations at Odds, Is It a Misalliance?" *New York Times*, February 15, 1999, p. A7.

39. Craig R. Whitney, "The French Aren't Alone in Having Gall," *New York Times*, December 6, 1998, section 4, p. 6.

40. "Rural France, up in arms," *The Economist*, September 11, 1999.

41. "France cool on Bush 'axis of evil' speech: Chirac aide," Agence France Presse, February 1, 2002.

42. Victor Mallet, "The French disconnection," *Financial Times*, February 26, 2002, p. 14.

43. Christophe de Roquefeuil, "US dismisses European charge of 'simplistic' world view," Agence France Presse, February 8, 2002. When U.S. Secretary of State Colin Powell heard Vedrine's comment, he accused the French foreign minister of "getting the vapors." David E. Sanger, "Allies Hear Sour Notes in 'Axis of Evil' Chorus," *New York Times*, February 17, 2002, p. A18.

44. Thierry Meyssan, *9/11: The Big Lie*, London: Carnot Publishing, 2002, p. 10.

45. Meyssan, p. 139.

46. Elaine Sciolino, "French Leader Offers Formula to Tackle Iraq," *New York Times*, September 9, 2002, p. A1.

47. "In Bush's Words: On Iraq, U.N. Must Face Up to Its Founding Purpose," *New York Times*, September 13, 2002, p. A10.

48. "Old Faithless," *Daily Telegraph*, May 23, 2003, p. 27.

49. David A. Bell, "The Napoleon Complex," *New Republic*, April 14, 2003, p. 27. Bell describes Villepin's prose style this way: "Icarus-like, the author swoops up toward the sun of Romantic lyricism, only to plummet, wings melted, headlong into the ocean of banality."

50. John Tagliabue, "France and Germany Agree on Iraq," *New York Times*, October 3, 2002, p. A16.

51. Karen DeYoung and Mike Allen, "Time Grows Short for Iraq Accord, Bush Warns," *Washington Post*, October 17, 2002, p. A14.

52. Julia Preston, "Shift Toward U.S. Stand on Iraq Is Noted in Council," *New York Times*, November 1, 2002, p. A20.

53. Maggie Farley and Paul Richter, "Move by France Ups the Stakes," *Los Angeles Times*, January 22, 2003, p. 1.

54. Glenn Kessler and Colum Lynch, "France Vows to Block Resolution on Iraq War," *Washington Post*, January 21, 2003, p. A1.

55. Kessler and Lynch, January 21, 2003.

56. Sonni Efron and Maggie Farley, "France Says It May Veto Use of Force in Iraq," *Washington Times*, January 21, 2003, part 1, p. 1.

57. Kessler and Lynch, January 21, 2003.

58. Kessler and Lynch, January 21, 2003.

59. Richard W. Stevenson and James Dao, "Bush Says Iraqis Are Still Resisting Demand to Disarm," *New York Times*, January 22, 2003, p. A1.

60. Steven R. Weisman, "U.S. Set to Demand That Allies Agree Iraq Is Defying U.N.," *New York Times*, January 23, 2003, p. A1.

61. Weisman, January 23, 2003.

62. Weisman, January 23, 2003.

63. Paul Ames, "Chirac blasts eastern Europeans over pro-American stance, warns on EU membership," Associated Press, February 17, 2003.

64. James Blitz and George Parker, "Blair and Chirac collide over 'new Europe,'" *Financial Times*, February 19, 2003, p. 8.

65. James Graff and Bruce Crumley, "'France Is Not a Pacifist Country,'" *Time*, February 24, 2003, p. 32.

66. Karen DeYoung, "Chirac Moves to Repair U.S. Ties," *Washington Post*, April 16, 2003, p. A1.

67. Thomas Fuller, "Chirac Pledges French Support for African Prosperity," *New York Times*, February 22, 2003, p. A2.

68. Sebastian Rotella, "The Men Behind the French 'Non,'" *Los Angeles Times*, March 17, 2003, part 1, p. 1.

69. Warren Hoge, "It's the 'moment of truth,' Bush says," *International Herald Tribune*, March 17, 2003, p. 1.

70. Robert J. McCartney, "France Denounces U.S. and Its Allies," *Washington Post*, March 18, 2003, p. A14.

71. "Chirac's View: 'A Heavy Responsibility,'" *New York Times*, March 19, 2003, p. A14.

72. Alan Cowell, "France Holds Out a Tentative Olive Branch, With Thorns, to the U.S.," *New York Times*, March 28, 2003, p. B10.

73. "After D-Day," *The Economist*, June 12, 2004, p. 48.

74. Elaine Sciolino, "France Works to Limit Damage From U.S. Anger," *New York Times*, April 25, 2003, p. A13.

75. Karen DeYoung, "U.S. Denies Campaign Against France," *Washington Post*, May 16, 2003, p. A23.

76. "Chirac again slams Iraq war, says US-Britain can't make peace alone," Agence France Presse, June 3, 2003.

CONCLUSION: THE FRENCH DECISION

1. Democratic Presidential Candidate Debate in Des Moines, Iowa, November 24, 2003.

2. Paul Betts, Andrew Gowers, and Robert Graham, "Next weekend, George W. Bush sets foot in France for the first time since the Iraq crisis," *Financial Times*, May 26, 2003, p. 15.

3. Jody M. Kelman, "French Ambassador Defends Country's Stance on Iraqi War," *Harvard Crimson*, October 30, 2003.

4. Speech at Harvard University, October 29, 2003.

5. Claire Shipman and Joy Kalfopulos, "No Amour for France," ABC News/Good Morning America, May 30, 2003. http://abcnews.go.com/sections/GMA/World/GMA030530French_campaign.html

6. Thomas L. Friedman, "Our War With France," *New York Times*, September 18, 2003, p. A31.

7. James Graff and Adam Smith, "The French Resistance," *Time International*, February 24, 2003, p. 22.

INDEX